Leadership and Partnership

A dialogue between
Western and Tanzanian Christian leaders

edition afem
mission academics 28

Ralph Schubert

This book ist part of the series edition afem – mission academics,
ed. by Klaus W. Müller, Bernd Brandl,
Thomas Schirrmacher and Thomas Mayer.
http://www.missiologie.org

Bibliographic information published by Die Deutsche Bibliothek
Die Deutsche Bibliothek lists this publication in the Deutsche National bibliografie; detailed bibliographic data are available on the Internet at http://dnb.ddb.de.

ISBN 978-3-937965-95-6 (VTR)
VTR Publications
Gogolstr. 33, 90475 Nürnberg, Germany, http://www.vtr-online.de

ISBN 978-3-938116-68-5
VKW (Culture and Science Publ.)
Friedrichstr. 38, 53111 Bonn, Germany, http://www.vkwonline.de

ISSN 0944-1077 (edition afem – mission academics)

© 2008 by Ralph Schubert

This publication is based on a dissertation for the degree of MTh in Theological Ethics at the University of South Africa.

All rights reserved.
No part of this book may be reproduced in any form or by any means without permission in writing from the publisher,
VTR Publications, Gogolstr. 33, 90475 Nürnberg, Germany,
info@vtr-online.de, http://www.vtr-online.de.

Cover Illustration: VTR
Photo: Debora Geißler. Used by permission.

Printed in the UK by Lightning Source

Table of Contents

Acknowledgement 5
Introduction 7

Chapter 1
Christian Ethics, Leadership and Culture: Some Key Issues 13
   1.1   Definition of Christian Ethics 13
   1.2   Leadership and Christian Ethics 21
      1.2.1   Leadership and Christian Norms and Values 23
      1.2.2   Leadership and the Vision of the Kingdom of God 28
      1.2.3   Leadership and Power 33
      1.2.4   Leadership and Christian Virtues 36
   1.3   Christian Leadership, the Gospel and Culture 42

Chapter 2
Research Design and Methodology 57
   2.1   Data Collection and Analysis of Leadership Styles 58
      2.1.1   Leadership and Cultural Norms and Values 64
   2.2   Dialogue and Evaluation of Leadership Styles 83
   2.3   Reflection, Practical Actions and Application in
            Christian Leadership 86

Chapter 3
The Cultural Contexts, Personal Background and Character
of Western, Particularly Germanic and Anglo-Saxon,
and Tanzanian Leadership 89
   3.1   Cultural Contexts and Leadership 89
      3.1.1   Western Context 90
      3.1.2   Tanzanian Context 90
   3.2   Personal Background and Leadership 93
   3.3   Character and Leadership 100
      3.3.1   Christ-like Leadership 106
      3.3.2   Christian Leadership and Culture 117

Chapter 4
Relationships, Power and Conflict in Western, Particularly
Germanic and Anglo-Saxon, and Tanzanian Leadership 124
   4.1   Relationships and Leadership 124
      4.1.1   Organisational Structure and Leadership 124
      4.1.2   Trust and Leadership 132
      4.1.3   Self-disclosure and Leadership 134
      4.1.4   Task, Time and Leadership 135
   4.2   Power and Leadership 139
      4.2.1   Women and Leadership 148

4.2.2		Use of Power and Leadership	150
4.2.3		Meetings and Leadership	157
4.2.4		Decision-making and Leadership	160
4.3		Conflict and Leadership	164

Chapter 5
A Christian-Ethical Dialogue and Evaluation of Western and Tanzanian Leadership Styles and their Impact on Cross-cultural Partnerships 173

5.1		A Dialogue of Western and Tanzanian Leadership Styles	174
	5.1.1	Differences between Western and Tanzanian Leadership	174
	5.1.2	Christ-like Leadership in the West and in Tanzania	178
	5.1.3	Strengths and Weaknesses of Western and Tanzanian Leadership	185
5.2		An Evaluation of Western and Tanzanian Leadership Styles in the Light of the Bible	192
	5.2.1	A Christian-ethical Evaluation	192
	5.2.2	Practical Action Steps Forward	196
5.3		Towards a Christian Leadership Style	199
	5.3.1	What Can Westerners Learn from Tanzanian Leaders?	200
	5.3.2	What Can Tanzanians Learn from Western Leaders?	203
5.4		Leadership Styles and their Impact on Partnerships	206
	5.4.1	Challenges and Hindrances for Partnerships	206
	5.4.2	A Way to Foster Partnerships	209

Conclusion 216

Appendix 222

Questionnaire: Leadership Styles in the West and in Tanzania 222

1.	Personal Information	222
2.	Character and Leadership	222
3.	Relationships and Leadership	223
4.	Power and Leadership	224
5.	Conflict and Leadership	226
6.	Assessment of Leadership	227
7.	Comments and Feedback	228

Bibliography 229

Acknowledgement

It has been a great privilege to conduct this research into Christian leadership. Although it would be impossible to thank and acknowledge every individual, I would like particularly to thank the following individuals and institutions who have enabled me to move this study from possibility to reality.

I am grateful to the leadership of Wycliffe Germany, the Uganda-Tanzania Branch and the Africa Area of SIL International who encouraged me to undertake this study. They have graciously given me extra time to focus on this study. I wish particularly to acknowledge my colleague, Ken Boothe, who believed in me when I first became interested in a leadership study and encouraged me to pursue this research.

I do appreciate my supervisors Prof. Louise Kretzschmar and Dr Volker Kessler who enthusiastically supported and persistently challenged me. I am grateful and indebted to both of them as they guided me patiently through this research process.

This study would have been impossible without the Church of Tanzania. It was this Church that invited SIL International to Tanzania to collaborate with her in the task of the Great Commission. Motivation for this study comes from many years of enjoyment getting to know and appreciate Christian leaders in Tanzania, my colleagues and other expatriates. So I am thankful for the many opportunities I have had to learn and gain insights into how the Church in Tanzania operates, ministers and serves the people of Tanzania.

I would like to take this opportunity also to thank the government of Tanzania for allowing me to live and work in Tanzania for more than twelve years.

This research would not have been possible without all the individuals who were willing to share their time, energy, experience and thinking with me during the interviews and group discussion. Thank you!

A number of Wycliffe Associates from the UK have made a tremendous contribution to this study by searching for books and articles, which would not have easily been accessible for me otherwise. I am especially grateful to Prof. Dr Peter Stratfold, who willingly gave his expertise as a writer and an editor to help me to edit my English. I also appreciate the assistance of Michael Nchimbi who proofread the Swahili quotes and their English translation.

I cannot say enough about the solid, emotional and spiritual support of my wife, Anette, who set aside time out of her extremely busy schedule to serve as a sounding board and to discuss challenging questions with me. She patiently helped me to clarify my thinking. I am also thankful for the encouragement of my two boys, Samuel and Simeon, who accepted the fact that I was not able to spend as much time with them as I would have wished during the past two years. From time to time they asked me with a great sense of humour: "Dad, how many pages of your book have you written now?"

A study like this is not done in a financial and spiritual vacuum. I am grateful for the financial and prayer support of the faithful ministry partners who have stood behind us for more than fifteen years. Especially during times when I have felt challenged and stretched, it has been so helpful to know there are people around the world who are praying.

Finally, I am eternally indebted to my Lord and Saviour, Jesus Christ, without whom none of life has meaning. My sincere prayer is that this study will reflect glory to him and not the author. It is my prayer that this dissertation will be a contribution to further the kingdom of God. I pray that God may bless the people of Tanzania and Africa as it is sung in the national anthem of Tanzania:

> *Mungu ibariki Afrika.*
> *Wabariki viongozi wake.*
> *Hekima, umoja na amani,*
> *hizi ni ngao zetu, Afrika na watu wake.*
> *Ibariki Afrika; ibariki Afrika.*
> *Tubariki, watoto wa Afrika.*
>
> *Mungu ibariki Tanzania.*
> *Dumisha uhuru na umoja,*
> *wake kwa waume na watoto,*
> *Mungu, ibariki Tanzania na watu wake.*
> *Ibariki Tanzania; ibariki Tanzania.*
> *Tubariki*, watoto wa Tanzania.[1]

---

[1] Translation from Swahili to English: God bless Africa. Bless her leaders. Wisdom, unity and peace, these are our shields, Africa and her people. Bless Africa; bless Africa. Bless us, the children of Africa. God bless Tanzania. Continue with freedom and unity, women with men and children, God bless Tanzania and its people. Bless Tanzania; bless Tanzania. Bless us, the children of Tanzania.

Introduction

This research into a Christian-ethical comparison of Western and Tanzanian leadership styles aims to result in a deeper understanding of the two different leadership styles. Understanding and comparing the context of these leadership styles helps to reveal similarities and differences. A dialogue and evaluation of these leadership styles may lead towards a more Christian leadership style in both contexts. It is also important to see in which way the differences in leadership potentially impact cross-cultural partnerships and how good leadership can lead to more fruitful collaboration. For the purpose of this study "Western" is mainly used for the Anglo-Saxon[2] and Germanic[3] countries.

In recent years, there has been a stronger emphasis around the world on partnerships[4] than there were 15 years ago. It has been recognised by many sections of the worldwide business and Christian communities that working in cooperation will create better results than working in isolation or in competition. In many cases, one organisation can hardly accomplish the task alone. We as Christians should be able to work together since God has created us to live and work in community. However, as mere humans, those who have worked in partnerships will readily recognise that they do not always see the wisdom or the benefit of cooperation. Working in partnership means that our working environment will become much more complex. It is my desire to facilitate mutual respect and appreciation and to explore possible ways of fostering and strengthening cross-cultural partnerships. As I have been actively engaged for a number of years in exploring, forming and operating in cross-cultural partnerships, I have observed that different values and leadership styles can result in misunderstandings and create tremendous tension and conflict. It is important to reduce conflicts as much as possible or at least understand where these originate from and how to deal with them in an appropriate way.

My basic thesis is that there are major differences between Western and Tanzanian leadership styles, which are influenced by culture, economic status, education, gender, age, occupation, urban or rural setting, theology and the character of the Christian leader. These differences have great potential for misunderstandings and conflict in cross-cultural partnerships. This research focuses on the areas of culture, theology and character as I consider them to be central to Christian leadership. The other aspects already mentioned are also important, but space prevents them from all being discussed fully in this study. A cross-

---

[2] For the purpose of this research, this includes countries such as the USA, UK, Canada and Australia.
[3] For the purpose of this research, this includes countries such as Germany, Austria and the Netherlands.
[4] The term partnership is used in the widest possible sense including networks, alliances, consultations, strategic partnerships, joint ventures and sponsorship agreement.

cultural dialogue in the light of Scripture will lead to a deeper understanding of Christian-ethical leadership and a more fruitful collaboration.

The purpose of this dissertation is that the reader will have an increased understanding of Western and Tanzanian culture in terms of leadership styles. Having a better knowledge of the different social values will hopefully lead to a deeper understanding of why tensions, misunderstandings and conflicts can occur from time to time and how to respond to them. The discussion between Western, Tanzanian and biblical leadership may result in a better understanding of what Christian leadership really means in a global environment.

A substantial amount of literature is available on leadership in the West. However, very little has been written on African leadership, and much less about how different leadership styles impact on cross-cultural collaboration.

This research will hopefully help to increase the SIL[5] members' self-awareness and other-awareness in their relationships with the people they serve and work with. However, it is my hope that the insights gained in this study will also benefit expatriates from other organisations as well as Tanzanian colleagues, friends and leaders. It may stimulate readers to rethink in what way their values and actions have a positive or negative impact on someone else and how these values and actions might need to be adjusted. Cross-cultural experience is a risk but it is also enriching. The North American Protestant theologian and ethicist Bernard Adeney (1995:43), who has extensive teaching experience in Indonesia, writes: "Cross-cultural experience opens the floodgates of new awareness. God's Spirit can help keep things in perspective. The fruit of the Spirit can help us adjust." Living and working in a different culture changes how a person thinks, feels and acts. Through this experience God can change a person's character and personality to become more like Him. This research is not designed to be a one-way but a two-way street, where it is hoped that exchange and cross-fertilization through dialogue will take place. Synergy might be created as people work together in partnership by increasing their understanding of different leadership styles, cultures and values.

Since 1993 I have worked with SIL International. SIL International is a partner organisation of Wycliffe Bible Translators International, dedicated to training, language research, translation and literacy. Most members of SIL International work in rather complex and diverse situations. Usually within the SIL community, there are several nationalities from many different denominations. Most workers find relating to one or two other cultures challenging enough. Among the thirty-nine members that make up the field personnel of SIL International in Tanzania, there are ten different nationalities.[6] In addition these SIL members work in a cross-cultural situation, speaking a second or even third language and relating to local citizens coming from a number of different ethnic groups from different denominations. Most of these people are confronted with a myriad of differences in terms of culture and values. This has

---

[5] SIL International is a partner organisation of Wycliffe Bible Translators International. (SIL used to stand for Summer Institute of Linguistics.)

[6] As of May 2005, these are American, British, German, Swiss, Canadian, Austrian, Swedish, Australian, Dutch and Chinese.

great potential for misunderstanding and miscommunication, which can create tension and conflict. Tensions very often occur because of conflicting values.

I was born in Tanzania and since I started to work in Tanzania more than ten years ago, I have had a strong interest and passion in encouraging collaboration between Christian ministries. My efforts in building relationships with Tanzanian leaders have been both encouraging and frustrating at times. Sometimes my ignorance has led to situations of misunderstanding. In my early years in Tanzania I had to supervise an employee who was quite a bit older than me. For a number of reasons it was difficult to give him instructions or constructive critique. First of all, I was a foreigner. Secondly, I was much younger than him. I assumed that because of the role which I filled, I had the authority. But that was not necessarily the case. His age had much more weight than my position. According to the Tanzanian value system, he deserved more respect than I did.

During the SIL International Conference and the Wycliffe Bible Translators International Convention in 1999 a joint resolution was passed, which is called Vision 2025[7] (SIL International Conference & Wycliffe Bible Translators Convention 1999). The aim is to have a Bible translation project started in every people group that needs it within this generation. This resolution calls for much closer collaboration than in the past, not only at the language program level but also at the organisational level.

A year later during the Amsterdam 2000 conference, the centrality and importance of the Bible in the local languages in relation to evangelism, Church planting and Church growth was recognised. This declaration calls for a close cooperation between SIL International, other Bible agencies and the Church.[8]

Most of the SIL teams in Tanzania are trained in linguistics, literacy, anthropology, exegesis and administration, according to their respective assignments. They are very often not trained in leadership or partnership. To collaborate well with the local Churches and other organisations, it is important to have a deep understanding and self-awareness of your own culture, leadership style, personal, ethical and partnership values. According to the North-American evangelical anthropologist Sherwood Lingenfelter (1996:9), Christian cross-cultural workers desire to be agents of biblical transformation.

---

[7] Motivated by the pressing need for all peoples to have access to the Word of God in a language that speaks to their hearts, and reaffirming our historic values and our trust in God to accomplish the impossible, we embrace the vision that by the year 2025 a Bible translation project will be in progress for every people group that needs it.

We acknowledge that this cannot be accomplished simply by our working harder or doing more of what we are now doing. It will require us to make significant changes in our attitudes and ways of working.

Our desire is to build capacity for sustainable Bible translation programmes and Scripture Use activities. Therefore, we urge each entity within our family of organisations **to give priority to strengthening present partnerships, forming additional strategic partnerships and working together to develop creative approaches appropriate to each context.**

To this end we commit ourselves to pray for the fulfilment of this vision, seeking God's guidance and obeying Him in whatever new directions He may lead (SIL International Conference & Wycliffe Bible Translators International Convention 1999; my emphasis).

[8] The Bible agencies are part of the worldwide Church.

Since everybody views the world through their own cultural glasses and works with a cultural bias, it requires significant self-awareness to become agents of transformation. Lingenfelter suggests,

> ... that self-awareness and other awareness in relationship to cultural bias is essential for effective cross-cultural service. Missionaries and Christian leaders who are unaware of their cultural biases and the biases of others will inevitably be ineffective as agents of transformation (1996:10).

As SIL International and Wycliffe Bible Translators International seek ways to strengthen present partnerships, form additional strategic partnerships and work together in new ways, therefore, it is essential to understand the various leadership styles employed by different people and organisations. Lingenfelter suggests:

> When we enter another culture we must examine the life and beliefs of those people; we must learn how to live good lives according to their standards; we must live in submission to their authorities; we must discover their significant questions; and we must search the Scriptures to find biblical answers to their questions and needs, recognizing the limitations of our own views (1998:20-21).

I only agree in part with Lingenfelter. Missionaries need to understand the values and culture of the other society. As visitors and guests they also need to submit to their authorities. But the question is whether they need to live good lives according to the host's standards, which might not necessarily be biblical standards. A distinction needs to be made whether the standard of the host is in conflict with biblical standards **as the missionary reads her/his Bible** or whether the standard of the host is in **real** tension to biblical standards. There should be a tension if missionaries are agents of transformation. So it is important to analyse and reflect on those values in the light of the Bible recognising that our biblical and ethical view is biased by our own culture. Adeney (1995:46) asks the important question: "How do we learn to live 'well' (or virtuously) in another culture?" His answer is "we learn through experience". When situations, accounts and actions are reflected upon they become experience. This experience in turn will help to adjust our actions. However, the first step is to gain a deeper understanding of our own values. Entering another culture helps us to see our own culture from a different perspective and in a different light. It may be an eye-opener to realize how other people see us. As Adeney (:24) points out: "Cross-cultural understanding comes with the shock of recognizing ourselves as others see us. An ability to adjust my own values in order to seek goodness in another cultural framework begins with understanding 'what' my own values are and 'why' I hold them." Before a person can be an agent of transformation s/he needs to be transformed. To be willing and open to reflect upon and possibly adjust our own norms, values and virtues is critical.

To facilitate this reflection, Western and Tanzanian leadership styles are examined in this study. As this research engages in a Christian-ethical comparison of leadership styles in the West and in Tanzania and their impact on cross-cultural partnerships the focus is on culture, theology and the character of a leader. I consider these three areas as core to Christian leadership. Every aspect of life is interwoven by culture, and so also is leadership. To contextualize Christian leadership appropriately it is essential to take culture and theology into account. A leader's theology and Christian faith impacts her/his thinking and behaviour. Leaders read the Bible through their own cultural lenses, which shapes their theology and understanding of Christian leadership. Culture and theology play a major part in the formation of a leader's character. Apart from culture and theology, one's character determines one's leadership behaviour. Focusing on culture, theology and the character will help to determine which leadership aspects are merely Western or Tanzanian and which are Christian. Other aspects like economic status, education, gender, age, occupation, urban or rural setting are part of the culture and taken into account but not discussed extensively as this would be beyond the scope of this research.

Chapter one discusses some key issues of Christian ethics, leadership and culture. The criteria of what constitutes good Christian leadership in terms of Christian norms, values and virtues are discussed. It also describes the vision of the kingdom of God, how Jesus practised leadership and exercised power. This chapter outlines what sorts of people Christian leaders need to be and how they can become such people. Finally, it describes how the gospel and culture interact towards a contextualized Christian leadership style. Chapter one provides a framework of Christian-ethical criteria, which is then employed in the dialogue and evaluation of the leadership styles in chapter five.

In chapter two the research design and methodology are discussed. This study is a combination of theoretical and empirical research. Data are obtained from observations, case studies, interviews, a group discussion and existing literature. A questionnaire is developed based on the two cultural value models by Hofstede, Trompenaars and Hampden-Turner. The criteria for interviewees are discussed. The two cultural value models by Hofstede, Trompenaars and Hampden-Turner are described at length and a synthesis is derived. These cultural value models are later applied in chapters three, four and five to analyse, interpret and compare the context of the two leadership styles. From the cultural models key themes are derived such as personal information and leadership, character and leadership, relationships and leadership, power and leadership, and conflict and leadership. The information obtained on these topics is presented and interpreted in chapters three and four. Furthermore, chapter two discusses how the data are analysed and evaluated and chapter five examines how practical actions and application in Christian leadership and partnership can be derived.

Chapters three and four describe the context of leadership styles in the West and in Tanzania in terms of personal information, character, relationships, power, and conflict based on collected data in the interviews and group discussion, participant observations, case studies and existing literature. For the interviews a questionnaire is used. The cultural models discussed in chapter two provide a means for the analysis, comparison and interpretation in chapters three and four.

In chapter five Westerners and Tanzanians enter into a cross-cultural dialogue through the questionnaire used in interviews and also through a group discussion on each other's leadership style and how they understand Christian leadership. The two leadership styles are evaluated from a cultural perspective applying the Christian norms, values, virtues and kingdom leadership discussed in chapter one. In the evaluation of the two leadership styles, the cultural values identified through the cultural models must be critiqued by the biblical norms and values discussed in chapter one. Through this dialogue it may emerge what is merely Western or Tanzanian and a deeper understanding of what Christian leadership style is will be reached. The final chapter also includes potential areas of misunderstandings and their impact on cross-cultural partnerships. Employing the theoretical framework of Christian ethics discussed in chapter one may clarify the nature of the ethical problems and suggest possible responses. Subsequently, the practical implications, actions and suggestions for Christian leadership and partnership are discussed.

A deeper knowledge and understanding of each other's leadership style can potentially reduce misunderstandings and tensions, and increase the effectiveness of the ministry and lead to healthier and more fruitful partnerships. Beyond this, the implication of this study is a deepening and strengthening of existing relationships among partners in Tanzania.

From this research it might be possible to draw some conclusions which could be relevant and applicable to Western-African partnerships in other parts of Africa as well. This must be evaluated and determined by my readers from situation to situation, since the African continent is so huge and diverse.

Chapter 1

Christian Ethics, Leadership and Culture: Some Key Issues

In this section a number of key issues relevant to Christian ethics, leadership and culture are discussed. These key issues include a definition of Christian ethics, and the Christian norms, values and virtues that make a good leader, kingdom leadership, the use of power, and in which way the gospel and culture influence the understanding of Christian leadership. The Christian-ethical criteria discussed in this chapter are applied in the analysis and evaluation of Western and Tanzanian leadership styles in chapter five. They also provide a means of giving direction to the reflection on leadership styles and to a proposal of some practical actions on how to move forward and foster better partnerships.

1.1 Definition of Christian Ethics

Since this study engages in a Christian-ethical dialogue of the two different leadership styles in the West and in Tanzania, it is essential to define what is understood by ethics in general and Christian ethics in particular.

Ethics has been defined in a number of different ways. Russell Connors and Patrick McCormick (1998:175), North American Catholic theologians, define ethics as "the study of moral experience; more specifically, it is the systematic and communal reflection on and analysis of moral experience". Arthur Dyck (in Kammer 1988:11-12) defines ethics in a general way as "systematic reflection upon human actions, institutions, and character". Dyck points out that ethics has to do with people's behaviour, how they shape communities, and who they are as persons. Klaus Nürnberger (1988:9), a South African theologian and ethicist, defines ethics as "*a reflection on what ought to be, and on how we can be liberated and motivated to bring it about*" [his emphasis]. South African Protestant ethicist Louise Kretzschmar defines ethics as follows:

> Ethics can also be defined as **our** understanding of what "ought" to be. Ethics is about the way in which **we** perceive certain actions or attitudes – some are perceived as wrong or bad, or we say that such actions or attitudes ought neither to be commended nor practised. Conversely, other actions or attitudes may be regarded as right or good, and people will be encouraged to imitate these actions or attitudes (1993:10). [my emphasis]

Kretzschmar's definition is more elaborate than Nürnberger's as it begins with how people perceive certain actions or attitudes. Ethics is not just a **reflection** of what ought to be but also **people's understanding** of how certain actions or attitudes are perceived. It is essential to clarify people's perception before an evaluation happens. Connors and McCormick separate morality and ethics in the following definition:

> Morality is concerned with persons becoming good, doing the right thing and building just communities. ... Ethics, which is the systematic and communal reflection on and analysis of moral experience, asks what "the good", "the right" and "the just" are. Ethics tries to show – based on reasoned reflection – why this character (and not that one) is good, why this action (and not that one) is right, and why this community (and not that one) is just (1998:13).

Connors and McCormick go a step further in their definition in that they not only reflect and analyse a certain action or attitude but also identify reasons why a person, an action or a community is good. That way they combine ethics with morality describing the situation *as it is*, then presenting the situation *as it should be*, and explaining *why* it ought to be that way.

Thus, these definitions call for a thorough description and analysis of a situation before it can be evaluated. However, ethics does not stop with the analysis and evaluation. Ethics moves a step further from the analysis calling for change and transformation of individuals and communities (Kretzschmar 1994:20). It can be argued, that in ethics analysis leads to action. Thus, the task of ethics is at least threefold (:17-22). First, the context and nature of the ethical problem needs to be understood. Secondly, the problem has to be addressed. Finally, people need to engage in practical action to promote liberation, salvation and transformation. Christian ethics must have an impact on society. Emmanuel Ngara (2004:92), a Catholic Christian from Zimbabwe, encourages Christians to take their responsibility to change the world seriously.

Christian ethics is *God* and *Christ* centred (Brown 1998:107-111, 115-121). The basis of any Christian ethics should be "the affirmation that God has decisively called and formed a people to serve him through Israel and the work of Christ" (Hauerwas 1981:9). David Jones (1994:14), a Presbyterian theologian from the USA, defines Christian ethics as "the study of the way of life that conforms to the will of God – the way of life that is good, that pleases God and fulfils human nature". British ethicist Colin Brown (1998:142) offers a helpful framework for Christian ethics: "First, **it is about seeing the world through God's eyes**. Second, **Christians ought to be committed to Jesus Christ as the Lord and exemplar of their moral life**" [his emphasis]. God and his basic loving character is core of Christian ethics. Christians have a personal, intimate relationship with God through Jesus Christ. **Jesus** is at the centre of Christian ethics (:115-119). As a person he embodies the unique standards of Christian ethics (:116). Jesus himself is and practises kingdom ethics. Jesus is **the** exemplar of moral life. Keith Ward (in Brown 1998:117) argues, "The moral way of life that is Christian can only be seen in Jesus. He embodies the right way of life and in him we are back to the source of what it is like to be a morally acceptable person". Christian leaders from the West and from Tanzania are called to be loyal to Jesus and imitate him in their leadership. Jesus' leadership may be interpreted and practised in different ways in each society and culture. Thus, a dialogue between Westerners and Tanzanians can lead to a Christian view of leadership as Christian leaders together seek "to understand Scripture under the guidance of the Holy Spirit, to help one another in dealing with problems they face in their particular contexts, and to check one another's cultural biases" (Hiebert 1999:113).

The Christian worldview is influenced and shaped by the Bible. In Christian ethics the *Bible* is regarded as a primary source, as the North American Protestant theologian Bruce Birch and ethicist Larry Rasmussen (1989:15) point out: "The Bible is formative and normative for the Christian moral life. Christian ethics is not Christian ethics apart from Scripture." Christians are expected to be loyal to the teaching of the Bible. The Bible provides guidance and direction in ethical decision-making for Christians.

Thus, Christian ethics can be defined as follows:

> An understanding of what ought to be, a willingness on the part of individual believers to be saved and to become disciples of Jesus Christ, and a commitment on the part of both individual believers and communities to preach and practise their faith with reference to human, social and physical reality (Kretzschmar 1994:3).

In other words, Christian ethics is the response to a moral vision, which is derived from the Scriptures and people's knowledge and experience of the will of God (Kretzschmar 2001:282). This definition of Christian ethics implies the double commandment in Matthew 22:37-39, loving God and your neighbour. It is an expression of the vertical relationship between humans and God and the horizontal relationship among people. Christian ethics recognizes "people need to be saved from sin, despair and oppression through the redeeming work of Christ in order that they may be empowered to be different and act differently" (Kretzschmar 1994:3). The task of Christian ethics is to transform individuals, communities, and societies.

According to Charles Kammer III (1988:17), a Lutheran theologian from the USA, our ethical view is created by a combination of factors, which he calls the "moralscape", based on the image of a landscape. The components of our *moralscape* are our worldview, loyalties, norms and values, experiential and empirical elements and mode of decision-making (:18).

Our *worldview* is created and shaped by the community in which we grow up and live. The Christian worldview is in addition influenced and formed by the Bible and the Church. The worldview is the broadest framework, which in part determines what kind of leader one becomes (:20-23). Since the worldview impacts the leadership style it is essential to scrutinize it in our ethical reflection (:23). Christian leaders are called to let their worldview be transformed, as Paul puts it: "Do not conform yourselves to the standards of this world but **let God transform you inwardly by a complete change of your mind**" (Romans 12:2) [my emphasis].[9]

A person's *loyalty* influences her/his character and behaviour. It may make a difference in leadership style whether a person is a Christian and loyal to the Bible or not. It may make a difference in a leader's decision whether s/he is loyal to the group or not. Kammer (1988:25) points out, "There is little doubt

---

[9] I generally use the Good News Bible for Scripture quotes. If a different version is used it is indicated.

that what we love shapes our lives both individually and collectively, both who we are and what we do".

Leaders' *norms and values* are shaped by their worldview and loyalties. Kammer (:72) defines values as "states or goods that we desire. They inform the affective motivations of our behaviour and development, and define the goals and ends of our action. Values represent that which we love and that to which we aspire." Norms he (:73) defines as "rules and principles, some formal and some informal, which provide guidelines for our behaviour and which help us operate in a world of conflicting interests and confusing loyalties". According to Kammer, values refer to a person's character, and norms are an expression of these values in a person's actions. The Catholic theologian Richard Gula's (in Connors & McCormick 1998:158) definition is similar as he defines moral norms as "the criteria for judging the sorts of person we ought to be and the sorts of actions we ought to perform in faithful response to God's call to be loving". Gula adds the Christian component of love as a criterion. Connors and McCormick offer a threefold definition of moral norms:

> To begin with, **moral norms are the general or specific instructions directing persons and communities toward virtue and/or right action.** ... Second, **moral norms teach the moral wisdom and experience of the community in short propositional statements prescribing or forbidding certain habits or actions.** ... And, third, **moral norms seek to preserve and protect those basic human goods or values which help make life fully human. They also seek to preserve a sane hierarchy or order to these values** (1998:156-157). [their emphasis]

According to this definition norms guide a person's or community's being and doing. Norms also provide guidance about which value prevails over the other. Birch and Rasmussen define the purpose of values as follows:

> "Values" in ethics *refer to moral goods to be realized in society.* They function as moral norms by which we judge both actions and the structures of society itself. Or, as we project our hopes into the future, they function as the standards by which we judge the kind of society we aspire to (1989:50). [their emphasis]

It seems that Birch and Rasmussen use the terms values and norms interchangeably. Values are used to examine the current behaviour of society and to determine the future character of society. Kretzschmar (2001:296) defines values as "those attitudes or actions that reveal what we esteem or rate highly, and according to which we make decisions. They reveal what we applaud and value as opposed to what we despise and reject". British ethicist and theologian Ian McDonald (1995:xvii) offers a helpful summary of values as "variously described as general guides to behaviour, as giving direction to life, as maturing and evolving with experience, as patterns of evaluating and behaving, or simply as goals". Management consultants Fons Trompenaars from the Netherlands and Charles Hampden-Turner from the USA define the difference between norms and values as follows:

Norms are the mutual sense a group has of what is "right" and "wrong". Norms can develop on a formal level as written laws, and on an informal level as social control. **Values**, on the other hand, determine the definition of "good and bad", are therefore closely related to the ideals shared in the group (2002:21-22). [their emphasis]

Trompenaars and Hampden-Turner define norms as deontological and values as teleological. According to the various definitions above there does not always seem to be a clear separation of norms and values. I prefer the definitions by Kammer and Trompenaars and Hampden-Turner, which are closely related. These two definitions seem to be clear and precise. Usually norms are an expression of values. A norm is how a person *should* behave. A value is how a person *aspires* or *desires* to behave.

Leaders in the West and in Tanzania have different experiences. These experiences "develop, test, and challenge our worldview, loyalties, norms, and values" (Kammer 1988:28). Leaders do not make ethical decisions in a vacuum. As part of the empirical world, leaders face moral situations and problems to which they must respond and which they must solve (:29). Leaders make their ethical decisions based on moral norms and values, moral consequences and goals, and moral character and conduct (Kretzschmar 2004:109). They make decisions based on deontology, teleology and virtues.

Deontological ethics defines what is right and wrong employing *norms* and *values* (Adeney 1995:146). This means, an action is right or wrong in itself no matter what the consequences are (Kretzschmar 1994:4). Deontology appeals to principles, commands, maxims, exhortations, laws and rules (McDonald 1995:6; Kammer 1988:31). It does not necessarily take into account what the effect on the environment is. This approach has the advantage that the criteria for decision-making are clearly defined. It provides clear guidelines for making ethical decisions. This is helpful where clear guidance is required. However, it can also be narrow in the sense of being restrictive not taking other important factors in the decision-making into account. I believe deontology may be more helpful if linked to teleology, as McDonald (1995:8) points out: "Rules and principles – narrow and wide deontology – have thus greater moral significance when linked to motive and inner disposition, to the awakening of moral and spiritual understanding (as they are in the biblical tradition), and to the particularities of cases." In other words, when deontological ethics is applied it may have greater impact when a situation is considered in the wider context rather than applying the norms rigidly.

Deontological ethics tends to be dichotomistic. Westerners who come from a guilt culture[10] and think analytically tend to see things in black and white. Thus, they may be able to relate well to deontological ethics.

---

[10] As a result of her studies in Japan, Ruth Benedict (1934; 1946) suggests that there are guilt and shame cultures. She (in Adeney 1995:251) suggests that people in guilt cultures internalize and associate right and wrong with personal sin. In a guilt-oriented culture the individual does everything to conform to the norm, which is *the justice and law* formulated by the culture, society, and group (Käser 1998:138).

The second philosophical stream is called *teleological* ethics. Teleological ethics is "concerned about realizing some end or goal (embodying some value). As such, they [teleologists] are deeply concerned about consequences and they measure morality by the ability of an action to accomplish a desired end" (Kammer 1988:31). It determines goodness by the outcome. In teleology, "No action is intrinsically right or wrong: it all depends on its consequences; in particular, the foreseeable consequences of the action" (McDonald 1995:14). The focus is on what effect somebody's action has on the world. The emphasis is not so much on inner quality but on goals, motive, consequences or results of an action (Adeney 1995:147). Teleological ethics seems to be able to deal well with a number of grey areas. Since leadership is very complex and has a lot to do with culture, theology, and character, teleology plays a significant part in the analysis. For Tanzanians who live in a shame culture[11] motives and consequences play an important role. Thus, I believe they may be able to relate well to teleological ethics.

These two different approaches of deontological and teleological ethics may seem somewhat contradictory. But they are not. They complement each other. Christians believe in biblical moral norms and values that reflect the character of God. These norms are good in themselves and universal. However, they might be expressed and emphasized differently in different places and times. But they are transcultural (:149). When these moral norms are lived out they will also have an effect on the environment. So the deontological and the teleological dimensions cannot always be completely separated. Each approach has its place.

Roman Catholics have developed the concept of *prima facie*[12], which was introduced by the British moral philosopher David Ross (Adeney 1995:153-156; Jones 1994:136). "[Ross] distinguishes between *actual* duty and *prima facie* duty, between what is *actually* right and what is *prima facie* right. What is actually right or obligatory is what we actually ought to do in a particular situation" (in Frankena 1973:26). This concept recognizes the fact of a fallen, sinful world where not everything is clearly defined as right or wrong. It also recognizes that norms and values may conflict with each other in certain situations (Jones 1994:137). Hence, actual duties are "determined by reference to the situation in its totality" (:137). There can be situations in which a compromise is necessary and appropriate in order to promote a higher value.

In the question about the Sabbath (Matthew 12:1-14) Jesus places the human physical needs over keeping the Sabbath law. In these two accounts of looking for food and healing a man, a decision was made based on a higher

---

[11] Benedict (in Adeney 1995:251) suggests that people in shame cultures associate right and wrong with disgrace or loss of face before the group. In a shame-oriented culture the individual does everything to conform to the norm, which is the *commonly accepted behaviour* recognized by the culture, society, and group (Käser 1998:138). It is most important not to violate the norm and to keep face, to protect prestige, and to maintain the relationship as being part of the group (:137-140).

[12] The translation of *prima facie* is "on the face of it" or "on first assessment" (Adeney 1995:153).

value, the actual duty instead of the *prima facie* duty, avoiding an effect that might have had implications, which might have been worse.

As people deal with cultural and biblical values in a certain situation, a person needs to decide which one carries more weight. In such a situation it may be more important to consider the consequences rather than making the right decision. *Prima facie* is teleological as it takes the consequences of an action into account. I can see the need for a compromise in some cases. However, this concept may place a person in a rather difficult situation and create some tension. The question is which value should prevail over another value and for what reason. Since leadership is influenced by culture, theology, and character in a certain situation the question may arise which of these three factors carries more weight and has a higher value. In the analysis of leadership styles in the West and in Tanzania this concept is helpful in discovering why leaders promote one value over another.

Virtue ethics, which deals with a leader's character and conduct, is discussed in more detail below in the section on leadership and Christian virtues. Character has to do with a leader's integrity. Thus character and spiritual formation are essential for every leader. However, here their relationship with norms-based and ends-based ethics can be noted. When a situation is examined and evaluated it is important to bear in mind:

> First, the *end* the agent seeks to realize must be good, intrinsically worthy of human spirit. Second, the *motive* of the agent must be good, so that the end is sought because it is worthwhile, the mark of a good character. Third, the *means* to the end must be good, conforming to the standard of what is right, since neither a good end nor a good motive is compatible with a bad means (Jones 1994:11). [my emphasis]

Based on Aquinas's teaching, goal, act and motive must all be good. As can be seen from the framework of the moralscape the individual, community and character, each play a significant role in creating one's ethical view. The community plays a central role in the moralscape as Kammer points out:

> Society is the source of our worldviews, makes claims upon our loyalties, provides us with rules for living together, and makes claims about what we should value. Society is also largely responsible for determining what empirical information is available to us and how we will interpret it. Our social setting will also determine the experiences we have that shape our personhood. It also seems likely that particular societies favour certain modes of decision-making (e.g., pragmatism in most modern Western societies) (1988:19).

Kammer (:127) continues, "Moral development requires recognition of these social influences and a conscious decision to either affirm or reject them".

In the final analysis, deontological and teleological elements and virtues need to be carefully considered. What is a good and a bad leader? What character traits should a good leader have? "How directly and forcefully do we communicate? How individualistic or communalistic are we in decision-making? How competitive are we? ... How authoritarian are we with our subordinates?" (Adeney 1995:156). In which way are power and authority used? How are meetings conducted? How do people deal with conflict? An individual's motivation behind a certain action can be *deontological* right or wrong in themselves regardless of their cultural effect in a given situation. However, no matter what the motivation of a certain action is, it is essential to consider the outcome. The outcome of an action always has an impact on somebody. The outcome and, in turn, the impact of this action may be considered good or bad in different cultures. In ethical terms this is called the *teleological* element.

Christian ethics is deontological, teleological and stresses personal virtue. It is deontological because of its strong reference to the Bible and its emphasis on norms and values such as love, justice, mercy, faithfulness and humility. It is teleological because it seeks to relate to the context and promote good outcomes. Christian ethics addresses a person's motives, character and actions. I do believe Christian ethics provides clear guidance in leadership matters. At the same time it leaves enough room to apply biblical values in this contemporary world. Christian ethics is concerned with virtue because Scripture emphasises the importance of character and becoming more like Christ.

The understanding of the concepts of deontology, teleology and virtue ethics are essential in Christian ethics and leadership. However, to do ethics in a responsible way, South African theologian Charles Villa-Vicencio suggests keeping three things in mind:

> First, the Christian tradition requires a Christological understanding of God's redemptive purpose for creation. ... Secondly, an ethic of responsibility involves a hierarchy of values and norms. ... Finally, it must take full recognition of human rationalisations and the inclination to self-justification (1994:86).

In other words, as we engage in a Christian-ethical comparison of leadership styles in the West and in Tanzania, we need to recognize the sinful nature of these societies. God's desire is to see these societies being transformed. Because parts of culture are sinful, biblical values and norms must prevail over cultural values. However, the cultural context needs to be taken into consideration since biblical values in terms of leadership may be understood and applied differently. On the other hand, human beings tend to rationalise and justify their actions. There can be a tendency to use the culture as an excuse for certain leadership behaviour, which is not necessarily compliant with Christian norms, values and virtues.

Since this research deals with leadership styles in two different societies with very different values, the area of *cross-cultural* ethics needs to be in focus. As different leadership styles in the West and in Tanzania are examined on the basis of a Christian-ethical comparison, cultural elements need to be seriously considered as they influence an individual's perception of good and bad. As Adeney relates values to cross-cultural ethics and how they play out in different cultures, he points out:

> Cross-cultural ethics is not simply a question of distinguishing relative and absolute values. Different cultures prioritize their values differently

in relation to the patterns of meaning relevant to the story of their people. Different priorities may require the understanding of "absolute" values differently in different contexts. Certain practices, for example truth-telling, may be correctly interpreted in a variety of ways in different cultures (1995:17-18).

A Western understanding of certain values like love, truth and justice may be understood and applied differently by a Tanzanian. Thus, moral character and conduct may be expressed in different ways according to the cultural values. As a result of this, goals and consequences may take different priorities. The means to reach these goals can also differ because of different values and virtues. Thus, it is the task of cross-cultural ethics to look at the deontological, teleological and virtue aspects of a leader's actions from a cultural perspective. So Westerners and Tanzanians can learn more about norms and values from each other.

This research seeks to understand the contexts of leadership in the West and in Tanzania. After the dimensions of the cultural contexts have been examined we will be able to "discover some of the biblical keys that will allow us to unlock the chains of our cultural habits and the gates of our cultural walls" (Lingenfelter 1998:21).

> Paul Hiebert (1985) argues that Christianity provides a new hermeneutic for cultural living. Every culture and every person must change in light of a new perspective – Jesus Christ, crucified, risen, and exalted. Jesus came to save not cultures but people, and he came to transform them into his likeness (in Lingenfelter 1998:18).

The gospel challenges the worldview of any Christian. Their lives are transformed through the Holy Spirit on the basis of Christian norms and values displayed in the Scriptures (2 Corinthians 3:18). As a result Christian norms and values are lived out in virtues. As leaders are transformed, they will be enabled to evaluate their culture in a new light and have an impact on their environment. Christians from different cultures can help each other to understand the Scriptures in the light of their particular contexts and to check one another's cultural bias in a cross-cultural dialogue (Hiebert 1999:113). Some relevant norms and values regarding Christian leadership are discussed in the next section.

1.2 Leadership and Christian Ethics

Leadership has to do with norms and values, goals and consequences and virtues. Thus, it is closely connected with Christian ethics. Biblical norms, values and virtues build the foundation of Christian leadership. These norms, values and virtues need to be interpreted in community under the guidance of the Holy Spirit.

As suggested above, the Bible is the primary source of Christian ethics (Kammer 1988:41; McDonald 1995:27). The teachings of the Bible shape and inform our Christian worldview, loyalties, attitudes, and intentions. Hauerwas (1981:56) argues, "for Christian ethics the Bible is not just a collection of texts but scripture that makes normative claims on a community". The Scriptures play a significant role "for teaching the truth, rebuking error, correcting faults, and giving instruction for right living, so that the person who serves God may be fully qualified and equipped to do every kind of good deed" (2 Timothy 3:16-17). Even though it is an ancient, historically conditioned book, the Bible is contemporary as it can be applied at any time in any situation and context.

The Bible is not an ethical textbook, but it is a rich source of moral norms, values and virtues (Brown 1998:167). The Bible consists of a variety of literary forms, including history, poems, songs, prophecy, stories and teaching (Kammer 1988:43). As a result it does not provide a single ethical vision (Connors & McCormick 1998:98-99). It also does not shape our moral vision in just one way. The Scriptures speak to people in a number of different ways at various times, as Spohn and others (in Connors & McCormick 1998:99) have argued: "[T]he Bible might serve as: (1) an expression of God's command in our lives, (2) a moral reminder, (3) a call to liberation, (4) a revelation of what God is doing in our world, (5) a call to discipleship and (6) an invitation to respond to God's love." Hauerwas (1981:66-69) makes the point that even though not everything in the Bible is narrative, the Scriptures need to be read as a **story** with a beginning and a progression. In this story, the character of God is reflected and revealed. I concur with Connors and McCormick (1998:101) as they conclude, "Acknowledging the narrative character of Scripture means that for Christians the primary moral significance of the Bible is to be found in the way it shapes and nurtures our personal and communal *character* [and actions]" [their emphasis]. Thus, biblical teaching shapes a leader's character and behaviour, the way people live together in community, and collaborate.

The important question is: What is Christian leadership, what is Western leadership and what is Tanzanian leadership? This question cannot be answered in isolation. The response to this question can be informed and challenged through a dialogue in community. Hauerwas (in Richardson 1994:93) argues, there can be no Christian ethics without Christian community. As can be seen in the Scriptures (Romans 12:4-8; 1 Corinthians 12:12-31; Ephesians 4:1-16; Philippians), "Community is at the heart of Christian faith itself" (Birch & Rasmussen 1989:19). Christians are part of the body of Christ. Human beings exist and live in relationships, as Birch and Rasmussen point out:

> Our lives ... are set within communities and are shaped by communities, all sorts of communities. We are not born into an undifferentiated schema of disconnected events and relations, but into corporate life already alive with communities which structure our social existence. The moral life cannot exist apart from these, and is only possible with a view to these communities. Whatever moral consciousness we possess does not exist prior to, apart from, or independent of social relatedness. Communities are the forms of our social relatedness and the material reality of the moral life (1989:19).

People cannot live without others. God created human beings from the very beginning to relate to one another (Genesis 2:18-23). Christian ethical behaviour is shaped in community. Christian ethics is what Birch and Rasmussen (1989:17-34) call "community ethics". The faith community plays an important part in Christian ethics in terms of being "a major source and resource for moral development", a "source of rich and varied content for member's ethics", and being a "framework of accountability for the Christian moral life" (:132). Discussing Western and Tanzanian leadership styles in community provides a source, resource, and a framework of accountability in developing a view of Christian-ethical leadership. As Western and Tanzanian societies interact within and with each other and the Scriptures, the power of the gospel can bring the transformation "that God seeks to bring about in our own personalities, our interpersonal relationships, our social context, our thoughts and paradigms, our churches and, indeed, in all of creation" (Kretzschmar 1994:19). Christian ethics must result in personal and social transformation, and also new perspectives on leadership.

Christians are called to be salt and light in this world (Matthew 5:13-16). Christians ought to bring a different taste into society. They should be visible within the society, as the German Protestant theologian and martyr Dietrich Bonhoeffer (1906-1945) puts it:

> The member of the Body of Christ has been delivered from the world and called out of it. **He must give the world a visible proof of his calling,** not only by sharing in the church's worship and discipline, but also through the new fellowship of brotherly living" (1959:258). [my emphasis]

Christians are responsible to have an impact in society. Bonhoeffer continues:

> Let the Christian remain in the world, not because of the good gifts of creation, nor because of his responsibility for the course of the world, but for the sake of the Body of the incarnate Christ and for the sake of the Church. Let him remain in the world to engage in frontal assault on it, and let him live the life of his secular calling in order to show himself as a stranger in this world all the more (1959:264).

Christians are called to make a difference in this world. They have a responsibility to challenge the values and norms of society. Christian leaders are called to apply values and norms that are possibly contrary to the culture.

What follows below is a discussion of biblical norms, values and virtues, the vision of kingdom leadership, and the use of power, which will be used as criteria to assess Western and Tanzanian leadership styles in chapters three, four, and five.

1.2.1 Leadership and Christian Norms and Values

Leaders act and make decisions based on norms and values. These norms and values are reflected in a leader's behaviour and conduct. They also have consequences and impact on other people. So the questions are: What constitutes Christian leadership? What makes a good leader? What are the relevant Christian norms and values, or, is there a right way to lead, given cultural differences? A number of values are mentioned in the Bible such as love, justice, mercy, faithfulness, humility, hope, which are expressed in the virtues of honesty, joy, peace, patience, kindness, gentleness, goodness, self-control, compassion, forgiveness, godliness, endurance and sobriety (Proverbs 11:1; Micah 6:8; Galatians 5:22; Colossians 3:12-15; 1 Timothy 3:2-7). For the purpose of this study, I will focus on *love, justice, mercy, faithfulness* and *humility,* as these norms and values seem to be core to leadership and partnership. Love is the centre of Christianity and thus must be the centre of our relationships and leadership. Justice, mercy, faithfulness and humility are the primary forms and expressions of love (Matthew 23:23; John 13). If leaders do not lead in justice, they oppress people. A leader who exercises justice is a fair person. Leaders without mercy have difficulties in forgiving others. Merciful leaders can forgive others who do not live up to their expectations, make mistakes or fail. Leaders must be committed to God, to the people and to the task. Thus, faithfulness is required of a leader. One of the leader's responsibilities is to enable and empower others. Leaders with humility are willing to humble themselves, serve others and make them successful. These values of love, justice, mercy, faithfulness and humility are all represented in the life and ministry of Jesus as a leader and reflect the norm of servant leadership. Therefore, they are essential for contemporary Christian leaders at any time and anywhere. These core values reflect God's character and so are trans-cultural. They also demonstrate our attitude toward God, toward others and toward self, which is also expressed in the double commandment in Matthew 22:37-39:

> 'Love the Lord your God with all your heart, with all your soul, and with all your mind.' This is the greatest and the most important commandment. The second most important commandment is like it: 'Love your neighbour as you love yourself.'

Love is central to Christian ethics, leadership and partnership. God is a God of love. He desires a loving relationship between him and people and among people. First and foremost Christian leaders must have a loving relationship with God. God desires to have that kind of reciprocal relationship with humankind (Exodus 20:6; Deuteronomy 6:5). As a result of this personal, intimate and loving relationship with God, he commands us to love one another. Jesus (John 13:34-35) instructed his disciples: "And now I give you a new commandment: love one another. As I have loved you, so you must love one another. If you have love for one another, then everyone will know that you are my disciples." Love is what Brown (1998:154) calls the "distinguishing characteristic" of Christians. So in Christian-ethical leadership love becomes one of the key criteria. Love must govern our behaviour and also our leadership styles. According to David Bennett (2005:11), a North American evangelical theologian, love for others, including other Christian leaders, is the primary mark of a Christ-like leader. This does not necessarily mean that leaders must consider love as more important than doing the right thing. Love is balanced by other norms and values such as justice, mercy and faithfulness. A loving Christian relationship can mean to point out wrong behaviour. A loving action "is characterized by listening and the sensitivity that is required to understand the other person's need. We have to put ourselves in the place of the other person in order to begin to discern what action we need to take" (Nthamburi 2003:112). Zablon Nthamburi, a Kenyan Protestant theologian, stresses the importance and meaning of Christian love:

> Within the Christian faith, love is not an optional injunction but an obligatory matter. Christian love does not offer an easy assurance that if you treat others nicely they in turn will reciprocate. But we are commanded to love. This means that we have some responsibility towards others and we share in the moral responsibility of our neighbour. Without putting emphasis on love, undue emphasis on equality can easily promote individualism and self-centredness. Love takes the first place among all other values (2003:113).

According to Bonhoeffer (1954:97-103), Christian love demands listening, active helpfulness, forbearing and forgiveness. These are important characteristics in leadership as well as partnership as people live and work in community.

It is interesting to note that even Joseph Fletcher, whose ethic is anti-absolutism and anti-deontological ethic, uses the norm of love to give direction to his situation ethics, which is teleological as it must lead to the result of love (Villa-Vicencio 1994:76-77).

Among other values mentioned above, love is the most important Christian value in all aspects of life that impacts peoples' ethical decisions. Especially in a cross-cultural situation, where certain behaviours may not always be understood immediately, a loving approach is most appropriate. Whereas Westerners may be sometimes perceived as not loving, Tanzanians have a strong desire for harmony, which often prevails over the moral decisions they make.

According to Jesus, justice, mercy and faithfulness are the primary faces of love (Matthew 23:23). Christian leaders have a responsibility to govern in *justice*. Justice recognizes the dignity of mankind. In the book of Amos, the importance of justice can be seen. The prophet calls the people of Israel to a life of justice:

> Make it your aim to do what is right, not what is evil, so that you may live. Then the Lord God Almighty really will be with you, as you claim he is. Hate what is evil, love what is right, and see that justice prevails in the courts. ... [L]et justice flow like a stream, and righteousness like a river that never goes dry (Amos 5:14-15a+24).

Leaders who are just and fair can count on the presence and the blessings of God. On the contrary, Amos points out the serious consequences of injustice such as darkness, gloom, death, destruction, disaster, and exile (Amos 5:18-6:14). Injustice leads to oppression and extortion as demonstrated in the life of Jehoiakim (Jeremiah 22:13+17). Justice results in dignity, liberty and freedom. Connor and McCormick distinguish between commutative, legal, distributive and social justice:

> Commutative justice deals with the fair exchange of goods and services between individuals, while distributive justice ensures that each person or group contributes and receives a fair (proportionate) share of the common good. Legal justice has to do with the individual's obligations to the larger society, while social justice looks to the establishment and maintenance of just and equitable systems and structures in the community. Social justice seeks to provide for the full and fair participation of all persons and groups in the governance of political, economic, cultural and social institutions, and aims at correcting any oppressive and alienating trends within the community (1998:66).

Social justice seems to be the key in reference to leadership. Social justice probably impacts commutative, legal and distributive justice.

Mercy is driven by love. God is a merciful father (2 Corinthians 1:3). God is merciful even when people are disobedient and sin (Nehemiah 9:17; Joel 2:13). Paul reminds us of God's mercy despite our sinful behaviour in a powerful way:

> For we ourselves were once foolish, disobedient, and wrong. We were slaves to passions and pleasures of all kinds. We spent our lives in malice and envy; others hated us and we hated them. But when the kindness and love of God our Saviour was revealed, he saved us. It was not because of any good deeds that we ourselves had done, **but because of his own mercy** that he saved us, through the Holy Spirit, who gives us new birth and new life by washing us. God poured out the Holy Spirit abundantly on us through Jesus Christ our Saviour, so that by his grace we might be put right with God and come into possession of the eternal life we hope for (Titus 3:3-7). [my emphasis]

God has shown mercy to us even though we did not deserve it. His mercy is so great that human beings can enter into a personal relationship with him and thus have eternal life. Jones (1994:92) points out, "The full revelation of God's mercy brings with it the full responsibility to practise mercy, to glorify God by living lives that reflect his mercy". God expects us to be merciful as he is (Luke 6:36). Christian leaders must be merciful in their leadership as they work with subordinates. Leaders who are merciful are compassionate. They express their solidarity with the oppressed. They see and understand the needs of others. They react to these needs in a selfless and sacrificial manner. They are willing to invest their time, energy and life for the sake of others. A merciful leader will also be shown mercy (Matthew 5:7).

God revealed himself to Moses as a *faithful* God who keeps his covenant (Deuteronomy 7:6-10). God demonstrates his love by being faithful to his promises. He makes and keeps his commitments (2 Samuel 7:15). Jesus is the fulfilment of God's promises as Paul puts it:

> As surely as God speaks the truth, my promise to you was not a "Yes" and a "No". For Jesus Christ, the Son of God, who was preached among you by Silas, Timothy, and myself, is not one who is "Yes" and "No".

On the contrary, he is God's "Yes"; **for it is he who is the "Yes" to all God's promises** (2 Corinthians 1:18-20a). [my emphasis]

God is faithful even in difficult times (1 Corinthians 10:13). Because God is faithful he is trustworthy. If Christians sin and confess it, he is still faithful and just and will forgive us our sins (1 John 1:9). God's faithfulness is a powerful motivation for Christian leaders also to be faithful and "practise the same in their own relationships and responsibilities" (Jones 1994:94). Servant leaders are expected to submit and be faithful to God (1 Corinthians 4:2). Faithful leaders are honest and committed to people and the task. Christian leaders are expected to handle worldly wealth, such as money and property, faithfully (Luke 16:10-12). They speak the truth and can be trusted. Leaders have been given a trust from God. He expects them to be faithful servants (Matthew 25:14-30).

Humility is an expression of serving others in love. Based on Benedict, Norvene Vest (2000:89), a Catholic theologian from the USA, defines humility as follows: "Humility is facing the truth about our human condition, accepting our limitations, and cheerfully depending on God. ... To look death and limitation in the face and *still* aspire to the greatness for which we are destined in Christ: this is humility" [his emphasis]. In other words, humility is recognizing God's strength in our own weaknesses (2 Corinthians 12:9). If Christian leaders are serious in imitating Jesus, they must be humble. Christians are asked to follow the example of Jesus and "wash one another's feet" (John 13:1-20). No matter whether rich or poor, educated or uneducated, man or woman, old or young, of high or low position, Western or Tanzanian, leader or follower, everybody must be humble, as Peter (1 Peter 5:5-6) writes: "And **all** of you must put on the apron of humility, to serve one another; for the scripture says, 'God resists the proud, but shows favour to the humble.' Humble yourselves, then, under God's mighty hand, so that he will lift you up in his own good time" [my emphasis]. Humble leaders consider others better than themselves, are selfless and look out for another's interest (Philippians 2:3-4). The whole issue of humility and servanthood is discussed below in more detail in the section on leadership and the vision of the kingdom of God.

These Christian norms and values, discussed above and derived from the Scriptures, are not only essential for good leadership, but also build the foundation for healthy and efficient collaboration among partners. When leaders act with a loving attitude, are fair, forgiving, committed to the relationship, and humble, it will affect how they communicate and work together with others. A loving leader is patient, kind, gentle and endures even if things do not go as expected. A just leader is fair and judges on a neutral basis without giving preference to anybody. A merciful leader is ready to forgive others for their mistakes. A faithful leader is godly, abiding in God, compassionate and committed to the other even in times when s/he is disappointed by the other. A humble leader considers the other's interest rather than her/his own and is willing to submit. These virtues enhance the ability of working together tremendously and make a huge difference in any relationship. By way of contrast, according to Paul, an unloving leader is jealous, conceited, proud, ill-mannered, selfish, irritable, keeps a record of wrongs, and gives up (1 Corinthians 13:4-7).

The Christian values of love, justice, mercy, faithfulness and humility are deontological in nature. However, they may be interpreted, understood and applied in different ways in the Western and Tanzanian contexts. As discussed below in the section on Christian leadership, the gospel and culture, I believe it is the task of contextual theology to identify in community, under the guidance of the Holy Spirit, and through dialogue the biblical norms and values which are trans-cultural and which are applied differently according to each cultural context. Christians from both groups learn more about Christian leadership in dialogue than separately.

1.2.2 Leadership and the Vision of the Kingdom of God

In Christian ethics, Jesus is the centre. He is **the** example modelling true Christian leadership. To become a Christian leader is to become like Jesus. With his life, Jesus provides a vision of the kingdom of God. He practises kingdom ethics and kingdom leadership. Christian leaders ought to become more like Jesus. It is God's desire to see people's lives "transformed, individually and collectively, by the Word of God as it penetrates deeply into the life of individuals and communities" (Scripture Impact Initiative 2004:2). Kingdom ethics calls for a life style that reflects God's character and righteousness and practices that are intrinsically good (Jones 1994:77). As leaders are transformed and become more Christ-like they will have an impact on their society. Kingdom ethics is the biblical teaching of the coming kingdom of God.[13] Kingdom ethics is what Bonhoeffer (in Kelly & Nelson 2003) calls "Christ-centred spirituality". It "provides the ethicist with a vision or goal that can guide ethical behaviour in the present" (Kretzschmar 1993:97). This vision is guided also by norms such as "love your neighbour" and values such as love, justice, mercy, faithfulness, humility and hope. So kingdom ethics offers a picture of what Christian leadership looks like, which is key to this research. According to Cook (in Kretzschmar 1993:97), "the incarnate life of Jesus is a living example of this kingdom ethic". Jesus embodied the kingdom values that he preached (Ngara 2004:15). Jesus lived a life of dissent and opposition (Whitehead & Whitehead 2000:93). He was willing to preach and act against the established religious practice of his times. He acted on the basis of love, mercy and humility in ways that contradicted norms and values of the society. Kingdom ethics liberates men and women from sinful behaviour. Lingenfelter points out:

> The gospel brings a contradictory message to the peoples of the world, challenging their social order and beliefs. ... The Scriptures show clearly that Jesus challenged the accepted society and worldview. Although he was living as a Jew in the Jewish world, he shattered that

---

[13] I am assuming here that the kingdom of God has already been inaugurated in the ministry of Jesus, but not yet fully consummated.

world with his preaching and teaching. His good news brought conflict and change (1998:17).

It is the Church's responsibility to model this kind of leadership as Ngara argues:

> For the Church to play its role effectively in the promotion of good leadership in society, it must be able to demonstrate within its own ranks a vibrant culture of good leadership, **a culture of leadership which reflects and projects the qualities and leadership style that Jesus stood for** (2004:10). [my emphasis]

Even though Christian leaders have been transformed into the image of Christ there seems to be a huge gap between reality and destiny. However, as Christian leaders grow and mature in their faith this gap becomes smaller and smaller. This is a life-long journey. Thus, Christian-ethical leadership is a growth process.

The analysis of this research shows how big the gap is and which aspects of leadership in the West and in Tanzania may be fully, partly or not at all compatible with the gospel. Kingdom ethics encourages and challenges Christian leaders to question certain behaviour and apply kingdom principles cross-culturally. That way traditional and cultural beliefs may be overturned and provoke social and religious conflict and dissent and may finally result in the transformation of individuals and communities. This can be a risky process within partnerships because it can also lead to breaking relationships.

For the purpose of this study it is essential to have a sound biblical understanding of leadership and power as it impacts other areas significantly like how leaders build relationships, make decisions, conduct meetings, and resolve conflicts. Additionally, sociological insights are needed to understand relationship and power because the Bible provides insights into leadership and power, but does not fully explain what leadership or power mean.

To understand what kingdom leadership means, it is essential to look at the life, teaching, and ministry of Jesus and the way he trained his disciples. Jesus represents kingdom leadership as *servanthood* and *stewardship,* as his focus is on attitudes and character formation. The ultimate purpose of Jesus' life is summarised in his servanthood and stewardship. He came to serve not to be served (Matthew 20:28). At the same time he fulfilled God's purpose for his life. Expressed in the life of Jesus, servanthood and stewardship demonstrate how Christian leaders ought to practise power, love, justice, mercy, faithfulness and humility.

With reference to the first of these, *servanthood*, a number of principles of how Jesus led can be observed in the gospels (Wilkes 1998:11-12):

(1) Jesus humbled himself and allowed God to exalt him.

(2) Jesus followed his Father's will rather than sought a position.

(3) Jesus took the risk and found greatness in serving others.

(4) Jesus practised relational leadership.

(5) Jesus shared responsibility and authority with those called to lead.

The attitude of *humility* is emphasised in a number of accounts, such as Jesus washing the disciple's feet (John 13:1-17), the discussion about who is the greatest (Mark 9:33-37; Matthew 18:1-5; 23:11-12; Luke 22:24-30), and the dispute about the requested positions of honour for James and John (Matthew 20:20-28). In all of these accounts, Jesus contrasted the practices of society with his new community of disciples. Jesus' teaching and his example were countercultural to the norms and values of his time. Jesus described himself as "gentle and humble in spirit" (Matthew 11:29). He also challenged the disciples to humble themselves like a child (Matthew 18:1-4). The Dutch Catholic theologian, Henri Nouwen (1932-1996), who lived a good part of his life in the USA, Latin America and Canada, drew the following conclusion for kingdom leadership:

> The way of the Christian leader is not the way of upward mobility in which our world has invested so much, but **the way of downward mobility ending on the cross**. This might sound morbid and masochistic, but for those who have heard the voice of the first love and said "yes" to it, the downward-moving way of Jesus is the way to the joy and the peace of God, a joy and peace that is not of this world. ... **It is not a leadership of power and control, but a leadership of powerlessness and humility in which the suffering servant of God, Jesus Christ, is made manifest** (1989:62-63). [my emphasis]

This does not mean that Jesus had no power and authority, but he was willing to give it up. Serving in humility means being willing to suffer and die as Jesus did rather than seeking a position of power and control (Matthew 20:28).

Jesus was willing to submit in humility and *to follow God's will rather than seek a position*. Jesus had an intimate relationship with his father. He spent extensive time in prayer seeking God's will (Mark 1:35-39). Jesus made his decisions prayerfully (Luke 6:12-16). In solitude he received directions for what lay ahead. Intimacy with God must be the primary focus of a leader's life. Bennett (2005:11) points out, "When leaders are genuinely listening to God, and keeping in step with the Spirit of God, they will naturally find themselves in tune with one another as well". Jesus did not want to suffer and die on the cross but he was willing to be obedient to the will of God (Matthew 26:39+42). He was not interested in a position. Two of the disciples, James and John, had other desires (Mark 10:35-45). They sought a position of honour. But the servant image used by Jesus is an expression of humility, and the willing withdrawal from the competition for status and power (Bennett 1993:28). Christ-like leaders must not intentionally seek status and power.

Jesus was able to take the risk and *serve others* because he was secure in himself and in God (John 13:3). The image of the servant is the most commonly used by Jesus. He used a number of words to express the concept, but most frequently διακονος (*diakonos*) and δουλος (*doulos*). These two words are used with a different emphasis, as Bennett observes:

> [W]hen the emphasis is on the task, the responsibility, on obeying orders and being under authority, the word used is *doulos*. But when the

emphasis is on the rendering of personal service, or when the stress is on the attitudes of humility and love which should inspire the service, then the word more likely used is *diakonos* (1993:22).

Whereas δουλος (*doulos*) stresses behaviour, the focus of διακονος (*diakonos*) is on character. Using διακονος (*diakonos*) Jesus stressed that "the attitude underlying every action was to be that of the humble servant" (:24). Jesus knew that to become a leader it is essential to be able to follow and serve others. Therefore, his emphasis in building his team was on attitudes and character versus status and personality. Jesus came to serve even though others wanted him to be a political Messiah (Wilkes 1998:160-161). However, he rejected peoples' expectations of their mental leadership model.

Jesus practised *relational* leadership, building a team of twelve disciples to carry out his vision and mission. Jesus called the disciples into an intimate personal relationship with him. However, Jesus was not only people-oriented but also task-oriented. In Mark 8:31-33, where Jesus spoke about his suffering and death, Jesus rebuked Peter. In that situation Jesus paid more attention to his task of going to and dying on the cross than to his relationship to Peter. It is interesting to note that Gene Wilkes, a Protestant theologian from the USA, does not list "rebuking his disciples" as being part of servant leadership. Maybe it does not fit into Wilkes picture of a good leader.

It is interesting to note that Jesus did not teach his disciples a lot about leadership but much more about 'followership'. Leadership and followership are closely interconnected. This is reflected in the various terms and images he used for his disciples, including brother or sister (*adelphos, adelphe*), apostle (*apostolos*), servant (*diakonos, doulos, hyperetes, oiketes, therapeia*), worker (*ergates*), son or child (*hyios, paidion, teknion, teknon*), disciple (*mathetes*), manager (*oikonomos*), friend (*philos*), shepherd (*poimen*) and sheep (*probaton*) (Bennett 1993:17-54). When Jesus used these terms, he put the stress on relationships.

The term *brother* is used most frequently by Jesus, especially in his teaching in the Sermon on the Mount regarding anger and reconciliation (Matthew 5:21-24), love for enemies (Matthew 5:43-48), and judging others (Matthew 7:1-5). In building a team, Jesus knew about the challenges of interpersonal relationships and the danger of competition. The word "brother" demonstrates a close connectedness of an egalitarian relationship (Bennett 1993:18). Jesus makes it plain that the disciples are all on the same level and submit to one master (Matthew 23:8). Later on, after his resurrection, he closed this gap by calling his disciples "brothers" (Matthew 28:10; John 20:17). This indicates that even though brothers are fundamentally peers, there can still be someone who exercises authority within their community as an elder, deacon, apostle or manager (Bennett 1993:18).

The word *son* or *child* is used by Jesus to illustrate that children of God share and imitate his character (Matthew 5:9+45-48; Luke 6:35-36), and have a sincere and simple faith (Luke 18:17).

In Luke 12 and John, 15 Jesus referred to the disciples as his *friends*. Friend is a term of affection and love, which denotes companionship, closeness and camaraderie (Bennett 1993:46). In John 15, Jesus expressed that true friendship means obeying his commands as an expression of love. Hence, Christian leaders must be obedient to God.

The qualifications of a disciple as team member are evidenced in Luke 14, John 8, 13 and 15. Jesus defined the qualifications of being a *disciple* as follows: a disciple must surrender unconditionally to him, be obedient, be willing to part with every material possession, undergo a transformation of character, love self-sacrificially, produce visible products and have a beneficial impact upon others (:38-39).

Jesus *shared responsibility and authority* with his disciples. Jesus was sent by God (Matthew 15:24; John 5:36) and the disciples were sent by Jesus (Matthew 10:5; John 17:18). Jesus appointed the twelve disciples as *apostles* (Mark 3:13-19; Luke 6:12-16). He also called them to preach and exercise authority (Mark 6:7). He empowered the disciples by pairing responsibility with authority (Matthew 28:18-20; Acts 1:8). Even though Jesus shared his authority with the disciples, they were still subordinate to Jesus (John 13:14-16). Bennett (1993:21) puts it like this: "Jesus reminds them that no matter how much authority the 'apostle' may have, he remains one who has been sent by another." Christian leaders receive their responsibility and authority from Jesus. They are also called to share their responsibility and authority and empower others.

Stewardship is based on servanthood because it exercises authority and responsibility with an attitude of humility. It is interesting to note that Jesus used the term *manager* only once to describe his followers (:43). The Greek word οικονομος (*oikonomos*) can also be translated as "steward" (Whitehead & Whitehead 2000:104). The parable of the faithful manager or steward (Luke 12:41-48) shows that a manager is one who holds a position of being in charge of people as well as possessions. The Whiteheads point out three characteristics of a steward:

> First, a steward acts as a servant rather than an owner or master. Second, the steward's chief strength is a seasoned reliability: an inner authority, developed on the job, on which both the steward and the community can depend. Third, the steward operates in a context of absence, making responsible decisions while the owner is away (2000:111).

It is important to note that in this parable of the faithful manager the manager is referred to as "servant". As s/he occupies a position of authority, at the same time s/he remains under authority. A steward basically re-distributes power. It can be argued, "The 'manager' (*oikonomos*) fulfils a particular function within the larger category of 'servant' (*doulos*)" (Bennett 1993:44). The Whiteheads observe:

> In the New Testament a steward is an authoritative servant. "Steward" is a translation of the Greek word *oikonomos*: the one who sees to the law (*nomos*) of the household (*oikos*). The steward oversees the domestic order: the rhythms, rules, and agreements by which a household or community thrives. In the New Testament and elsewhere, stewardship describes a leadership position reserved for experienced, capable per-

sons. Stewards exercise considerable authority, but not in their own name. Stewardship links power with service (of the community) and authority with dependence (on the Lord) (2000:104).

Bennett (1993:31) rightly observes "the image of '*worker*' is associated with a task to be done with submission and accountability to the Lord's authority, and with prospect of ultimate reward" [my emphasis]. When Jesus spoke about the large harvest and the need for workers he stressed the task, as well as the link of accountability between the workers and the Lord of the harvest (Matthew 9:37-38).

According to Wilkes (1998:20), Jesus led with a vision of the kingdom (Mark 1:14) and he served with a mission as the Messiah (Luke 4:16-20). Jesus was a *servant* who *leads* and at the same time he was a *leader* who *serves*.

Kingdom leadership is expressed in servanthood and stewardship. Robert Dale, a Baptist theologian from the USA, has produced this useful summary of kingdom leadership:

> Servants [Stewards] lead out of relationships, not by coercion;
> Servants [Stewards] lead by support, not by control;
> Servants [Stewards] lead by developing others, not by doing all the ministry themselves;
> Servants [Stewards] guide people, not drive them;
> Servants [Stewards] lead from love, not domination;
> Servants [Stewards] seek growth, not position (1986:34).

Thus, I would argue kingdom leadership is more than just servanthood. It is *stewardship*. Even though Dale does not mention that a steward also suffers, stewardship represents the idea of a leader who exercises authority with a serving attitude. Servanthood and stewardship are virtuous expressions of love and humility. Western and Tanzanian leadership behaviour must be measured in chapter five against this kingdom leadership exercised by Jesus.

1.2.3 Leadership and Power

Leadership and power are closely connected. The following provides a biblical ethical perspective of power as it relates to kingdom ethics. Hence, the focus is on how Jesus receives and uses power. Power plays a significant role especially in the area of leadership. The way power is exercised and perceived affects relationships, how decisions are made, meetings conducted, conflicts resolved, and organisations shaped.

The New Testament uses a number of different words in reference to power: δυναμις (*dynamis*), εξουσια (*exousia*), and θρονος (*thronos*) (Betz in Coenen, Beyreuther & Bietenhard 1971:922-935; Kretzschmar 1995:198). δυναμις (*dynamis*) is the word most often used. It means ability, power, and might. It may be exercised in a number of spheres including the physical, spiritual, political, or military (Luke 9:1; Ephesians 1:21; Romans 8:38). εξουσια (*exousia*) is mainly used in reference to people who hold positions of power and exercise authority (Mark 1:22; Luke 12:11; Romans 13:1-5). θρονος (*thronos*) refers to the physical area from which power is exercised (Matthew 5:34; 19:28; Revelation 5:6).

In the accounts mentioned above, it becomes clear that power and authority is given by God to be exercised on his behalf. Therefore, power is subject to the authority and will of God. Power and authority derive from God. God is the source of power.

The following discussion on power is based on the Whiteheads (2000:115-127; 2003:149-162) and an article by Kretzschmar (2002:51-53). Their structure and arguments have been used with reference to the way Jesus used power.

Jesus is **the** exemplar for the proper use of power. The personal power represented in the life and ministry of Jesus can wear at least five faces:

FACES OF PERSONAL POWER		
MODE	EXPERIENCED AS	NEEDED IN
Power on	initiative and influence	adult competence
Power over	coordination and control	organizational leadership
Power against	competition and conflict	assertion and negotiation
Power for	service and nurturance	parenthood and ministry
Power with	mutuality and collaboration	interdependence and dependability

Figure 1.1 (Whitehead & Whitehead 2003:151)

This chart emphasises that there are different kinds of power. These different types of power are reflected in the life and ministry of Jesus.

Jesus received his power from God (Matthew 3:16). This power gave him a sense of autonomy and adequacy. Jesus could not have relinquished power (Philippians 2:1-11), if he had not first received and exercised personal power (Kretzschmar 2002:52). Jesus knew where his power came from. He knew where he had come from and where he was returning to (John 13:3). Thus, Jesus had *power on* or *in* himself. He had power over his life and within himself (John 10:17-18). Because God gave him power he was able to give it up again. By exercising his power Jesus had an impact on people's lives. Christian leaders receive spiritual authority not by position but from God.

Jesus had *power over* the disciples, which is implied in the act of giving them a different name (John 1:42; Mark 3:17) (Bennett 1993:20). Jesus did not give many instructions about how to structure and organise the church. But he passed his power on to his disciples (Matthew 28:18-20; John 20:21; Acts 1:8). Jesus promised the disciples the Holy Spirit to guide them according to God's will. Christian leaders exercise power over others.

Jesus exercised his *power against* the Pharisees, which created conflict and dissent (Matthew 12:1-8; 16:1-4; 23). He confronted the evil spirits (Luke 4:31-37). Jesus negotiated with the wife of Zebedee and the other ten disciples

(Matthew 20:20-28). Jesus confronted his disciples when he asked them to pray together with him in Gethsemane (Mark 14:32-42). He always told the truth (John 8:40+45; 14:6). Sometimes it is necessary and appropriate for a Christian leader to confront and exercise power against others to further God's kingdom. This can create conflict. It is important to deal with conflict in an appropriate and biblical manner. When Jesus confronted people, for instance when he chased away the sellers in the temple (Matthew 21:12-13), he was emotional and even angry. Hence, there is a place to show "holy anger". However, there is a fine line between "holy" and "sinful" anger. Jesus acted with godly authority. Human anger without godly authority is sinful because it "does not achieve God's righteous purpose" (James 1:20). Generally, Christians ought to be "slow to become angry" (James 1:19). God's ultimate purpose is reconciliation with him and others. Jesus promoted both approaches of conflict resolution individually (Matthew 18:15) and as a group (Matthew 18:16-17). The key principle is that no matter which approach is used the conflict should not escalate and people are reconciled again with each other. If this is not possible, Jesus went even so far as potentially terminating the relationship.

Jesus was given *power for* others. He exercised this power for his nurturing, serving and caring ministry. He listened, counselled, healed, forgave sin, encouraged and enabled others (Matthew 5-7; 9:1-8; Luke 7:36-50; 13:10-17). His power was revealed in many signs and wonders (Matthew 14:13-36; Acts 2:22). Jesus came to "proclaim good news to the poor, set captives free, recover the sight of the blind, set at liberty those who are oppressed, [and] proclaim 'the year of the Lord's favour' [Luke 4:16-21]" (Linthicum 2003:58). This was Jesus' mission. Jesus came to transform society. His power for others is an expression of his self-sacrificing love. The Whiteheads (2003:88) observe: "Power, he [Jesus] sought to persuade them [the disciples], comes as a gift from God that we are to develop and then give away in care for others." Christian leaders must therefore use their power to care for others.

Jesus shared his *power with* the disciples (Luke 9:1; Matthew 28:18-20; John 20:21; Acts 1:8). Thus, power is not a possession but a social transaction, a way of relating (Whitehead & Whitehead 2003:150-151). In the New Testament, the Whiteheads observe,

> Power is not a commodity possessed by a few leaders but the dynamic interaction – for better or for worse – that moves through a group of people. ... Through the New Testament we see God's power moving through Jesus to arouse hope, heal illness, and confront destructive patterns of domination (2000:17).

Jesus enabled and empowered his disciples. He gave them power over evil spirits, sickness, the dead, demons, snakes, scorpions and the Enemy (Matthew 10:1-8; Luke 10:19-21). Power is a gift that Jesus shared in his interactions with the disciples. Christian leaders must empower others. Jesus exercised his personal power *within* and shared it *with* the community. Over the years the relationship between Jesus and the disciples had grown to a stage of true collaboration and interdependence, in which he did not call them servants anymore but friends (John 15:1-17). This interdependence is reflected in accountability and obedience (John 5:19-29).

This understanding of how Jesus exercised power has significant consequences and is key to Christian-ethical leadership. When authority is misunderstood as a private possession, authority becomes unaccountable, a special status, and self-serving (Whitehead & Whitehead 2003:169). In contrast, leaders with a sound biblical understanding of power are accountable to God and view themselves as stewards and servants of God for others. When this personal and relational power demonstrated by Jesus is properly understood and implemented, it will enable Christians to grow in four phases: (1) receive power and become mature; (2) achieve personal autonomy and celebrate self-reliance; (3) express power in the form of ideas, making demands on others, assuming responsibility, and taking charge; and (4) share power and enjoy mutual influence and empowerment (Whitehead & Whitehead 2000:115-127). This growth process is part of a leader's character formation. Depending on how much leaders have already grown in these areas, it will have a major impact on how they deal with power, make decisions, contribute in meetings, handle conflict, and the way in which they collaborate with others. How leaders grow and mature and which character traits are important for a leader are discussed in the next section.

1.2.4 Leadership and Christian Virtues

Christian ethics is also about *character* (Brown 1998:137-147). When virtues are practised they form a person's moral character. A person's moral character is the foundation for Christian-ethical leadership. For Christians character formation takes place individually, in community, and through engaging with the Scriptures. As this study examines leadership issues in a Christian-ethical perspective, *virtue ethics* becomes essential. Virtue ethics is the link between deontological criteria like right norms and values and teleological criteria like good goals and consequences. A good leader's actions are based on right norms and values like love, justice, mercy, faithfulness and humility. A leader with a moral character does what is right. S/he is concerned about good goals and consequences. A leader's moral motives determine her/his goals.

Virtues can be defined as "those good moral habits, affections, attitudes and beliefs that lead to genuine human fulfilment, even perfection, on both personal and social levels" (Connors & McCormick 1998:25) [their emphasis]. Virtues are not only good actions, but they also include the attitudes, affections, and beliefs from which actions flow. Thus, virtues are norms and values lived out. William Frankena (1973:64), a philosopher and ethicist from the USA, defines virtue as "a disposition, habit, quality, or trait of the person or soul, which an individual either has or seeks to have". Virtue ethics not only addresses the question of what should be done but also why and how. Virtue ethics "goes deeper than merely responding to a given situation and deciding what to do about it: it asks questions about **what kind of person we want to be, or to become,** and **what attitudes we ought to have to life"**

(Brown 1998:137) [his emphasis]. It looks at a deeper level beneath the surface at the motives and intentions of a person, which are based on the norms and values one follows (Connors & McCormick 1998:48).

During the course of history a number of virtues have been listed. Based on the Christian theologian Thomas Aquinas (in Frankena 1973:64), traditionally Christianity has seven cardinal virtues. Faith, hope and love are the theological virtues. Prudence, fortitude, temperance, and justice are called the human virtues. In the Bible, we find Christian virtues such as honesty, compassion, kindness, humility, gentleness, patience, tolerance, forgiveness, joy, peace, kindness, goodness, faithfulness, self-control, knowledge, endurance, godliness, brotherly affection, hospitality, and generosity (Colossians 3:12-15; Galatians 5:22; 2 Peter 1:5-7). Other virtues mentioned by the apostle Paul are "faith, hope, and love; and the greatest of these is love" (1 Corinthians 13:13). With reference to the Christian values stressed above, love, justice, mercy, faithfulness and humility, the Christian virtues stressed in this study on leadership are: being loving, just, merciful, faithful and humble. Other virtues mentioned above such as patience, self-control, knowledge and endurance are also important leadership virtues. However, because of the limitations and constraints of this research, the focus is on the five virtues of being loving, just, merciful, faithful and humble. These virtues are core to leadership and also lead towards better partnerships. They are an expression of a leader's norms and values. These virtues also impact the way people live and work together in community. However, these individual virtues may be relative to different cultural and societal contexts.

1.2.4.1 Leadership and Character

Character and personality play a significant role in leadership. A North American Protestant leadership expert Robert Clinton (1996) is deeply convinced that a good character is **the** key to good leadership. Laurenti Magesa (2002:66), a Tanzanian Catholic theologian and ethicist supports this wholeheartedly: "Personal character is an indispensable element of good leadership." North American management consultant Stephen Covey (1989; 1991) also stresses the importance of character and leadership.

Character can be defined as "the moral being of a person or group as that is forged into a distinctive constellation" (Birch & Rasmussen 1989:74). Connors and McCormick (1998:18) define character as "*the core, unique, self-chosen and integral moral identity of a person*" [their emphasis]. Character has to do with basic principles and values, which people learn and integrate into their basic character (Covey 1989:18). According to Birch and Rasmussen (1989:190), "Character includes our basic moral perception – how we see and understand things – as well as our fundamental dispositions, intentions, and motives". Character is a person's mind and heart.

The aim of character ethics is to move towards what Covey (1989:32-35) calls a "principle-centred" paradigm based on norms and values. He (:35) defines principles as "guidelines for human conduct that are proven to have enduring, permanent value". According to Covey (1991:95-96), principles are not values but territories. Values are maps, which describe or represent the territory. When a leader's personality or "map" matches with her/his character or "territory" s/he is a person of integrity. This indicates there is a close connection between values and virtues. A leader's values are expressed in virtues. Virtues in turn are reflected in her/his behaviour. The behaviour of a person of integrity is consistent with her/his character. This person lives what s/he believes. Ngara (2004:43) describes a leader of integrity as somebody who is "guided by a code of ethical conduct and must demonstrate a high degree of consistency between the story he or she tells and his or her behaviour". The virtue of life-style consistency supports the building of trust, which girds a trusting relationship. A leader of integrity and honesty is trustworthy. Demonstrating "good living and life-style" are most likely culturally defined in different ways. However, no matter where we are in the world, most people watch our **actions** much more closely than our **words**. There is an old saying: "Actions speak louder than words", or "Walk the talk". Whitehead and Whitehead (2000:80-83) describe an authentic religious leader as a genuine person who adopts a non-defensive leadership style and is willing to exercise spiritual leadership. A genuine leader is available to the people and spiritual (:81). Non-defensive leaders are comfortable with themselves (:82). They do not need to cover up their weaknesses and present a different image of who they are. Christian leaders are recognized as spiritual leaders when they help people find meaning in their own lives (:82).

A consistent life-style grows out of a person's spiritual maturity. An important factor for Christians is the level of *spiritual maturity*, which is the core of a consistent life-style and a key aspect of a Christian leader's character (Ngara 2004:17). Kretzschmar (2001:285) defines Christian spirituality as "the actual experience of a believer, and communities of believers, of God and a willingness to deliberately deepen and give expression to this ongoing interaction between the believer and God in daily life". Kretzschmar (:285) argues that spirituality becomes the source of our ethical norms and values because there is no conflict between God's will and God's character. Spiritual maturity certainly has a great impact on people's ethical norms and values. However, spirituality is not the only source of our ethical norms and values. I would argue that people's ethical norms and values are not only influenced by their spirituality but also by other elements like the social environment, personal history and culture. In spiritual formation, one's likeness to Christ grows as one interacts with one's environment and one's character and actions become more Christ-like.

Whereas virtues are character traits, *personality* is an expression of how someone functions and relates to others (Frankena 1973:63). People can be shy or warm, introvert or extrovert, polite or harsh. Personality has to do with a person's public image, attitudes, behaviour, skills and techniques, which can be observed in human interaction (Covey 1989:19). A leader's character is expressed in her/his personality. Thus, it is essential for a good leader to continually grow and to become more mature in her/his character and also spiritually. The development of a leader's character leads to the transformation of her/his personality. For instance, an introvert remains an introvert, but can develop the extrovert part of her/his personality and express his/her faith in different ways like up front leadership or quiet, behind the scenes leadership.

Leaders' character and personality affect their leadership styles and how they collaborate. Thus, ongoing character formation is essential in Christian leadership.

1.2.4.2 Christian Leadership and Character Formation

Character formation is core to Christian leadership. At the same time the formation of a godly character is one of the biggest challenges for a Christian leader (Clinton 1996:57). McDonald stresses the importance of character formation:

> Personal growth presupposes moral development, which is inseparable from growth in moral awareness and sensitivity towards others. The agent is seen to be much more than a thinking machine: she or he is a person who feels, is capable of empathy, exercises will power and takes responsibilities for actions (1995:49).

Moral leaders are relational and take their authority and responsibility seriously. They are committed and practice courageous leadership. The question is: How does one become a good leader?

In his book *The Making of a Leader* Clinton (1988) focuses on the formation of a leader's character. He (1996:44-47) argues that a leader goes basically through six phases during his life: Foundation, internal growth, ministry maturity, life maturity, convergence, and resonance. God sets the foundation in a leader's life early on through a number of influences such as family, social environment and historical events. During the second phase of internal growth the focus is on the leader's spiritual growth. His/her personal relationship with God is fostered through prayer and Scripture meditation. During this time the leader is also challenged through difficulties. Through these challenges God prepares the leader for the future. As the leader becomes more mature in ministry s/he discovers her/his gifts and skills and how to use them effectively. During the phase of life maturity, the leader's sensitivity increases and s/he is better able to set the right priorities according to her/his gifts. The relationship with God becomes more important than success in ministry. During the time of convergence the leader takes on a role that fits her/his profile, gifts and experience well. Some leaders may have the privilege of experiencing the last phase of resonance. During this time they do not have any specific responsible leadership role. They receive recognition, and are able to enjoy, and celebrate the fruits of their life-long ministry. Even though they do not fill a specific role they still have some influence through the relationships, experience and wisdom they have built over the years. These six phases also indicate that leaders go through a life-long growth process.

The foundation of a leader's character is already set during early childhood and even before birth. However, this does not mean that certain character traits cannot be changed. Birch and Rasmussen (1989:190) define character formation as "the learning and internalizing of a way of life formative of our own moral identity. It is our moral 'being', the expression of who we are". To change leadership behaviour at its root, a person's character needs to be changed. It requires work on the basic paradigms (Covey 1989:31). It is essential to work on one's character to become a good leader.

Christian virtues must be acquired by teaching and practice as well as by grace, as Frankena (1973:63) points out. Christian virtues are a gift from God as God offers them to all (2 Peter 1:3-8). However, Christians also have a responsibility to ask God for these gifts and practise them as Peter (2 Peter 1:5-7) and Paul (Colossians 3:12b) point out: "[Y]ou must clothe yourselves with compassion, kindness, humility, gentleness, and patience." According to Aristotle (in Hauerwas 1981:122), character formation takes place by putting received virtues into practice and making them a habit to bring them to completion and fulfilment. He (in Birch & Rasmussen 1989:42) writes, "We become just by doing just acts, temperate by doing temperate acts, brave by doing brave acts." As Christian leaders practise moral virtues regularly they become a good habit and finally result in a good moral character. Birch and Rasmussen (1989:46) point out: "Virtues are 'internal', a matter of character, but they are moral goods internally related to *practices*; they are habits of behaviour nurtured in conduct ..." [their emphasis]. In order to make something a habit, according to Covey (1989:47), it requires "the intersection of *knowledge, skill*, and *desire*. Knowledge is the theoretical paradigm, the *what to do* and the *why*. Skill is the *how to do*. And desire is the motivation, the *want to do*. In order to make something a habit in our lives, we have to have all three" [his emphasis]. So leaders need to have the knowledge, skill, and desire to develop moral virtues as they impact their motives and actions. Connors and McCormick point out the significant impact habits have on character formation in contrast to individual acts:

> As the repeated actions or patterns that we develop over a long period of time, habits express and shape our character more deeply and permanently than isolated, individual acts. Habits are important because they are deeply ingrained into our personality, and so they tend to define how we can be expected to behave over the long haul. Habits are our particular and personal character traits (1998:42-43).

It takes time to make virtues a habit and consequently an integral part of one's character. But it is worth the effort. Developing habits is like a journey, which has a major impact on how a leader thinks, feels, and behaves.

Virtues are acquired and character is formed individually, in community, and through engagement with the Scriptures. Character formation takes place in a number of different ways including through the agency of one's family, childhood, school, peers, the impact of a person's social experience, and church community.

Hauerwas (1981:130) argues, a leader's Christian moral character is "not one of 'development' but of conversion". A Christian moral character is certainly a matter of conversion. I believe that Christian moral formation begins with conversion as a person acknowledges her/his sin, repents, and experiences God's forgiveness. The ongoing transformation of one's attitudes, values, and actions is then a result of conversion. This is a life long learning and growth process. It is important that leaders take responsibility for their actions and their character. Responsibility demonstrates accountability and integrity in a leader (Connors & McCormick 1998:30-31). As leaders take responsibility for their actions, personal growth takes place (Hauerwas 1981:147). Leaders acquire virtues by increasing their self-awareness through self-examination, self-reflection, and receiving constructive feedback from others. That way they learn more about their own personalities, strengths and weaknesses. As leaders reflect on their life stories, certain patterns may be discovered. Engaging with the Scriptures, solitude, silence and contemplative prayer provide helpful means in this process, which is not only character formation but also spiritual formation.

As already noted, character and spiritual formation are intimately connected. A Christian leader is called not only to grow morally but also spiritually. Spiritual maturity develops through spiritual formation. Spiritual formation and maturity are essential for the moral character formation of a Christian leader. It is the process of becoming more like Christ (2 Corinthians 3:18). Spiritual formation is a shared responsibility by God and the person being formed. It is initiated and sustained by God (Amirtham & Pryor 1989:163). The person's responsibility is a response to God's initiative. As Bonhoeffer (in Kelly & Nelson 2003:36) puts it, "It is not we who change ourselves into the image of God. Rather, it is the very image of God, the form of Christ, which seeks to take shape within us (Gal. 4:19)". Spiritual formation is fostered through solitude, personal and communal prayer, contemplation, discipleship, community, and life experience. Spiritual formation is a lifelong journey. Spiritual maturity is personal as well as collectivist. The Catholic theologians Loughlan Sofield and Carrol Juliano (1987:58-59) call for a spirituality that "1. integrates the total person; 2. nurtures through reflection; 3. contains a shared or communal dimension; 4. is balanced; 5. moves him or her to compassionate action".

Spiritual formation is influenced by a number of contributing factors such as culture, sexuality, physical health, age, personality, and psychological development (:59). Thus, when talking about spiritual formation it is important to look at the whole person.

Character and spiritual formation take place individually and collectively. The individual does not exist in isolation. People always live in social relationships. Character formation takes also place in community. Birch and Rasmussen (1989:67) argue "character formation and community dynamics go hand-in-hand". Connors and McCormick describe the dynamic and interdependent relationships among character, actions, and communities well:

> 1. The character of persons is affected by the communities they live in and the actions they perform; and that character in turn shapes future actions and impacts the evolving shape of the community.
>
> 2. The actions we choose flow from our character and are influenced by our community. At the same time these actions modify our character and impact the evolving shape of the community.

3. The communities we live in are a fruit of our past deeds and character, while their structures and systems in turn influence our developing character and the actions we may perform (1998:12).

Character is shaped by the community and, reciprocally, a person's character contributes to the kind of community of which s/he is part (Richardson 1994:93; Brown 1998:68; Kammer 1988:141). Consequently, leaders make ethical decisions that are informed by the community and also impact community. Birch and Rasmussen (1989:81) conclude: "*Character is the chief architect of our decisions and actions. ... Community is the chief architect of character*" [their emphasis]. Hauerwas (1981:116) goes so far as to say, "Our capacity to be virtuous depends on the existence of communities which have been formed by narratives faithful to the character of reality".

When people engage with the Scriptures, individually and collectively, virtues are developed and characters shaped and transformed. When people read, meditate and reflect on the Scriptures, a conversation between their own stories and the biblical stories takes place. Consequently, they are transformed by the Holy Spirit. The Bible, and particularly the New Testament, lays special emphasis on character formation (Mark 7:15; 2 Peter 1:3-11). These virtues equip Christian leaders in two ways. First, these virtues enable Christian leaders to live a godly life. Second, they make Christian leaders effective and productive in their families, communities, and ministries. That way they are a witness to the world.

Community life and the Scriptures thus play a significant part in character formation as Birch and Rasmussen (1989:45) point out: "To belong to a people of God means *the formation and transformation of personal moral identity in keeping with the faith identity of the community*" [their emphasis]. The character of a Christian leader is not only formed but also transformed by the grace and power of God. It is important to bear in mind, "Character is always in the process of formation, always growing and becoming: 'not that I have attained, but I press on...' (Phil. 3:12)" (McDonald 1995:62). Character formation is a lifelong work in progress.

Moral formation through the development of virtues results in moral character. Character and personality are essential to the way in which leaders function and how they make decisions. A leader "'with character' is someone with judgement to know what is right and courage to do what is good. 'Character', in other words, is the mark of those who are morally discerning and committed to acting on their convictions" (Birch & Rasmussen 1989:74). Leaders with moral character have moral conviction, commitment, and the courage to act. Christian leaders ought to be people who reflect Jesus, not just in what they do, but in the kind of people they are (Brown 1998:180). Virtue ethics provides a means to gain a better understanding of a leader's motives, attitudes, and character which affect her/his behaviour.

1.3 Christian Leadership, the Gospel and Culture

Christian leadership may be understood and applied differently in the West and in Tanzania. This has to do with the influence of culture and how the

Scripture is understood in different contexts. The challenge is to understand what it means to be a Christ-like leader appropriate to each cultural context (Bennett 2005:13-15). What does kingdom leadership look like in Tanzania and the West? How will Christ-like character be expressed? As mentioned above, in Christian ethics it is important to understand the context in which we live and work. Our worldview and culture shape our norms and values, on the basis of which we make decisions. If the contexts are understood well, it is possible to gain a good grasp of the ethical problems and challenges that arise from these contexts. As this study deals with cross-cultural leadership issues, it is essential to take the ethics of contextual theology into serious consideration. According to Stephen Bevans (2002:4), a North American Catholic theologian and missiologist, contextual theology "realizes that culture, history, contemporary thought forms, and so forth are to be considered, along with scripture and tradition, as valid sources for theological expression". Thus, doing theology contextually takes into account not only the Scripture and tradition as the faith experience of the past, but also the context, which is the present human experience expressed in culture, history, and contemporary thought forms (:4-5). Contextual theology recognizes the impact that tradition and culture have on the understanding of the gospel and one's Christian faith.

According to the author's personal faith, there are some non-negotiable biblical norms like "do not murder" and values such as love, justice, mercy, faithfulness and humility. However, I believe that biblical values "may need to be *applied* differently in different cultures" (Adeney 1995:20) [his emphasis]. Charles Kraft (1979), a North American evangelical anthropologist, has developed a model of how to do biblical theologising in a cross-cultural setting. He seeks appropriate ways of contextualising theology and applying biblical norms and values in a cross-cultural context.

In the past often theologising was done by applying a theological perspective to Scripture (:8). For a long time this was only done by Western theologians. The insights gained by these theologians were, in turn, transferred into another culture without necessarily considering that a Westerner might ask different theological questions than an African or give different answers to those questions. So Kraft attempts to do theology from a cross-cultural, anthropological perspective by asking questions instead of presenting solutions.

The way people understand and interpret the Bible is influenced and conditioned by their culture and worldview, as we have seen earlier in reference to Kammer's moralscape. Each person reads and interprets the Bible through her/his cultural glasses. So a person's Christian faith and biblical understanding are biased by her/his culture. The missionary's challenge is to apply biblical values in a cross-cultural situation. The challenge for the individual is to transfer biblical values, as s/he understands them, from her/his cultural perspective into another culture. To make it even more complicated a third culture, which is biblical culture, is added to the two already existing cultures. As Kraft (:9) points out "the Bible is a multicultural book, much of it directed to Hebrew audiences, while some of the latter portions were directed to audiences whose primary language was Greek". In a cross-cultural situation there are at least three different cultures in dialogue in an interactive, dynamic process, as shown in my figure 1.2 below.

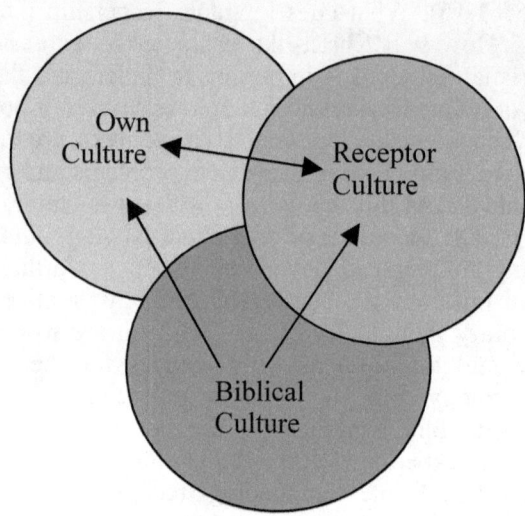

Figure 1.2

The person's own culture and the receptor culture are influenced by other cultures. Whereas the biblical culture, as an ancient culture, does not change: it potentially impacts other cultures. However, as a person's own culture is influenced by other cultures, her/his interpretation of the Scripture may change. In other words,

> A cross-cultural Christian is in dialogue with at least three different communities. First there is the community of faith, which spans the authors of Scripture, the exemplars of the church through history and the living members of the church in all cultures today. Finally there are the adopted culture and subcultures that the person has entered (Adeney 1995:63).

Kraft's (1979:12-13) aim is not to make a biblical value, which might be valid within Western culture, absolute for every culture. Instead, he attempts to develop a broader, cross-culturally valid theological perspective, which he calls "Christian Ethnotheology". He (:21) argues, "Theology should, however, be culturally relevant – whether that culture be African or American". However, Kraft uses a rather Western approach in the way he looks at and analyses culture. Coming from behavioural science, he (:47) believes that culture is created by human beings. Furthermore, he considers cultural forms as neutral vehicles, which are used by people to express functions and meanings. In this way God uses culture as a means to interact with people. I agree with Lingenfelter (1998:16) who rejects the idea that culture is a neutral vehicle when he writes, "Analogies such as Kraft's map or 'a tool for communication and interaction' (Lingenfelter & Mayers 1986: 122) are inadequate to capture the pervasive presence of sin in the lives and thought of human beings". Culture cannot be neutral since it was created by humans who are both sinful and good (Romans 11:30-32; Galatians 3:22). Thus culture is a confusing mix of good and evil.

As leadership in the West and in Tanzania is examined and evaluated, the context and the culture must be taken into consideration. In each context leadership may be practised differently but may still be compatible with Scripture. Questions that need to be looked at are: What does servant leadership in each context mean? How are love, justice, mercy, faithfulness, and humility practised? What is the view of status and role? How are power and authority exercised? How are conflicts dealt with? What is the concept of confrontation versus harmony? What is the understanding of time? The answers to these questions may help to increase people's understanding of the social environment, unlock cultural chains and open a path to more fruitful collaboration and successful partnerships.

In his book *Christ and Culture* North American Protestant theologian and ethicist H Richard Niebuhr (1894-1962) (1951) offers a framework of five different options, which describe the interrelationship between Christianity and culture:

- ❖ Christ against culture
- ❖ The Christ of culture
- ❖ Christ above culture
- ❖ Christ and culture in paradox
- ❖ Christ the transformer of culture

The first two options seem to be two extreme opposite views. The last three options are mediating positions, which lie between the first two. It seems that in some ways all of the five types are sometimes appropriate. Niebuhr adopts the last option "Christ the transformer of culture". This view is only acceptable to those who believe that Christ is Lord of all – even of culture. It recognizes that each culture has negative and positive aspects. As Christians we cannot separate ourselves from culture. Christians must evaluate their culture in the light of Scripture. Cultures must be transformed by the power of the Holy Spirit based on biblical norms and values. I agree with Niebuhr's last position that Christ transforms culture. Christians are agents of personal and social transformation. I strongly believe in the transforming power of the gospel. Christians have a responsibility to challenge the culture in which they live as the apostle Paul appeals to the Romans 12:2: "Do not conform yourselves to the standards of this world but **let God transform you inwardly by a complete change of mind**. Then you will be able to know the will of God – what is good and is pleasing to him and perfect" [my emphasis]. As a leader's mind is transformed her/his attitude and behaviour will also change.

Kraft refers only to the first three of Niebuhr's five positions. Generally, Kraft's position is indebted to Niebuhr and similar to his in many respects, but charts a slightly different course at a number of points, as Kraft (1979:104) himself points out. For the purpose of defining biblical values, the Christ-above-culture position seems to be most relevant and is mainly discussed at this point. Kraft has redefined Niebuhr's *Christ-above-culture* position to the *God-above-but-through-culture* position. Kraft states:

> Culture consists of forms, functions, meanings, and usage...Culture is seen as a kind of road map made up of various forms designed to get people where they need to go. These forms and the functions they are intended to serve are seen, with few exceptions, as neutral with respect to the interaction between God and man. Cultural patterning, organizing, and structuring of life, the functions they are intended to serve, and the processes cultures make available to human beings are not seen as inherently evil or good in themselves (1979:113).

Kraft uses a dichotomistic approach. As a result of his Western-influenced thinking he separates theory from practice. The core of culture is its values. These values are expressed through various practices like rituals, heroes and symbols. The cultural system is so interwoven as a part of the human being that in essence it cannot be separated into different parts.

I suggest taking Kraft's God-above-but-through-culture position even a step further to a *God-above-but-through-and-in-culture* position. As can be seen in the Scripture God is *above* culture. He came into this world as man (John 1:1-16; Philippians 2:6-11). God works *through* culture. God uses culture to communicate with people. God not only communicates through culture. He is as Christ also part of culture. So he is *in* culture. When God created the world he put awareness of him into people's hearts and minds (Romans 1:18-23; 2:14-15). Because God is in culture through Christ and the Church, the gospel is able to transform culture from within. This is in agreement with what Adeney suggests:

> Nothing that we think, say or do is exempt from the influence of our culture. Nothing we believe is exempt from the influence of our race, class, age and gender. Faith does not free us from culture, because culture is the environment in which what we believe takes shape. "There is no space which is not cultural space." Not only our personal practices but also our social institutions, our economic policies and our political practices reflect and influence the beliefs of our culture (1995:21).

One of the best examples of the God-above-but-through-and-in-culture position is the incarnation. Jesus, the Son of God, came into this world as a human being. Because Christ was *in* culture he was able to transform culture from *within*.

David Bosch (1929-1992) (1991:455), a pre-eminent South African Protestant missiologist, argued, that there are some aspects of culture, which are fully compatible with the gospel. Other aspects of culture are only partly or not compatible at all with the gospel. For this reason the gospel is always in creative tension with any culture. "The primary task for the Christian church and Christians is the critical function of continually discerning what is compatible with the Gospel in contemporary culture" (Mwikamba 2003:104).

Part of this dissertation aims to identify which aspects of leadership in the West and in Tanzania are fully, partly or not compatible at all with the gospel. It is God's desire to see individual people and whole communities transformed. It is the Christians' responsibility to identify the nature and causes of ethical problems, to speak out and engage in practical action to facilitate change where necessary and appropriate.

Since culture is made by human beings, it "is the pen of disobedience" (Lingenfelter 1998:17). This is what Lingenfelter (:21) calls "being prisoners" of our own culture. The responsibility of a Christian is to

> ... discover some of the biblical keys that will allow us to unlock the chains of our [negative] cultural habits and the gates to our cultural walls. ... We must look through multiple windows if we are to genuinely apprehend the transforming power of the gospel and apply kingdom principles interculturally (Lingenfelter 1998:21).

The challenge is to find out and to know what the kingdom principles are, since "we who are not part of the biblical cultures cannot *trust* our interpretational reflexes to give us the meanings that the original authors intended", as Kraft (1979:133) points out. Because we deal with a set of at least three different cultures,

> ... we need to look beyond each command to discover how the word and custom symbols were understood by the authors and those to whom they were originally written. That is, we need to look for the supracultural meaning in each by getting beyond our own cultural conditioning (with its "plain meanings") to the interpretation of each within its original cultural context (Kraft 1979:138).

The supra-cultural meaning and the kingdom principles, which are biblical values that are not culturally bound, can be identified through a dialectic process when a cross-cultural, theological dialogue between the biblical culture, the receptor culture and the own culture takes place. As this study looks at the notion of leadership in the West and in Tanzania in relation to the Bible, a dialectic process takes place. Based on the German philosopher Hegel, Adeney describes this dialectical process as follows:

> When a thesis is presented in a given culture, it provokes an antithesis (a contradiction), which comes to conflict with the thesis. Through the dialectic between thesis and antithesis, eventually a new synthesis is formed out of the opposing ideas. The synthesis becomes a new thesis provoking its own antithesis, and the round continues, with each step coming closer to Truth (1995:64-65).

Through this process we come closer to "Truth". This process is presented in figure 1.3.

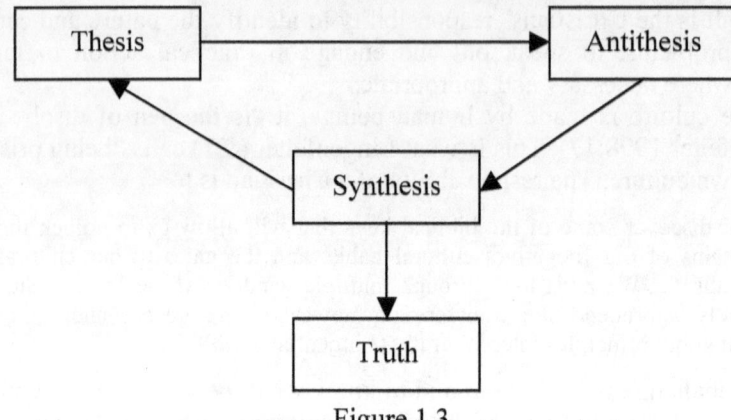

Figure 1.3

However, Adeney (:65) challenges Hegel's view since "Dialectical thinking can be wishy-washy and avoid the unpleasant fact that sometimes when there are opposing views, one is true and the other is false". He (:65) further points out, "The truth is often bigger than any one person's ability to grasp". Two different concepts may be coherent in their cultural contexts. Thus, Adeney (1995:65) suggests: "By dialogue between two internally coherent truths we may come closer to an understanding of ontological Truth. But this cannot be done alone. It is the product of community." This is shown in the following figure 1.4.

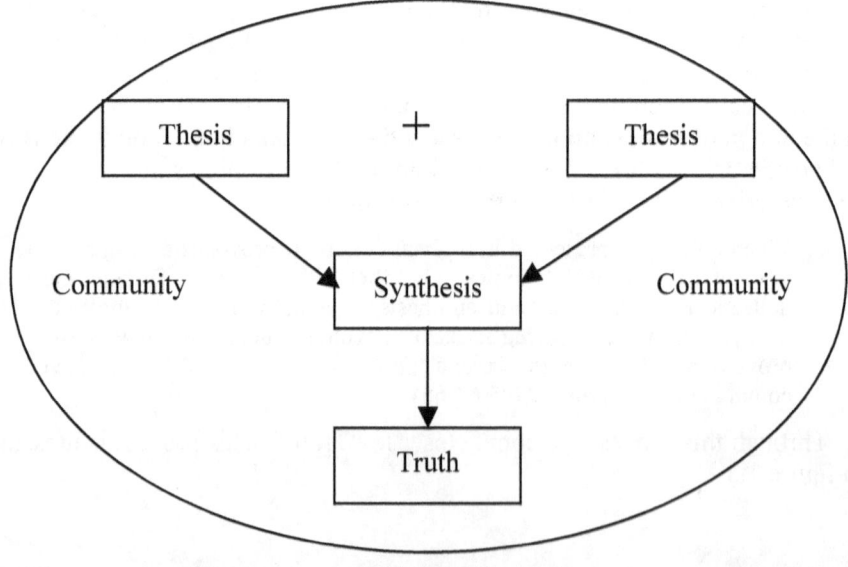

Figure 1.4

When people from two or more different cultures come together with their concept and another concept, which both may contain some truth in their own societies a dialogue begins. This dialogue cannot be done alone but must be done in community. From my own cross-cultural experience, I believe that the latter approach is much closer to reality. Truth is not necessarily absolute. It may be defined in different ways according to the context. There may be good reasons for certain leadership behaviours in the West and in Tanzania that are appropriate and acceptable in Tanzania, but not in the West, and vice versa. However, through the dialogue of these two leadership styles and taking the Scripture into account, we may come closer to a Christian-ethical understanding of leadership. Through this dialogue within community we may come closer to truth and consequently possibly to a better understanding of what the supra-cultural biblical value is.

Adeney also suggests three steps on how to approach and apply biblical values in a healthy way:

> A first step in overcoming ethnocentrism is the recognition that my own values are not necessarily the same as God's. All Christians hold many values derived from their culture. A second step is to understand that our own interpretation of Scripture comes from a particular cultural context. A third step is to see that God's values may be "enfleshed" differently in another culture from how they are in my own (1995:23).

Adeney takes the process of contextualization a step further than Kraft and Lingenfelter when he writes:

> We do not translate the Bible directly into a new cultural setting. Nor do we even "transculturate" it, as if the message of the gospel were an abstraction that could simply be expressed in different cultural forms. It is the Bible, not an abstract interpretation of its message, that is authoritative. The message of the Bible can be understood only as it is perceived from a specific cultural standpoint. God's word is always incarnated, and different parts of the church may incarnate it differently. In other words, the content of the gospel cannot be separated from its cultural form (1995:102).

God speaks to people in different ways at different times in different places. This is a very pragmatic approach in which biblical and theological understanding is developed through experience. Norms and values are important and can be useful tools. However, it is important to see how these norms and values are applied in daily life. "The goal of biblical understanding is not the formulation of some transcultural set of ethical principles but obedience to God in a particular time and place" (:97).

The North American evangelical missiologist Keith Eitel takes a different approach to contextualization. His concern with the models of some anthropologists like Kraft and Adeney is that Scripture is compromised and this will result in syncretism. Eitel's concept of contextualization is: "Stripping the Bible of its temporal cultural applications in order to expose its absolute supracultural truth and translate it into the familiar cultural context of a recipient people-group is the crux of contextualization." (Eitel 1986:4) His view of the Bible is strong, absolute and normative using a historical-grammatical-contextual method of exegesis (:44). It seems oversimplified when Eitel suggests, "Scripture is to be used as a normative guide for faith and practice". As a result he tries to derive absolute, normative, ethical principles from Scripture. Eitel (:14-17) regards the Bible as the inspired, authoritative Word of God, which is the core guide for Christians. However, to discover the supracultural meaning of the Bible, he tries to separate the text from the culture. This is not possible since "God used the knowledge, experience and cultural background of the authors" (Lausanne Committee for World Evangelization 1978). However, Eitel (1986:47) admits that it is "difficult at times to minimize the demands of culture". But he (:62) expects a person to surpass cultural demands in obedience to God. The important question is how biblical values can be incorporated in a culture in a meaningful and appropriate way without neglecting the culture and compromising the Scripture. He (:38-40) claims that the universal elements in Scripture must be transferred with the appropriate attitude by using a formal correspondence model.[14]

It appears that this model is rather ethnocentric, with the receptor culture only considered at a very late stage. The Bible being in dialogue with the culture does not necessarily mean it is critiqued by the culture. "Culture must always be judged and tested by Scripture" (Lausanne I 1974). Taking the culture seriously does not mean that culture's values cannot be evaluated by biblical standards. Biblical and ethical norms do exist. However, in the end Eitel agrees at least to some degree with Kraft and Adeney:

> Since the national and the missionary are from differing cultural backgrounds, they may, indeed, arrive at different conclusions regarding the ethical decisions or the process of evaluating issues, but the missionary and national would both be remiss if they did not help each other gain better understanding in light of God's word (1986:85-86).

These differences have mainly to do with the way Scripture is viewed. Biblical norms in practice may play out in different ways according to differing cultural backgrounds, as Byang Kato (1936-1975) (1985:23), an evangelical theologian from Nigeria, confirms: "Since the Gospel message is inspired but the mode of its expression is not, contextualization of the modes of expression is not only right but necessary."

In conclusion, it is important to find the right balance, as it was expressed in the Willowbank Report by the Lausanne Committee for World Evangelization (1978): "[T]he right response is neither a slavishly literal obedience nor an irresponsible disregard, but rather first a critical discernment of the text's inner meaning and then a translation of it into our own culture."

For the purpose of this research, I agree in principle with Kraft, Niebuhr, Lingenfelter and Adeney that it is necessary to use a contextual approach that takes the cultural context as well as the biblical text seriously. The former general secretary of the Association of Evangelicals of Africa and Madagascar

---

[14] According to Eitel (1986:39-40), the formal correspondence model includes five stages:
    a.   The translation of scripture
    b.   The communication of information
    c.   The enhancement of the second stage
    d.   The application of insights gained
    e.   Hearers becoming evangelists

and vice-president of the World Evangelical Fellowship, Byang Kato, from Nigeria appeals:

> Africans need to formulate theological concepts in the language of Africa. But theology itself in its essence must be left alone. The Bible must remain the basic source of Christian theology. Evangelical Christians know of only one theology – Biblical theology – though it may be expressed in the context of each cultural milieu (1985:12).

I agree with Kato that it is necessary to contextualize theology in Africa. However, I do not think it is possible to produce a pure biblical theology without dialogue with other Christians. Biblical theology can be developed through a contextual approach, which recognizes that a dialogue between the cultural context and the biblical text must develop. A contextual approach takes both the culture and the Bible seriously. Through this dialogue, people's culturally conditioned understanding of the Bible is being challenged and corrected. The result will be a deeper understanding of the biblical meaning and consequently lead to a biblical theology. Christians come to a biblical theology as they help each other understand how God's Word contradicts their thinking and their way of life (Lingenfelter 1998:22). Marvin Mayers, a North American Protestant anthropologist, points out:

> This is not an approach of compromise, but of enrichment. To compromise is to abandon principle, however much or little. *To extend one's range of variation of lifestyle is to incorporate as many lifestyles into [her/]his own as possible without producing destructive tension or causing abandonment of principle or absolute* (1987:559). [his emphasis]

This research provides such a dialogue. As the tension between the two different leadership styles in the West and in Tanzania is discovered in terms of the understanding of time, the view of status and role, and confrontation versus harmony, it will lead towards a discussion of what Christian-ethical leadership in each context means.

An example of the need to configure culture is the fact that only very few women in Africa are employed in leadership positions. This problem has been recognized by a number of women and also a few men. Women's potential leadership role has not been recognized (Bam 1991:364). Ruth Muthei James (2003:161), a theologian from Kenya, observes women are often only given a low level or middle level management position. There are very few societies in Africa that are matrilineal, where women occupy the positions of authority in society, family and religion (Kayonga 2003:142; Nthamburi 1991:18). However, the majority of women have been oppressed by patriarchal systems, as Nthamburi points out:

> The crucial sphere of life where women have felt overwhelmingly disadvantaged was in relation to decision-making, planning and policy formation. Despite the fact that women account for more than fifty per cent of Africa's population, they have in effect, been under-represented or not represented at all in forums that determine their future destinies (1991:19).

This is also echoed by Anna Mary Mukamwezi Kayonga, a Catholic theologian from Uganda:

> The church is a patriarchal structure allied to those who wield power. Women do not participate at the level of church decision-making. The ecclesial structure, which is hierarchical and masculine, is a model of the oppressive man-woman relationship. At the level of conscience and faith the male dictates what a woman is supposed to believe and practise (2003:145).

So far women have been denied full participation in decision-making, which is controlled by male authority (Mncube 1991:358). Mercy Amba Oduyoye, a Methodist theologian from Ghana, offers two reasons for this situation:

> **Visualising God as male** and **experiencing leadership as a male prerogative**, have blinded the church to the absence or presence of women. It has made it difficult – and indeed, in some churches, impossible – to conceive of women priests and women leaders (1986:93). [my emphasis]

It becomes clear that some of the contributing factors for the exclusion of women from leadership include socio-cultural norms and value systems, structures and policies of organisations, the influence of churches, lack of training, and women's multiple roles (James 2003:63-169). James (:160) calls for a substantial increase in the number of women at all levels of management and decision-making since women can make an enormous contribution to the development of society. It can be observed that in a number of African countries, more and more women are employed in leadership positions. But there is still a long way to go. I do believe it is essential and just for women to be recognized as leaders in society and the church. Women have played key roles in history. Jesus recognized the importance of women, as Kayonga (2003:147) observes: "Ahead of his culture, tradition and time, Jesus is quick to recognize women's goodness and potentiality and he utilizes them for the greater glory of his father. Women are involved at the beginning, in the middle and at the end of Jesus' life." The revelation of the incarnation was given to Mary and Elizabeth (Luke 1:26-45). Jesus' mother asked him for more wine at the wedding of Cana and he performed a miracle (John 2:3). The first witnesses of the resurrection of Jesus were women (Matthew 28:19-20).

So cultural norms and values, structures and policies must be challenged on a biblical basis. Women ought to have a place in society, like men, to take on leadership roles because "Woman like man has equal personal dignity; she has inalienable rights and responsibilities proper to the human person" (Kayonga 2003:139). Oduyoye goes even further saying:

> Whatever is keeping subordination of women alive in the church cannot be the Spirit of God. ... Where leadership and initiative are seen as contrary to the female spirit (or are viewed as characteristics only of rebellious women) and are not encouraged or supported, we can suspect the Spirit of God is being ignored. The pyramids of power that exist in African culture have found companions in Christianity (1986:97).

Entering into a dialogue of contextual theology in reference to Christian leadership, the gospel and culture, it is essential to understand the nature of African Christian ethics. It is important to keep in mind that most ethical theories have historically been developed in the West. Since this study deals with leadership issues in the West and in Tanzania, African ethics needs to be taken into account as much as Western ethics. Peter Kasenene (1994:140), a theologian from Swaziland, argues that African ethics is different from Western ethics because of different value systems. Africans are not so much influenced by the philosophies of Plato and Aristotle as Westerners. African Christian ethics grows out of African theology, as Kasenene argues:

> When the gospel is applied to a specific situation, it produces a relevant theology for the local people. African theology must be understood in this context, as incarnating the Christian faith in the culture and situation in which African people live. African people have problems and concerns, cultures and world-views which are unique to them. Theology made elsewhere cannot provide relevant and meaningful answers to Africans (1994:139).

It is true that each society has its own challenges. Thus, theology must be relevant to the local situation in addressing these issues. However, Christians from the West may have theological insights, which may also be helpful and at least in part applicable in Africa, and vice versa. These insights may need to be adjusted through dialogue to make them fully relevant and meaningful in each context. I do believe that there is a place where we can learn and benefit from each other and also critique one another in an appropriate way. I agree with Paul Hiebert, a North American evangelical missiologist, who calls for an international theological dialogue:

> [T]he global church must become an international hermeneutical community in which Christian leaders from around the world become partners in hermeneutics – seeking to understand Scripture under the guidance of the Holy Spirit, to help one another in dealing with the problems they face in their particular contexts, and to check one another's cultural biases. Out of this process there can emerge a global theology that is increasingly freed from the influences of specific human contexts (1999:113).

Kasenene further observes:

> Whereas the Christian faith is universal and the gospel of Christ is the same for all churches, societies, communities and times, the language and mode of proclaiming the gospel must be suited to the culture, thought-system and experience of the people who profess it (1994:139).

It is the task of this study to explore which aspects of Christian leadership are universal and must be applied universally and which aspects can be applied in a culturally appropriate way without violating biblical norms.

According to Kasenene (1994:140) and others (Mugambi & Nasimiyu-Wasike 2003:2), in Africa, religion and ethics cannot be separated. Because "life is seen as an integral whole, and religion is the fabric that binds life together" (:2), thus "Ethics is an integral part of religion and of theology" (Kasenene 1994:140). Hannah Kinoti, a Kenyan theologian who died in 2001, points out,

> ... that traditionally African peoples have held the strong belief that spiritual powers are deeply concerned about the moral conduct of individuals and communities alike. ... African peoples have traditionally believed that the laws and rules that govern society were initially given by God (2003:79).

Hence, it could be argued that in African societies, spirituality and religion cannot be separated from ethics. However, ethics is the critical reflection of ethos. Christian ethics must critique culture. In Africa unethical behaviour is noticed not only by the society, peer group, family or self but also by the supernatural realities (:79-80). According to Kasenene (1994:140), African ethics is built around vitalism, communalism, and holism. From these three values, a number of virtues are derived, such as benevolence, hospitality, respect for seniors, charity, honesty, bravery, sharing and fairness (:140). The challenge of this study is to determine which form these virtues take in African ethics as Tanzanian leadership is considered.

Vitalism is important in African societies (:140). Various rites and rituals demonstrate what a precious gift of God life is (:140). This respect for life is expressed in generosity and caring for one another, which promotes the wellbeing of the community (:141). Leaders are expected to care for the wellbeing of their subordinates.

Community in Africa consists of individuals who exist corporately in terms of the family, clan and whole ethic group. An individual **is** because s/he **belongs,** as John Mbiti (1974:136), a Kenyan theologian and missiologist living in Switzerland, points out: "Only because of the other person the individual becomes aware of his own being, his own duties, his privileges, and responsibilities he has for himself and for others. ... The individual can only say: "I am because we are, and because we are I am."[15] Because the individual receives her/his identity from the group s/he is responsible "for the promotion of the community's welfare by doing good and avoiding evil" (Kasenene 1994:142).

In African thinking life cannot be separated from the extended family community. Thus, "It is this sense of belonging together, of being a community of related persons, that makes it possible for members of traditional society to share what they have with the needy in that community" (Moyo 2003:53). This sense of community creates an attitude of caring, generosity, and benevolence. The community values are much stronger in rural areas than in the cities, where they are slowly deteriorating. During the years I have lived in Tanzania, I have seen both. There are people who are willing to help, give

---

[15] All translations in this dissertation from German to English are my own translations.
Translated from the original German: Der einzelne wird sich nur im Hinblick of andere Menschen seiner Eigenart, seiner Pflichten, Vorrechte und Verantwortlichkeiten sich selbst und anderen gegenüber bewußt. Das Individuum kann nur sagen: „Ich bin, weil wir sind, und weil wir sind, bin ich".

and share with those who are needy especially within the family community. This of course can be misused and some people exploit their relatives. There are also others who have benefited from family and friends in the past, but are not willing to give anything back when they are able. Wilbur O'Donovan (2000:15), a North American Protestant theologian who has lived in Africa for over 30 years, points out, "Because of the sinful nature of all human beings, even some of the best community values of African culture are often corrupted by attitudes of tribalism, prejudice, political oppression, financial corruption and other evils". Since communal identity and life are so important in Africa it may be a real challenge for an individual to criticise another individual or group on the basis of Christian ethics without being excluded from the group. They may be excluded, but hopefully find a new identity within the Christian community.

Vitalism and communalism are a *holistic view* of the sacred and the profane, the physical and the spiritual, the religious and the moral (Kasenene 1994:142). According to Kasenene (:142), the well-being of the community "is attained when there is personal integration, environmental equilibrium, social harmony, and harmony between the individual and both the environment and the community". The negative aspect of holism is that there is no clear distinction between church and society, church and my community, and church and family. Since "African theology takes people holistically in their spiritual, social, economic and political dimensions" (:143), Kasenene (:142) argues, African ethics "must be holistic, aiming at the liberation of the whole person and whole communities and freeing humanity from political, social, economic, religious, mental, psychological and physical deprivation". This requires change based on ethical norms and values.

It is normal for any society to change. Like Western societies African societies have changed. These changes affect the values and virtues of a society. Mwikamba (2003:84), a theologian from Kenya, observes, "African traditional values and virtues of charity, honesty, hospitality, generosity, loyalty, truthfulness, solidarity, respect for elders, respect for nature and respect for God are fading away". It cannot be denied that many traditional values have been undermined by the early missionaries, as well as colonial and postcolonial regimes (Magesa 2002:93-110; Bell 2002:66). More recently these values may be changing due to a higher level of education, globalization, and the influence of the mass media.

As the Tanzanian leadership style is examined in chapters three, four and five, we will see how the contemporary leadership style in Tanzania is influenced not only by traditional values but also by the missionary and colonial era and how leadership has changed over time.

The task of African ethics as well as Western ethics is twofold: (1) Cultures need to be constructively criticized in order to improve them, not to undermine or destroy them (Mugambi 2003:26). "Just as Jesus fulfilled the Torah, so should the Gospel help every Christian in every culture to enrich his or her cultural heritage" (:26-27). (2) Cultures need to be challenged by the Gospel to transform the norms of this world into ideals that are consistent with the promises of the kingdom of God (:18). The challenge of this study is to identify the basis of Christian ethics in terms of leadership in the West as well as in Tanzania. This is possible because "Christian ethics, like African ethics, is concerned with both the relationships between people and the relationship between people and God" (Kasenene 1994:144). The core of these relationships is love, "expressed not in terms of duty alone, but in terms of affection which builds community" (:144).

African ethics has a strong teleological emphasis because good relationships are key. People usually think about what affect and consequences a certain action may have on the relationship. However, it also has a deontological component in the sense that the values of the community become somewhat normative. For instance, harmony prevents confrontation. The group interest is more important than the individual's need. An older person may be given a certain position because of her/his age even though s/he may not have the capability to fill the role.

To summarize, in this chapter, the key issues of Christian ethics, leadership and culture have been discussed as they are closely related. The task of Christian ethics is to understand the context of leadership, analyse and evaluate it, and propose possible changes or actions. To analyse and evaluate Western and Tanzanian leadership styles in chapters three, four and five criteria of Christian norms, values and virtues have been identified. Thus, a good Christian leader is loving, just, merciful, faithful, and humble. As leaders act on these values, and virtues it will impact their relationships with colleagues and staff and enhance cross-cultural relationships. Thus, it is essential for a leader continually to grow morally and spiritually. Since leaders have responsibility and exercise authority, the use of power is key to leadership. Christian leadership is also influenced by one's understanding of the Scripture and the social context in which a person lives. So a cross-cultural dialogue will help to come to a better biblical understanding of what Christian leadership really means in this contemporary world.

Leadership behaviour is strongly influenced by culture. Thus, the cultural models discussed in chapter two will help us to understand the African and Western contexts and their influence on the different leadership styles in chapters three and four. In chapter five the Christian-ethical criteria of love, justice, mercy, faithfulness and humility, kingdom leadership, and the use of power are applied to evaluate, challenge and criticise Western and Tanzanian leadership styles.

Chapter 2
Research Design and Methodology

The previous chapter has shown that the task of Christian ethics is to understand the context, to analyse and evaluate the nature of ethical problems, and to elicit suggestions and propose practical actions. Leaders base their actions on norms and values. To evaluate a leader's behaviour the biblical values of love, justice, mercy, faithfulness and humility are key. Jesus is the example modelling true Christian leadership. Thus, in terms of providing leadership and exercising power, Christian leaders ought to follow the example of Jesus who set out the vision of the kingdom of God. We have seen in chapter one that for Christian leaders it is important to have a sound biblical understanding of leadership, and that leadership style is influenced by a person's character, culture and theology. Therefore, it is essential to be aware of a leader's character and its formation process. It is also important to understand the cultural context of a leader as it influences her/his actions. To gain a better understanding of what Christian leadership means, a cross-cultural dialogue is useful. To evaluate leadership styles in chapters three, four and five the Christian-ethical values outlined in chapter one, such as love, justice, mercy, faithfulness and humility, are employed. These criteria, together with the vision of kingdom leadership in reference to servanthood and stewardship, the biblical use of power and the importance of virtues and character formation of a leader will help to identify and propose possible changes and actions in chapter five.

The purpose of this chapter is to describe the research design and methodological approach used in this study. Since this research relates to different cultures, a combination of different methods and data sources must be employed to facilitate sound data collection appropriate to each cultural context. This study combines *theoretical* and *empirical qualitative* research in a dialectical process. The theory applied to general observations and experience of more than ten years leads to a hypothesis, which is stated at the beginning of chapter three. The hypothesis is measured against the data sources. The main data sources are literature, especially books and articles, and participant observations, case studies, informal and semi-structured interviews, and a group discussion, which illustrate the theoretical argument (Mason 2002:126 & 176). The qualitative data provide contextual information and uncover emic views[16] (Guba & Lincoln 1994:106). The combined picture of theory and generated data is measured against the Christian-ethical framework of chapter one.

These different methods are complementary. This combination of various methods is important in generating valid and reliable data; the argument is empirically and theoretically grounded. British sociologist Jennifer Mason distinguishes between *generating* and *collecting* data because a researcher cannot be

---

[16] Emic views are insider views provided by people from within a society.

... a completely neutral collector of information about the social world. Instead, the researcher is seen as actively constructing knowledge about the world according to certain principles and using certain methods derived from, or which express, their epistemological position (2002:52).

Thus the researcher generates data from the chosen data sources through her/his subjective lens. An empirical world does exist, but it can only be known and understood interpretatively (:179). So there is no neutral collector nor objective view of the environment or situation.

The main approach of this qualitative research is *ethnographic*. The immersion of the researcher into the cross-cultural setting provides the basis for this research. Participant observations over a period of more than ten years, including exercising a role in the society as a leader, provide the necessary credibility and trust enabling the researcher to conduct interviews.

In this chapter I describe how the two leadership styles are analysed, interpreted, evaluated, reflected, and practical actions considered. Below in section 2.1 "Data Collection and Analysis of Leadership Styles", there is a discussion about which research methods, such as participant observations, case studies, interviews and group discussion are used to generate data for the analysis. How these research methods are employed to collect data about the leadership styles is explained. After discussing the research methods, it is laid out why culture is important for this study. Leadership behaviour is influenced by culture. A definition of culture is given, and two cultural value models by Hofstede, Trompenaars and Hampden-Turner are discussed at length. A synthesis is derived from these two models and key themes are drawn for this study. The cultural value models are used as a basis for the design of parts of the questionnaire for the interviews, and to analyse, interpret and position the leadership styles culturally. Once the cultural value models have been discussed, section 2.2 "Dialogue and Evaluation of Leadership Styles" describes how a dialogue among Westerners and Tanzanians takes places in the form of a comparison of leadership styles, presenting their view of each other's leadership and a group discussion. How the leadership styles are evaluated in the light of the Scriptures, as outlined in chapter one is then described. Finally, from the analysis of the generated data and an evaluation of the cross-cultural dialogue there is a discussion of how practical actions and application for Christian leadership can be considered.

2.1 Data Collection and Analysis of Leadership Styles

It is important that both Westerners and Tanzanians understand and accept their cultural roots so that they can be transcended and transformed by the gospel. This research examines the different leadership styles, in the West and in Tanzania. To reflect and analyse the leadership styles it is necessary to understand the empirical context of a particular situation (Kammer 1988:84). The particular situation can then be related to the broader aspects of the worldview. Kammer (:85) points out: "Our method of moral decision-making must begin with a careful description of the context to which we are responding. We need to know something about its history, the persons involved, and the social forces at work." To collect information and generate data the methods of participant observations, case studies, and semi-structured individual interviews and a group discussion are used. The collected information is later described and analysed in chapters three, four and five.

Participant observations have the benefit that deep insights can be gained over a period of time through the comparison of different events. Having lived and worked for more than ten years in Tanzania, I am in the favoured situation of being able to use a research approach, which the Christian North American linguist Kenneth Pike (1912-2000) (1996:32-33) calls *etic* and *emic*. Some of the characteristics of an etical view include alien, cross-cultural, comparing systems, classificatory, typological, approaches to a new situation with units prepared in advance, such as a questionnaire, and criteria for the evaluation such as norms and values which are absolute and are frequently the creation of the analyst. Some of the characteristics of an emicital view include domestic, mono-cultural, structural, leads towards the definition of units, which are known only after a situation has been analyzed, criteria are relative, contrastive, and observable only in reference to differential responses, and are discovered by the analyst. As an outsider to Tanzanian society, I have a detached etic observer view. As a Westerner, I have an alien and cross-cultural view of the Tanzanian leadership style. Thus, I am in a position to compare the two different leadership styles. On the other hand, having lived in Tanzania and learned Swahili, the national language of Tanzania, I also have a partially emic view, being a participant in Tanzanian society.

In participant observations the researcher can experience and observe at first hand a range of dimensions of social actions, behaviour, interactions, relationships, events, as well as spatial, locational and temporal dimensions (Mason 2002:84). These observations, and the way people interpret them and act on them are central to this research. Knowledge of Western and Tanzanian leadership styles can be generated through experiencing real-life settings, which can reveal data in multidimensional ways (:85). This immersion into the culture allows the researcher to be active and reflexive in the research process. Certain information, such as interactions in meetings, can only be obtained through observations. These observations are not only my own but also those of others gathered in the interviews. To prove my thesis, it is important that observations are selected where the Western and Tanzanian leadership styles are both similar and different. These observations were also checked with other observers who may have drawn different conclusions. Therefore, chapters three and four were each proofread by a Westerner and a Tanzanian.

My observational environment is in Tanzania, where I have worked with both expatriates from different nationalities and with Tanzanians from different organisations and churches. Over the years, I have been involved in various leadership roles and thus have been recognized as a leader in Tanzania. Settings relevant for this research include informal visits, work situations, meetings, and consultations. Observations have been recorded as soon as possible after the event. Since a number of events have been recalled over a longer period of time, certain details may have been omitted.

Case studies are part of participant observations. When using case studies as data sources, it is important to ensure that the appropriate range of data has been generated to permit a full and meaningful analysis of the case in question (:37).

Both participant observations and case studies are appropriate complementary research methods to the interviews since leadership issues can be complex. Through the combination of these various methods, an in-depth picture can be gained.

This research includes an interactional dialogue between Westerners and Tanzanians on leadership issues in a relatively informal style and topic-centred approach. Through the structured interviews, the relevant context is brought into focus so that situated knowledge can be produced (:62). Therefore, the *semi-structured interview* and *group discussion* methods are adopted. To examine Western and Tanzanian leadership styles, interview questions are designed to learn about the cultural values and also how Christian norms, values and virtues are understood and applied in each society. The questions were designed using the cultural models discussed below in this chapter, the Christian-ethical framework developed in chapter one, personal observations and knowledge gained from existing literature. The complete questionnaire is attached as an appendix.

Since I am interested in how Westerners and Tanzanians practise and perceive leadership styles, it is essential to draw on their knowledge, views, understanding, interpretations, experiences, and interactions as meaningful properties of the social reality, through semi-structured interviews (:63-66). Talking interactively by asking questions and listening is a meaningful way to generate data. Knowledge is situational. Therefore, a qualitative interview should be as contextual as possible in the sense that it draws on the social experiences of the interviewees. They are encouraged to tell stories and give examples. These stories make them feel more comfortable and allow for a more accurate categorization of their views in the analysis. Since context and situation cannot be controlled nor ignored, it is important to take it into account and ask questions for clarification during the interview. The purpose of the interviews is to gain an in-depth understanding of the leadership styles in different social contexts. Through the interview method the researcher is actively and reflexively engaged in the process. Hardly anything has been written about leadership in Tanzania. Thus, data need to be generated through interviews, which are not easily obtained through other means.

The interviews were conducted with ten Westerners and ten Tanzanians. The number of interviews was limited to twenty because of the restricted space and time within research constraints of a Master of Theology as compared to a Doctor of Theology degree. The interviews are supplemented by participant observations, case studies and a group discussion. In addition, the empirical part is supplemented by the theoretical studies from many written sources. Informed consent was obtained from the interviewees to their participation. A cross-section of males and females was interviewed of different ages, educational levels, occupations, and denominations, to see if there are any differences in practice and perception. People from different categories may have different perspectives and experiences regarding leadership issues.

A mixture of Christian leaders and followers were interviewed. Leadership behaviour is often determined by the followers' mental leadership model, as research suggests (Avery 2004:10-11). Thus leadership style is closely interconnected with follower perceptions. Therefore, it is important to also examine leadership from the followers' perspective.

Interviewees were selected according to the following criteria from each society: at least two female, not more than five persons under thirty years, at least three persons who are not in a top leadership position, people from at least five different denominations. These criteria ensure a broad cross-section of interviewees. It is essential not only to have a male but also female perspective on leadership issues. Often people take leadership positions when they are thirty years or older. Younger people may have a different perception of leadership than older people. Leaders' behaviour is often determined by followers' expectations. Thus, it is important to interview not only leaders but also followers. The church background of the interviewees may influence their theological understanding of leadership since Christian teachings vary. Thus, interviewees from different denominations may have different perspectives on Christian leadership. These selection criteria help in examining the way leadership is influenced by culture, theology, and character. Depending on the social class of the interviewees, they may have a different view on leadership. Their level of education may also influence the interviewees' understanding of theology and of leadership.

Five Western interviewees from Anglo-Saxon and five from Germanic countries were selected, so as to have a broad spectrum. Tanzanians from different ethnic groups were interviewed. Most of them come from urban areas. Some interviews with Westerners were conducted face-to-face. Others responded by e-mail because of geographical distance. The interviews with Tanzanians were always done face-to-face. This is important since Tanzania is an oral society, whereas Westerners respond well to questionnaires in writing. The questions were usually not asked in isolation. Since a semi-structured interview was used as one of the methods, the questions were clarified if necessary to be sure they were communicated clearly with the particular person interviewed, especially since a number of the Western interviewees speak English as a second language. The semi-structured interview method allows enough flexibility to ask follow-up questions such as "What do you mean by that?" for better understanding or moving to a deeper level. The Tanzanians were interviewed in Swahili for better communication. Therefore, all the questions had to be translated into Swahili. One of the challenges for an expatriate to interview Tanzanians is that one may be given the responses s/he desires to hear. The Tanzanians interviewed are people who I have personally known for a long time and have a trusting personal relationship with them. Most of these interviewees also have had intensive interactions with other expatriates or have been involved in research before. For cultural appropriateness a female research assistant was employed to interview Tanzanian women who are leaders in the church and at work. Women may have a different perception of leadership than men. Thus, by including female interviewees, a gendered perspective on leadership is elicited. Tanzanian women may not necessarily feel comfortable speaking up if the interviewer is a male, since Tanzania is a male dominated society. The interviewers need to have a high proficiency in both languages: English and Swahili.

The interviewees were asked to think about a specific situation, like a church or work setting, when they responded to the questions. The interviews were audio recorded and later transcribed carefully. This allowed for interaction during the interview. The interviewee did not have to wait until the responses were transcribed. The answers to these questions, which are recorded in chapters three, four and five, were checked with the interviewees. The Swahili is translated into English for the purposes of this dissertation. Non-verbal aspects of the interview are recorded in a separate section, as are observations, interpretations, and experiences.

To facilitate a cross-cultural dialogue on Christian leadership issues, in chapter five, in addition to the individual interviews, one *group discussion* was also conducted. For the group discussion, three Western and three Tanzanian senior leaders from different organisations and churches were invited in order to have a broad representation. Tanzanian senior leaders often have had a good amount of exposure to Western leadership within and outside of Tanzania. Tanzanian senior leaders are more confident and open than junior and middle leaders because they are not necessarily as dependent on senior Westerners for continued employment. This way it was possible to enter into a more equal dialogue between Westerners and Tanzanians. It was important to have female representation since women may have a different perspective on leadership issues. Thus, one Western and one Tanzanian female leader were invited. Unfortunately the Tanzanian woman was not able to come. The group was intentionally small to make an in-depth discussion possible. It was important for them to be comfortable with each other and to discuss the matter freely and creatively. Some, but not all, of the participants in the group discussion had been interviewed individually. As the individual interviews were conducted first, their comments could be checked on their own and in this group. The group discussion also helps in the comparative section in the last chapter to detect the "blind spots" of both groups. Some questions for the group discussion were chosen from the questionnaire such as *"How would you describe a good Christian leader?"* and *"How do you understand servant leadership?"* to provide a deeper discussion. Other questions were aimed at gaining clarification on different responses and why there is a dissonance between the ideal and actual practice such as: *"Why is there such a dissonance between the ideal and actual practice? Why is power exercised in different ways? Which is the dominant experience – a positive or negative experience of power? Why are some good and others bad leaders? Is the church any different? Why not?"* Other questions aimed at finding solutions for what needs to change, such as: *"How can bad leadership in terms of character and culture be changed? How can leaders from the West and Tanzania draw on the strengths rather than the weaknesses of their cultural paradigms and model recognisably Christian leadership in their contexts?"* There was an open, relaxed and trusting atmosphere from the very beginning of the group discussion. All participants were engaged and listened to each other. The participants felt comfortable to critique each other's leadership style. Everybody recognised that it is important to learn from each other.

To prepare the data gained in the interviews for analysis, it was sorted according to topics such as personal information, character, relationships, power, conflict and assessment of leadership, and indexed cross-sectional according to the following ethical values: love, justice, mercy, faithfulness, and humility. These are the biblical values selected in chapter one as part of the evaluation criteria for this study. In addition, the data are compared in terms of gender, age, educational level, occupation, denominations, leaders and followers. Using the same set of indexing categories facilitates the exploration of patterns and themes, which occur across the data.

It is important to sort data and build explanations based on alternative ways, cross-sectional and non-cross-sectional, to complement each other (Mason 2002:165-166). The cross-sectional data indexing uses the same set of indexing categories across the whole data set. The same lens is used to explore patterns and themes, which occur across the data. The non-cross-sectional approach of data organisation involves a way of looking at and sorting the data, which does not necessarily use the same lens across the whole. This holistic way of looking at data is especially useful for data generated by observations, case studies and stories offered by the interviewees. It emphasises the context to see how things work in particular settings. Using only cross-sectional categories may be too limiting since one looks only through a specific set of glasses. The holistic approach enables the researcher to make comparisons and build explanations in a distinctive way. Therefore, for the purpose of this research, the data are sorted and looked at in both ways, cross-sectional and non-cross-sectional.

The data generated by the various methods are mainly read interpretively by the researcher applying his knowledge about the culture through experience and theory. The samples are used illustratively rather than being representative of a wider population as the latter can be questionable (:125-127). This is important since the interviewees do not necessarily always represent the general public and the researcher's reflection and interpretation of the data may be subjective. This combination of empirical and theoretical research ensures that the argument is as well supported as possible.

The responses of the interviewees, the observations and case studies are described and interpreted in chapters three, four and five. Out of all the collected information, the similar and complementary responses are grouped together and summarized to confirm and illustrate or to correct the theoretical argument from the literature. The analysis of the information comprises three steps: first, extrapolating the major themes from each section and analysing them. Second, linking the responses of the interviews with the information in the existing literature. Third, drawing out the similarities and differences to identify which leadership aspects are merely Western or Tanzanian and which could be said to be essentially Christian.

The Dutch researcher Geert Hofstede, and the management consultants Fons Trompenaars from the Netherlands and Charles Hampden-Turner from the USA have developed a cultural value system as a result from their extensive research. These cultural value systems described below are applied to interpret and analyse the data generated through the interviews, group discussion, observations and case studies. This is essential first to understand fully where each society is coming from before any evaluation can be made. Douglas (in Lingenfelter 1996:10) and others argue, "All human beings are constrained by cultural bias inherent in the particular social environment in which they live and work. From these structural arrangements people embrace a particular set of values and foundational premises regarding nature, society, and others". Based on Romans 11:30-32 Lingenfelter takes it a step further arguing that we are all prisoners of our own culture. Thus, "The first task is understanding our prison and the cultural prison of others" (Lingenfelter 1998:19). Once Westerners and Tanzanians understand their cultural roots, they can enter into a dialogue with each other and the Bible to unlock the "cultural chains". To facilitate this cultural understanding, the cultural norms and values according to Hofstede, Trompenaars and Hampden-Turner are discussed below.

2.1.1 Leadership and Cultural Norms and Values

As suggested in chapter one, Christian leadership is influenced by culture, theology, and character. Leaders act and make decisions based on norms, values and virtues. The social environment, in which somebody grows up and lives, in turn shapes these norms, values and virtues.[17] As we have seen in chapter one, ethical decisions are influenced by our worldview, loyalties, norms and values, and experience. Thus each individual lives with a cultural, theological, and personal bias, as Lingenfelter (1998:34) suggests: "The social games that we play are much more than games. They reflect a particular bias that we have about the best and right way to live our collective life of faith." Individuals in a society adopt a related set of assumptions and values, which are elaborated in their worldview. These assumptions and values are called *cultural bias*. This cultural bias is an interactive and dynamic process of a person's culture, theology, and character, as presented in figure 2.1.

---

[17] The social environment consists at least of the areas of family, work, colleagues, study, media, economy, church and friends.

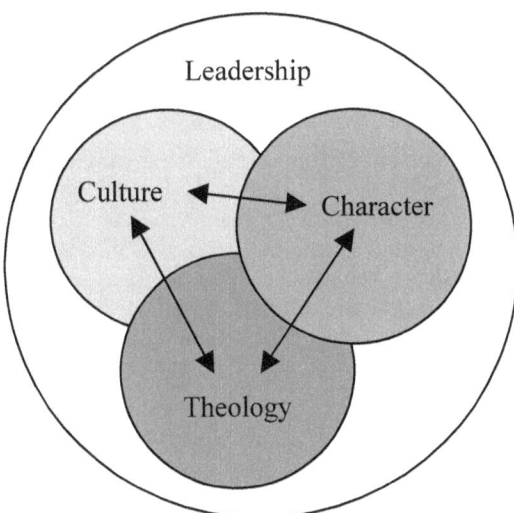

Figure 2.1

As we have seen in chapter one, Christian leadership, the gospel and culture interact. Thus, contextual theology takes the Scripture, the tradition and the context into account. In other words, culture plays a significant role in contextualizing theology. Hence, it is essential to understand the context and culture in which leaders live and work. People read the Bible through their own cultural lenses, which shapes their theology and understanding of the Christian norms and values. It impacts the valid use versus the abuse of power. The cultural models discussed below help one to understand where Westerners and Tanzanians are coming from, and how their theological understanding and Christian faith have been influenced by cultural norms and values. Scripture in turn challenges culture. Cultural norms and values are evaluated and criticised by biblical norms and values such as love, justice, mercy, faithfulness and humility. A leader's character is formed by culture and by Scripture. As leaders grow and mature as Christians, their character will change and thus their theological understanding of the Scripture will also change. When a person grows and matures spiritually s/he may in turn question and challenge certain aspects of their own or another's culture.

2.1.1.1 Definition of Culture

In this section cultural norms and values that may affect leadership behaviour are discussed. A number of anthropologists have defined culture in different ways. This indicates how difficult it is to come to terms with the concept of culture. The German evangelical ethnologist Lothar Käser (1998:35-38) suggests that culture is a strategy to survive. He (:37) defines culture simply but precisely: "*Cultures are strategies to design human existence.* And because existence in a cultural reality often must be designed under difficult circumstances, the following sentence is reality: *Cultures are strategies to cope with life*" [his emphasis].[18] Among many definitions the Willowbank Report of the Lausanne Committee provides the following helpful definition for the purpose of this research, as it connects beliefs, values and customs in an integrative way:

> Culture is an integrated system of beliefs (about God or reality or ultimate meaning), of values (about what is true, good, beautiful and normative), of customs (how to behave, relate to others, talk, pray, dress, work, play, trade, farm, eat, etc.), and of institutions which express these beliefs, values and customs (government, law courts, temples or churches, family, schools, hospitals, factories, shops, unions, clubs, etc.), which binds a society together and gives it a sense of identity, dignity, security, and continuity (Lausanne Committee for World Evangelization 1978).

This definition adds a theological perspective to culture. Culture is not only a system of values and customs but also has to do with beliefs.

Culture is influenced and shaped by several factors like history, religion, language and climate as shown in figure 2.2. These factors in turn lead to how a society is organised (Lewis 2003:67).

---

[18] Translated from the original German: ***Kulturen sind Strategien zur Gestaltung des menschlichen Daseins.*** Und weil das Dasein in der kulturellen Wirklichkeit häufig unter schwierigen Umständen gestaltet werden muß, gilt der Satz: ***Kulturen sind Strategien zur Daseinsbewältigung.***

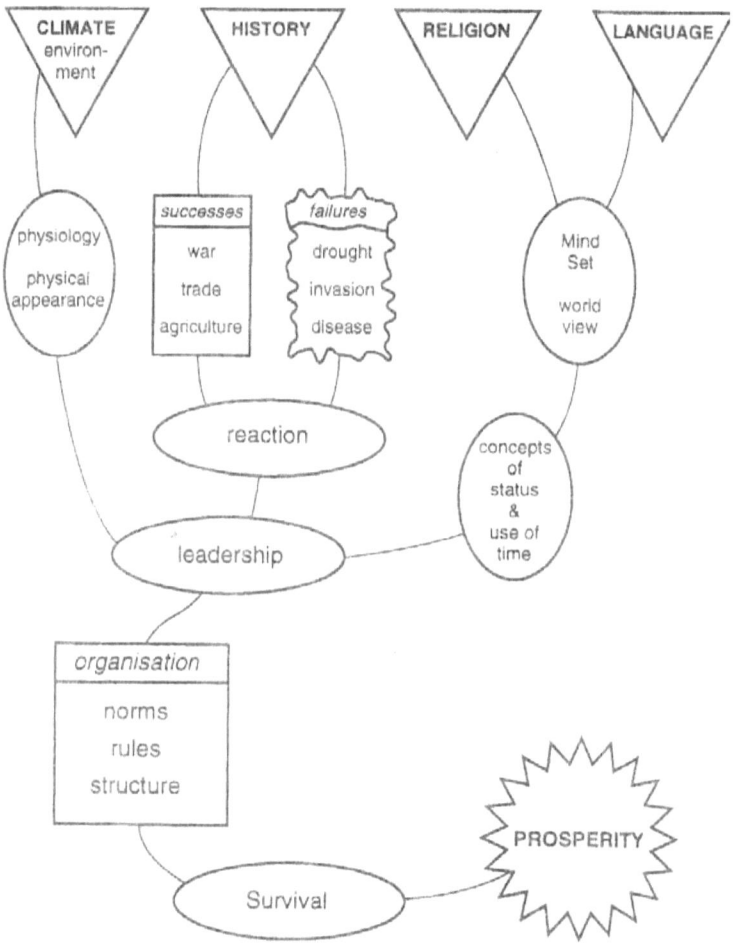

Figure 2.2 (Lewis 2003:67)

The diagram above shows how different factors such as climate, history, religion and language influence cultural values so that people cannot only survive but also prosper in a certain environment. Religion and language form to a great degree a person's worldview. Religion determines a person's loyalty. It also influences the perception of gender, which is then in turn reflected in the use of language. Climate and history carry experimental and empirical elements. Successes such as war, trade and agriculture and failures like drought, invasion and disease impact the economic realities of a society. All these factors in combination form the norms and values of a society. Thus, they affect leadership behaviour in various ways. How people relate to the climate and the physical environment in which they live makes a difference to their attitudes. However, in the diagram it seems that the different factors of climate, history, religion and language all carry the same weight concerning how they influence a society. Some factors like history and religion may be more important than the climate and the language. In fact, language is not a source of one's worldview and mindset, but an expression of it.

People's experience with leaders in the past influences their current and future leadership behaviour, how they make decisions, and deal with power. British linguist and management consultant Richard Lewis (2003:64) claims: "The behaviour of members of any cultural group is dependent, almost entirely, on the history of the people in that society." History certainly plays an important role in the way a society has been shaped over the years, decades and centuries. However, the influence of other factors, including climate, religion, language and character, should not be underestimated in people's ethical behaviour. I believe that religion and language are very much dependent on history. As can be observed, religion and language change over time. There is also a degree of interdependence between history and religion. History influences religion and vice versa.

Culture is like an onion that has different layers, as can be seen in figure 2.3.

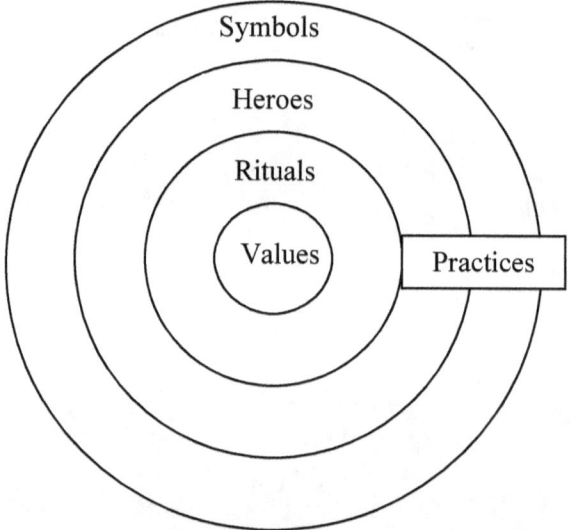

Figure 2.3 (Hofstede 1997:9)

This diagram above demonstrates how culture manifests itself at different levels of depth. The outer layers are what can be observed in any society as practices such as symbols, heroes and rituals.

Symbols are language, food, buildings, agriculture, dress, hairstyles, markets, fashions, art, flags and status symbols. These are symbols of a deeper level of culture, the norms and values of a specific group.

Between symbols and values are the heroes and rituals. Every society has people, alive or dead, who serve as models for behaviour. They possess certain characteristics that are admired by the individuals of the society. These people are called *heroes* who can be male and female.

Every society practises certain collective and social activities, which are called *rituals*. These rituals are performed to reach a desired end in itself.

They are an expression of cultural values and help people create a common identity.

The core consists of the *norms* and *values* of a society. Values deal with questions like what is bad or good, dirty or clean, ugly or beautiful, unnatural or natural, abnormal or normal, paradoxical or logical, irrational or rational. Values are the core of the onion, which is usually an unquestioned reality. Cultural values are the very heart of a person what Hofstede (1997) calls the "software of the mind". As much as a computer does not work without an operating system, a person cannot function without culture. Mayers (1987:98) claims, "that every thought a person thinks, every hope [s/]he has, every step [s/]he takes, every belief [s/]he holds, and every interaction [s/]he undertakes, is controlled by [her/]his culture. Every move [s/]he makes is programmed into [her/]him by [her/]his culture." Culture certainly plays a significant role. However, in my view, culture, Christian faith and character are interrelated. Thus, Christian leaders have a moral responsibility and must choose on which norms, values and virtues they base their actions. Therefore, they first need to be aware of their responsibility and be willing to make conscious, right choices based on biblical norms, values and virtues, even if this conflicts with cultural expectations.

The different layers of culture are connected and complementary. There is a connection between the values and rituals, heroes and the symbols. The rituals, heroes and symbols, what a person does, who s/he admires and how a person behaves, are expressions of her/his values.

Trompenaars and Hampden-Turner (2002:1) argue that cultures can never be completely understood. I agree that we might not be able fully and completely to understand another culture. There may always be certain areas, which need an explanation. Westerners may not be able to think and express themselves like Tanzanians, and vice versa. However, I believe missionaries and others who work in a cross-cultural context must make an effort to understand their own culture and the other culture in which they work. Adeney shows a way the cross-cultural worker needs to take to understand the values of a strange culture:

> In order to understand the values of a foreign culture, a person must suspend judgement and "place him or herself imaginatively within the scene of belief inhabited by those whose allegiance is to the rival tradition, so as to perceive and conceive the natural and social worlds as they perceive and conceive them." This is not always very comfortable. It requires that a person give up rigid categories in which the truth is always black and white (1995:117).

This is a tremendous challenge. It may take somebody many years to understand and have a feeling for a strange culture in such depth. Part of the aims of this study is to understand and describe Western and Tanzanian leadership styles. If it is understood why leaders act in a certain way, we are able to evaluate and challenge this behaviour based on biblical values such as love, justice, mercy, faithfulness and humility.

A number of different studies of leadership and culture exist, which were conducted by different researchers such as Hall (1981a; 1981b; 1982), Lingenfelter (1996; 1998), Lane, DiStefano and Maznevski (2000), Rodrigues (2001), Harris and the Morans (2004), House, Hanges, Javidan, Dorfman and Gupta (2004), Hofstede (1997; 2001), and Trompenaars and Hampden-Turner (2000; 2002).[19] It is interesting to note that many of these researchers base their research approach on Hofstede's model. Some combine a variety of models according to their purpose. Thus, it seems that Hofstede has developed probably the most extensively researched framework. His model has been used by many others and has proved to be extremely useful in developing a better understanding of leadership styles in different societies.

In a different context Hofstede (1997; 2001) and Trompenaars and Hampden-Turner (2000; 2002) have developed a useful concept of value orientations. The two models complement each other. In fact, Trompenaars and Hampden-Turner follow Hofstede, but incorporate more dimensions developed in sociology and anthropology. Only the set of individualism versus collectivism overlaps. These models are applied in this research to analyse and compare the cultural contexts of leadership styles in the West and in Tanzania and position them on the value continuum. Leadership in the West and in Tanzania should not be seen as watertight categories. Certainly there are differences, but there may also be some similarities. We may find leaders in the West who are authoritarian and hierarchical. At the same time, we may also find leaders in Tanzania who are much more participative. However, over the years I have observed some major differences in leadership styles in the West and in Tanzania. Recognizing that there are always exceptions, general tendencies in the different societies are presented in this study.

Hofstede (1997:13) did some extensive empirical research for IBM, examining different cultures in more than fifty countries spread across the globe. Since all of his interviewees were employees of one cooperation, it could be argued that the results may have a corporate ethos. However, it is striking that Hofstede's results covered amazingly well the same areas predicted by other anthropologists, sociologists, and psychologists (:14). So Hofstede's empirical research is strongly supported by a broad survey of literature on national culture. Thus, this demonstrates that even though the interviewees were from one multinational cooperation, differences in national value systems could be identified through the analysis. In fact, Hofstede (:13) observes, "from one country to another they [the interviewees] represent almost perfectly matched samples: they are similar in all respects except nationality, which makes the effect of nationality differences in their answers stand out unusually clearly". Hofstede (1997:23-138; 2001:234-248) has identified a set of five distinctive values to examine society: power distance, individualism versus collectivism, assertiveness versus modesty, uncertainty avoidance, and short-term orientation versus long-term orientation. These are discussed below.

The other model I use is that of Trompenaars and Hampden-Turner (2002:1-2), who did fifteen years of academic and field research. More than a

---

[19] I am not aware of any cultural models that have been developed by Africans or Asians.

thousand cross-cultural training programmes in over twenty countries were conducted, which provided material on the different cultural values. In addition, thirty companies in fifty different countries made a contribution to the research.[20] The interviewees were presented with relevant case studies and a set of possible responses from which they chose one. The analysis of the answers shows to what extent the respondent identifies with one of the opposing values. Trompenaars and Hampden-Turner (2000; 2002) try to understand cultural diversity in business using fourteen patterns that may be grouped into seven pairs of polarities as follows: universalism versus particularism, individualism versus communitarianism, specificity versus diffuseness, achieved versus ascribed status, neutral versus affective, sequential versus synchronous time, and inner direction versus outer direction. These are discussed below. These values are based on the work of Talcott Parsons and Edward Shils (1951) on how people relate to each other. So Trompenaars and Hampden-Turner combine theory and empirical research to support and substantiate their results.

Each model has its limitations. There is no one best way to analyse culture, as it is such a complex system. Even though a list of values might oversimplify and have the danger of stereotyping, it has the advantage of greater specificity and descriptiveness. These two models are Western models being very dichotomistic and contrast-oriented. For practical reasons, to keep it simple, the categories are divided into two polar cultural value orientations. These should not be seen as two different poles but rather as the two ends of a continuum. There is no black and white in culture but a scale of different grey shades. These categories may also be mixed to a certain degree since societies are usually in transition. Nevertheless, the clarity of these models makes them helpful for the purpose of this research.

Using Hofstede's model and that of Trompenaars and Hampden-Turner discussed below in this chapter will help the understanding of the different cultures with their leadership styles and how this potentially impacts any collaboration. The cultural value categories described by these authors were used in formulating questions for the interviews. Through the questionnaire, data were collected during the interviews to determine towards which cultural value each society is leaning.

After the two models have been described and compared, I explain how they are used in interviews, group discussion, case studies and observations. Then a synthesis is drawn from both models and key themes relevant to leadership are extracted (see 2.2 Dialogue and Evaluation of Leadership Styles). Additional information relevant to these themes is obtained through the questionnaire used in the interviews. These key themes are then explored in chapters three and four.

These cultural models are dynamic and not static. This is important for this cross-cultural research, as culture is alive and dynamic. So we need to be careful not to paralyse ourselves through analysis. Analysis might help to gain a better understanding of what the preferred value orientations in each culture

---

[20] A large database with 30,000 participants exists (Trompenaars & Hampden-Turner 2002:2).

are. The purpose is to peel off the skin and get to the very heart of the society with its cultural values. The aim is to identify Western and Tanzanian leadership styles based on cultural values.

2.1.1.2 Hofstede's Model

Hofstede (1997:23-138; 2001:234-248) uses a set of five distinctive values to examine society:

- ❖ Power distance
- ❖ Individualism versus collectivism
- ❖ Assertiveness versus modesty
- ❖ Uncertainty avoidance
- ❖ Short-term orientation versus long-term orientation

Using these five values, he examines different areas such as social class, education level, occupation, family, school, workplace, state and ideas. For the purpose of this research, especially the areas of social class, occupation, family, workplace, state and ideas are considered.

2.1.1.2.1 Power distance

Inequality versus equality relate to the level of *power distance*. Hofstede (1997:28) defines power distance as "The extent to which the less powerful members of institutions and organisations within a country expect and accept that power is distributed unequally". Whereas institutions are units of people like the family, school, church, and the community, organisations are the places where people work. Power distance informs us how close the relationships among the individuals in a given society are.

To examine the level of power distance in the West and in Tanzania, both groups of people, bosses and subordinates, leaders and followers, need to be interviewed. Whereas power distance is explained from the value systems of those being led, the way power is distributed is usually explained from the behaviour of the leaders.

Inequality within a society can be seen in the existence of different social classes. This is more obvious in some countries, such as Britain, than in others. Which class somebody is from determines her/his language, level of education and therefore also her/his occupation. These three areas are mutually dependent.

Small power distance societies tend to be more egalitarian and individualistic. In large power societies, status, symbols and dependency are common characteristics.

To collect information specifically on power distance in both societies, the following questions for the interviews were designed: "What do you expect from your employer? What attitudes and actions do followers expect from leaders? What kinds of people have more power than others? In your context, how are women perceived as leaders in terms of their status and role? How are authority and accountability exercised? How do leaders relate to their subordinates? As a subordinate do you expect to be consulted or told what to do? Can you think of an instance where power was exercised positively? How often is the abuse of power an issue in the West and in Tanzania? How is power abused? How are decisions made?"

2.1.1.2.2   Individualism versus collectivism

It is interesting that most people in this world live in societies which are much more group oriented than focused on the interest of the individual. These societies are called *collectivist* societies. In collectivist societies, the extended family plays an important role. The power rests with the group rather than with the individual.

In comparison fewer people are part of *individualist* societies. Here the interests of the individual have more weight than the interests of the group. Small family units characterize these societies. The difference between individualism and collectivism is defined as follows:

> Individualism pertains to societies in which the ties between individuals are loose: everyone is expected to look after himself or herself and his or her immediate family. Collectivism as its opposite pertains to societies in which people from birth onwards are integrated into strong, cohesive in-groups, which throughout people's lifetime continue to protect them in exchange for unquestioning loyalty (Hofstede 1997:51).

Whereas Westerners tend to be individualistic, Tanzanians are group oriented. Thus, leaders and followers from the different societies may have different expectations and responsibilities. It becomes clear that individualism is the opposite pole to collectivism. In a work setting, enough personal time, considerable freedom, and a challenge where something can be achieved are important for the individualist.

In contrast, training opportunities, good physical working conditions, and the full use of skills and abilities on the job play an important role for the collectivist to be content in her/his work (:51-52).

As was discussed in chapter one, in individualist societies, a guilt culture can be observed, while the collectivist society is shame-oriented.

To collect information specifically on individualism versus collectivism in both societies, the following questions for the interviews were designed: "How would you describe a good Christian leader? Who do you consider to be a good leader? How does one become a good leader? Describe the structure of the organisation or church in which you work. What roles exist? How do the various roles interrelate? Who jokes with whom? Is getting the job done or are the people involved more important? What do you expect from your employer? Which is more important to you, success and progress or caring for others? How are tasks and goals achieved? What attitudes and actions do followers expect from leaders? What is the task of a representative[21] before, during and after a meeting?"

---

[21] The meaning of "representative" was not well understood by some interviewees. However, in all cases it could be clarified. It would have been more appropriate to use the word "delegate"

2.1.1.2.3 Assertiveness versus modesty

Hofstede (1997:79-108) categorizes societies as masculine and feminine societies. This is an unfortunate categorization using a gender terminology. It cannot be justified that some characteristics are male and others are female. A more appropriate terminology is to say that some societies are more *assertive* than others, which are more *modest* (:79-80).

In a work setting, a person from an assertive society expects opportunities for high salaries, recognition for quality performance, opportunities for promotion, and also a challenge where something can be achieved (:81-82).

In contrast, a person of a modest society expects to have a good working relationship with the supervisor, to cooperate with colleagues in harmony, a living situation that is desirable, and job security (:82).

To collect information specifically on assertiveness versus modesty in both societies, the following questions for the interviews were designed: "What do you expect from your employer? Which is more important to you, success and progress or caring for others? How are tasks and goals achieved? If somebody expresses a different opinion in a meeting, what do you think is the best way of dealing with it? How do you restore peace after a disagreement or conflict? Are harmony and consensus ultimate goals? Should aggression[22] and emotions be shown or not? May they be ventilated at proper times and places? If you have a different opinion, is it important to keep face and be willing to submit for a certain purpose? What form should a leader's communication take?"

2.1.1.2.4 Uncertainty avoidance

The factor of *avoidance of uncertainty* addresses the question to what degree a society is open and welcomes change. "Uncertainty avoidance can therefore be defined as the extent to which the members of a culture feel threatened by uncertain or unknown situations" (Hofstede 1997:113).

People with weak uncertainty avoidance are fairly comfortable in ambiguous situations. Direct emotional confrontation is avoided.

Members of a society with a strong uncertainty avoidance often experience high stress and anxiety. They are time and achievement oriented. They need to have laws and rules to guide their daily life.

The uncertainty avoidance factor influences the way people are willing to change their leadership behaviour. Uncertainty avoidance has to do with the culture in which a leader lives but also with a leader's personality.

To collect information specifically regarding uncertainty avoidance in both societies, the following questions for the interviews were designed: "If you had a contract with someone and the circumstances changed what would you

---

instead of "representative". That way it would have been consistent with question 4.16 "What authority do delegates have in a meeting? In which way are delegates empowered?".

[22] The word "aggression" was not meaningful during the interviews since in more or less all societies, showing aggression is considered to be rude behaviour. Aggression is usually associated with angry and inappropriate physical behaviour.

do? If you had an appointment and a visitor came to see you unexpectedly, what would you do? Should aggression and emotions be shown or not? May they be ventilated at proper times and places? If you have a different opinion, is it important to keep face and be willing to submit for a certain purpose?"[23]

2.1.1.2.5   Short-term versus long-term orientation

Based on Confucianism, Hofstede (1997:164-170; 2001:234-248) describes the fifth dimension of short-term orientation versus long-term orientation.

The values of a *long-term* oriented society are persistence, perseverance, adaptation of traditions to a modern context, respect for social and status obligations within limits, and a willingness to subordinate oneself for a purpose (Hofstede 1997:165 & 173). According to Hofstede (2001:237), long-term orientation looks towards the future and is dynamic.

A *short-term* oriented society is more past and present oriented and more static. Its values are personal steadiness and stability, protecting your 'face', respect for tradition, respect for social and status obligations regardless of cost, and the reciprocation of greetings, favours, and gifts (Hofstede 1997:166 & 173).

Whether leaders are future oriented or more focused on the present and past affects how leaders make decisions and collaborate. These differences can result in enormous tensions in partnerships.

To collect information specifically regarding short-term versus long-term orientation in both societies, the following questions for the interviews were designed: "Is getting the job done or are the people involved more important? If you had an appointment and a visitor came to see you unexpectedly, what would you do?"

2.1.1.3   Trompenaars and Hampden-Turner's Model

Trompenaars and Hampden-Turner (2000; 2002) try to understand cultural diversity in business using fourteen patterns that may be grouped into seven pairs of polarities as follows:

- ❖ Universalism versus particularism: rules and relationships
- ❖ Individualism versus communitarianism: the individual and the group
- ❖ Specificity versus diffuseness: how far to get involved
- ❖ Achieved versus ascribed status: how status is accorded
- ❖ Neutral versus affective: feelings and relationships
- ❖ Sequential versus synchronous time: how time is managed
- ❖ Inner direction versus outer direction: how to relate to nature

These sets of values need to be seen on a continuum. Even though values may have a minus and a plus side not all of these values can be seen as oppo-

---

[23] Some questions were used for more than one purpose.

site poles since they are somewhat interconnected as reflected in the questionnaire. If somebody wants to see the similarities s/he also needs to recognize the differences. An individualist lives in community and needs a relationship with others. A collectivist, on the other hand, may also need time alone.

Finally, at the end of this section the different types of organisational culture are discussed.

2.1.1.3.1 Universalism versus particularism

Universalism (Hampden-Turner & Trompenaars 2000:13) is defined by playing by the rules, codes and laws. It tends to generalize situations.

On the opposite, *particularism* (:13) makes exceptions and considers the circumstances before a decision is made. The relationship plays a much more important role than what the rule says. Hampden-Turner and Trompenaars define this dimension of universalism and particularism precisely:

> Universalism searches for sameness and similarity and tries to subject all members of class or universe to the laws of their commonality. Particularism searches for differences, for unique and exceptional forms of distinction that render phenomena incomparable and of matchless quality (2000:14).

Relationships are essential in leadership. However, they may play a different role and take a different place in the West than in Tanzania.

To collect information specifically regarding universalism versus particularism in both societies, the following questions for the interviews were designed: "How do you build trust? How do you know that you can trust a person? How is trust breached? If you had a contract with someone and the circumstances changed, what would you do?"

2.1.1.3.2 Individualism versus communitarianism

Hofstede and Trompenaars and Hampden-Turner have basically included the same values of individualism versus collectivism or communitarianism in their value sets. *Individualism* focuses on the individual person. An individualistic society is characterized by competition, self-reliance, self-interest and personal growth and fulfilment (Hampden-Turner & Trompenaars 2000:68-69). Ideas come from the individual. They are the result of her/his choice and voluntary commitment.

In *communitarian* societies the interests of the group prevail over the interests of the individual. Cooperation, social concern, altruism, public service and societal legacy are important characteristics. Ideas are created through shared knowledge, communal values, and mutual supportiveness.

Individualism and communitarianism are defined as follows:

> Individualism seeks to locate the origins of value in the creative, feeling, inquiring, and discovering person who seeks fulfilment and is solely responsible for choices made and convictions formed. Communitarianism seeks to locate the origins of value within the social discourse

of the living society, which nurtures, educates and takes responsibility for the spirit engendered among its members (Hampden-Turner & Trompenaars 2000:69-70).

Since this category is basically identical to Hofstede's category of individualism versus collectivism, the same questions can be applied as above.

2.1.1.3.3   Specificity versus diffuseness

One of the most distinctive contrasts of a *specific* and *diffuse* society is *private* and *public* life space, which might be one of the sources for this dimension (Hampden-Turner & Trompenaars 2000:156-158). This dimension is defined as "the degree to which we engage others in **specific** areas of life and single levels of personality, or **diffusely** in multiple areas of our lives and at several levels of personality at the same time" (Trompenaars & Hampden-Turner 2002:81) [their emphasis]. Specific cultures have large public spaces in comparison to diffuse cultures. People from specific cultures are very willing to share their personal belongings and experiences with other people. They tend to be direct, precise and blunt.

People from a diffuse culture keep things rather close to themselves. They tend to be indirect, tactful, and somewhat ambiguous.

Specific and diffuse cultures are sometimes also referred to as *low* and *high context* (:89-90). This has to do with how much information somebody has to have before effective communication can take place. In societies with a high context, information sharing needs to take place before business can be properly discussed.

Specificity and diffuseness plays an important role in how much and what kinds of information people are willing to disclose, which impacts how people lead, make decisions and conduct meetings.

To collect information regarding specificity versus diffuseness in both societies, the following questions for the interviews were designed: "If you have a conversation with somebody, are there certain things you share more easily than others? If yes, what kind of information do you feel more or less comfortable in disclosing? If you had a contract with someone and the circumstances changed what would you do?"

2.1.1.3.4   Achieved versus ascribed status

In an *achieving* society the individual has a certain reputation because s/he has accomplished something. S/he fills a certain position because s/he has achieved it. In other societies, a person has been given a certain position or reputation. This is called *ascribed* status (Hampden-Turner & Trompenaars 2000: 189-191). "While achieved status refers to **doing**, ascribed status refers to **being**" (Trompenaars & Hampden-Turner 2002:102) [their emphasis]. Both achieved and ascribed status are important for ethics and spirituality and thus for leadership.

Titles play an important role in an ascribing society, as they clarify the status in the organisation. In an achieving society, titles are only used when they are relevant to the competence somebody brings to the task.

To collect information specifically regarding achieved versus ascribed status in both societies, the following questions for the interviews were designed: "What gives a person power? What kinds of people have more power than others? What is the role of the chairperson in a meeting? Do you always introduce someone using their title? What authority do delegates have in a meeting? In which way are delegates empowered? What is the task of a representative before, during and after a meeting?"

2.1.1.3.5   Neutral versus affective

Whether a society is more neutral or affective is indicated by the use of *reasons* and *emotions* (Trompenaars & Hampden-Turner 2002:69). A *neutral* society tends to separate emotions from reasoning. In an *affective* culture, feelings are more freely expressed than in a neutral culture. A key distinction of neutral and affective society is whether people communicate more verbally than non-verbally (:74-76). Whether people are more neutral or affective impacts on how they communicate. Communication plays a central role in leadership and partnership.

To collect information specifically regarding neutral versus affective in both societies, the following questions for the interviews were designed: "Should aggression and emotions be shown or not? May they be ventilated at proper times and places? If you have a different opinion, is it important to keep face and be willing to submit for a certain purpose? What form should a leader's communication take?"

2.1.1.3.6   Sequential versus synchronous time

In a society where people value *sequential* time, it is regarded as an arrow or a line in terms of seconds, minutes, hours, days, months, and years (Hampden-Turner & Trompenaars 2000:295). Once time is past, it is lost forever. "The cultures concerned with sequential time tend to see relationships as more instrumental" (Trompenaars & Hampden-Turner 2002:131). Relationships tend to be in focus as much as they help achieving the goal.

Synchronous time in contrast is circular (Hampden-Turner & Trompenaars 2000:295). Societies that value synchronous time are event-oriented. Events and opportunities repeat themselves. The past is important and carried through the present into the future (Trompenaars & Hampden-Turner 2002:133). Change is difficult unless people are assured that their heritage is safe (:133). Personal relationships play an important role (:131). Whereas in societies with sequential time the relationships tend to be seen as a means to achieve an end, in societies with synchronous time orientation, the other person is important and valued as a person in her/himself. In other words, the relationship outweighs the outcome.

According to Hampden-Turner and Trompenaars (2000:307), sequential people like to do one thing at a time and have difficulties handling unexpected happenings; synchronous people do many things at a time. Different perspectives of time can lead to different value systems and consequently create misunderstandings.

Regarding sequential versus synchronous time, the same questions are used as listed under Hofstede's category of short-term versus long-term orientation.

2.1.1.3.7 Inner versus outer direction

Whether a society tends more towards inner or outer direction can be observed by how people relate to nature, whether they try to control nature or let it take its course. While *inner-directed* societies "believe that they can and should control nature by imposing their will upon it", *outer-directed* societies "believe that man [human beings] is part of nature and must go along with its laws, directions, and forces" (Trompenaars & Hampden-Turner 2002:141). Actions and decisions are controlled either internally or externally. Inner and outer direction is defined as follows:

> Inner direction conceives of virtue as *inside* each of us – in our souls, wills, convictions, principles, and core beliefs – in the triumph of conscious purpose. Outer direction conceives of virtue as *outside* each of us in natural rhythms, in the beauties and power of nature, in aesthetic environments and relationships (Hampden-Turner & Trompenaars 2000:234). [their emphasis]

People from inner-directed societies tend to have a dominating attitude. Convictions are expressed openly.

Outer-directed people are flexible and peaceful. Harmonic relationships are important. They try to avoid conflict. They are able to adjust well as circumstances change.

It can be observed that inner-directed cultures are more self-conscious, which means guilt-oriented than outer-directed cultures, which are more shame-oriented. It is interesting to note that there is a close connection to being focused on the individual or being group-oriented.

To collect information specifically regarding inner versus outer direction in both societies the following questions for the interviews were designed: "How would you describe a good Christian leader? Who do you consider to be a good leader? Which is more important to you, success and progress or caring for others? If somebody expresses a different opinion in a meeting, what do you think is the best way of dealing with it? How do you restore peace after a disagreement or conflict? Are harmony and consensus ultimate goals? Should aggression and emotions be shown or not? May they be ventilated at proper times and places? If you have a different opinion, is it important to keep face and be willing to submit for a certain purpose?"

Leaders who act based on a combination of certain cultural values as discussed above influence the culture of an organisation. Which values leaders employ will determine the organisational culture. Thus, what follows is a discussion of different organisational cultures that can be found in different societies and places.

2.1.1.3.8 Organisational culture

The individuals who are part of the organisation influence organisational culture. Trompenaars and Hampden-Turner point out three aspects, which are important in determining organisational culture:

- ❖ The general relationship between employees and their organisation.
- ❖ The vertical or hierarchical system of authority defining superiors and subordinates.
- ❖ The general views of employees about the organisation's destiny, purpose and goals and their places in this (2002:157).

To describe organisations the two criteria equality-hierarchy and orientation to the person versus orientation to the task are used. This results basically in four different types of organisational culture (:158-177):

- ❖ The family
- ❖ The Eiffel Tower
- ❖ The guided missile
- ❖ The incubator

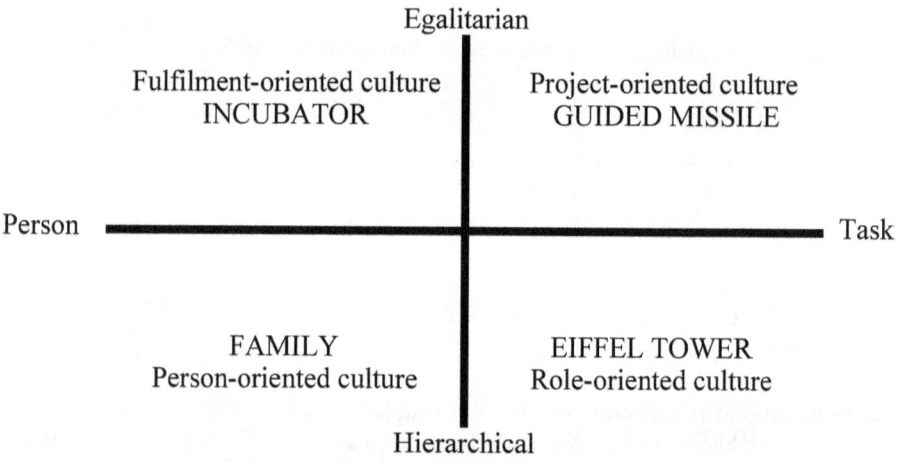

Figure 2.4 (Trompenaars & Hampden-Turner 2002:159)

In the *family* organisation, personal relationships are important. There is also a strong hierarchy, in which the leader is seen as the caring father. It is as much a person-oriented as a power-oriented culture. Power is ascribed to the leader. The authority of the leader is not questioned. Status is ascribed by age. The family-style culture tends to be high context. The individual receives pressure from the group. Relationships are more diffuse than specific. The family organisation is more concerned with their people than with objectives. Employees are rewarded by praise and appreciation more than by money. In this organisation, it is important to do the right things rather than doing things right.

In the *Eiffel Tower* organisation, the boss is at the very top. Employees act per instruction. Status is ascribed and relationships are specific. Status depends on the role somebody has. So it is impossible to challenge somebody's authority. The Eiffel Tower culture is very much role-oriented. In the Eiffel Tower organisation, people are expected to fulfil their given roles and follow set procedures rather than working through relationships.

In comparison to the family and the Eiffel Tower, the *guided missile* organisation is egalitarian. Performance and contribution to the desired outcome are the key distinctions in the guided missile culture. Members are committed to the task. Teamwork is greatly valued. This organisation welcomes change.

The fulfilment of the individual member is more important than the organisation in the *incubator* organisation. The incubator culture has a flat structure, in which the individual is important. The organisation should be an incubator for self-expression and self-fulfilment of the individual person. This organisation is characterized by an atmosphere of freedom for creating and innovating. Leadership is achieved. A potential leader must demonstrate quality performance producing results.

Trompenaars and Hampden-Turner do not take into account that the purpose of an organisation influences its character, like sales as opposed to research or welfare service. Various organisations exist for different purposes. An organisation that sells books has a different focus and character than one that does linguistic research or health care. Different purposes of an organisation may require different structures.

Because leaders influence the organisational culture different types of organisational culture have been discussed above. However, because of the constraints of space, in this research I will not be able to examine organisational culture in depth. At the same time, it cannot be completely excluded from the discussion. Thus, I will touch only briefly on organisational culture in chapter four. Therefore, only the following questions address the issue of organisational culture: "Describe the structure of the organisation or church in which you work. What roles exist? How do the various roles interrelate? Who jokes with whom?"

2.1.1.4   A Comparison of Hofstede's and Trompenaars and Hampden-Turner's Models

As noted earlier, Trompenaars and Hampden-Turner follow Hofstede in their model. Thus, the different criteria of Hofstede and Trompenaars and Hampden-Turner complement each other well, as presented below in figure 2.5.

COMPARISON OF BOTH MODELS	
HOFSTEDE	TROMPENAARS AND HAMPDEN-TURNER
Power distance	Achieved versus ascribed status
Individualism versus collectivism	Individualism versus communitarianism
Assertiveness versus modesty	Universalism versus particularism Specificity versus diffuseness Neutral versus affective
Uncertainty avoidance	Inner versus outer direction
Short-term versus long-term orientation	Sequential versus synchronous time

Figure 2.5

The diagram above indicates that the two value sets of Hofstede and Trompenaars and Hampden-Turner are slightly different but certain connections can be made. Whereas Hofstede measures power distance, Trompenaars and Hampden-Turner describe in which way status and power are received. Whereas power distance describes the end, achieved and ascribed status describes the means by which power distance is created. Individualism versus collectivism or communitarianism is basically the same in both models. The comparison is more complex in terms of assertiveness versus modesty. Assertiveness has elements of universalism, specificity and being neutral, like focusing on rules rather than relationships, being task-oriented and direct, and showing emotion being perceived as weakness. Modesty has elements of particularism, diffuseness and being affective (like a focus on relationships and expressing emotions freely). Uncertainty avoidance can be linked to inner versus outer direction. Inner-directed societies may avoid uncertainty more than outer-directed societies. The uncertainty avoidance factor is influenced by the way in which people relate to nature. People with strong uncertainty avoidance are inner-directed with a desire to control nature as much as they can. Whereas inner-directed people try to control actions and decisions to avoid uncertainty, outer-directed people are able to live with a high level of ambiguity and uncertainty. Outer-directed people tend to be flexible, which helps them to cope well with a high uncertainty factor. In a short-term oriented society, people tend to view time synchronously. Both short-term and synchronous time orientation are event oriented, with an emphasis on the past and present. Relationships prevail over the task. On the other hand, both long-term and sequential time oriented people look towards the future where relationships are less important than the task.

These cultural values and approaches are applied in chapters three, four and five to interpret the data generated through the questionnaires, case studies, personal observations and group discussion. The different categories are applied to understand the cultural context and position them culturally so that the two leadership styles can be compared to understand the cultural differences and similarities. It is important to understand these differences and similarities as a basis for the evaluation of leadership styles and how they may impact partnerships. In the dialogue these cultural values are used not only to interpret the information but also the group dynamics that take place during group discussion.

2.2 Dialogue and Evaluation of Leadership Styles

All cultural values discussed in this chapter influence leadership styles in one way or another. To facilitate a dialogue between Westerners and Tanzanians, the following key issues are drawn from the two models discussed above, as shown in figure 2.6: Personal information and leadership, character and leadership, relationships and leadership, power and leadership, and conflict and leadership. These key issues form the basis as themes of my questionnaire to obtain information for the next two chapters.

KEY ISSUES DERIVED FROM BOTH MODELS		
HOFSTEDE	TROMPENAARS AND HAMPDEN-TURNER	KEY ISSUES
Power distance	Achieved versus ascribed status	Power and leadership
Individualism versus collectivism	Individualism versus communitarianism	Character and leadership Relationships and leadership
Assertiveness versus modesty	Universalism versus particularism Specificity versus diffuseness Neutral versus affective	Conflict and leadership
Uncertainty avoidance	Inner versus outer direction	Conflict and leadership Character and leadership
Short-term versus long-term orientation	Sequential versus synchronous time	Relationship and leadership

Figure 2.6

The personal information (subsection 1 of the questionnaire) is essential as people from different age groups may have different cultural perspectives. Their church background may influence their theological understanding of leadership. People's educational level, their current occupation and work experience may influence how they exercise power, conduct meetings, make decisions and solve conflicts. The personal information of the interviewees helps to determine how big the gap is between the desired leadership style and reality.

Character and leadership (subsection 2 of the questionnaire) is closely related to individualism and collectivism and also inner versus outer direction. Character may be shaped differently whether a leader grew up in an individualistic or collectivist society. Individualistic societies may have different expectations from a leader than communitarian people. Individualists may value different character traits of a leader than those valued by collectivists. Whether leaders are more inner or outer directed may impact their behaviour, which in turn shapes their character, as has been discussed in chapter one.

Individualism and collectivism is the main focus on the whole area of relationships (subsection 3 of the questionnaire). For an individualist, the task prevails over the relationship, whereas for a collectivist the relationship is in focus. Leaders from individualist societies tend to have a different kind of relationship with their subordinates and other leaders than leaders from collectivist societies. Group-oriented subordinates have different expectations of their superiors than individualists. The importance of relationships is also reflected in a leader's time orientation.

Power and leadership are closely connected. How leaders exercise power depends on the level of power distance and whether power is ascribed or achieved. Power distance (subsection 4 of the questionnaire) varies from society to society. The level of power distance and how power is obtained and exercised are key to leadership. The way power is obtained, expressed and exercised basically impacts on all areas of leadership, including how meetings are conducted and decisions made.

Leaders also need to handle many conflict situations, hence the theme of "conflict and leadership". The way they deal with conflict depends on how assertive or modest, inner or outer directed, universal or particular, specific or diffuse, neutral or affective they are. An assertive, universal and specific leader may confront somebody directly, whereas a modest, particular and diffuse leader may desire harmony. Different communication styles can often result in conflict. Leaders from a neutral society may have difficulties reading many non-verbal clues an affective leader gives. This information is collected in subsection five of the questionnaire.

The information gained on these key issues through the literature, questionnaires, observations and case studies is described in chapters three and four. The generated data is then analysed and interpreted applying the cultural models discussed above.

Christian ethics is an ethics of both the individual person and the community. Ethical views and decisions need to be discussed, formed and made in community. The data generated from literature, interviews, case studies and observations inform chapters three and four. The two leadership styles are described, compared and interpreted to identify the major differences and similarities. After different leadership contexts have been described, compared and interpreted in chapters three and four, Westerners and Tanzanians enter into a cross-cultural dialogue in chapter five. The dialogue of the two groups, Westerners and Tanzanians, in chapter five is an expansion of the information presented in chapters three and four to identify differences, strengths and weaknesses of both leadership styles. Tanzanians present their view of Western leadership and, in turn, Westerners comment on Tanzanian leadership as they experience it. Both groups also discuss their views of Christian leadership in a group discussion. The different leadership styles are openly discussed and debated in the light of the Scriptures. Such a dialogue requires "that 'I' may be open and receptive to the 'other's' being in his or her world. Furthermore, such openness and receptiveness imply that I listen and see the other as a partner in dialogue" (Bell 2002:19). This dialogue also requires that everybody listen carefully, as North American philosopher Richard Bell further points out:

> We must learn how to listen and give detailed attention to the faintest cries of insult and oppression. This requires looking injustice in the eye and developing a capacity to listen to other voices as well as one's own, and cultivating a moral sensibility that goes beyond local thinking, self-interest, and greed (2002:57).

Good listening skills are essential in such a discussion to understand the underlying thinking, motivations, and feelings. Through this dialogue Westerners and Tanzanians learn together from each other and the Bible. Through this process, potential areas of misunderstandings and their impact in cross-cultural partnerships are discovered, potential blind spots may be detected, and the "cultural chains" are unlocked. This cross-cultural dialogue may result in a deeper and better understanding of Christian-ethical leadership so that the respective leadership styles are transformed by the Holy Spirit, based on Christian values such as love, justice, mercy, faithfulness and humility, and virtues such as honesty, stewardship, godliness, self-control, compassion and being forgiving. Thus, a more fruitful collaboration is fostered. In reality, these discussions need to be seen as a contribution of an ongoing long-term learning process.

After this cross-cultural dialogue, both leadership styles are critiqued in the light of Christian norms, values and virtues derived from the Bible. During this step, the various Christian-ethical criteria relevant to this study of leadership styles discussed in chapter one are employed as outlined below. As the evaluation of leadership styles takes place, the cultural values discussed above, such as power distance, individualism versus collectivism, assertiveness versus modesty, universalism versus particularism, specificity versus diffuseness, neutral versus affective, uncertainty avoidance, inner versus outer direction and time are also taken into consideration. This is because a certain act may be seen as loving from a Tanzanian perspective, but not honest from a Western viewpoint. However, these culturally conditioned perspectives must be challenged by the biblical norms, values, and virtues, as outlined in chapter one. Jesus provided the example of biblical leadership in the way he exercised love, justice, mercy, faithfulness, humility and power. Christian leaders are called to follow the footsteps of Jesus, despite living in many different cultural contexts.

As suggested in chapter one, in examining a situation ethically, the agent's goal, motivation, and means must be good. Therefore, as the two leadership styles are evaluated in chapter five, I begin by looking at the *character* of the actor or actors and the motivation of their behaviour (Kammer 1988:86). Does the leader act out of love? Does the leader behave justly, mercifully, faithfully and humbly? What virtues are applied? Is s/he honest, godly, self-controlled, compassionate, and forgiving? To discover real motivation can be difficult at times, as there may be a hidden motivation. Thus, the agent's *intentions* are also considered. Kammer (:86) suggests, "One way of unmasking our actual motivations is to look at the ends we are actually seeking". Looking at the intentions and ends sought requires a Christian-ethical reflection applying the biblical norms, values, and virtues. Then the nature of the act itself, the *means*, is considered (:87). Are the leader's actions based on love, justice, mercy, faithfulness and humility? Is the leader's use of power compliant with how Jesus exercised power, taking the Jewish context into consideration? Does the leader behave with a Christ-like character? Are the leader's actions compliant with the mission of Jesus of bringing good news to the poor, setting free the oppressed, proclaiming liberty and bringing salvation? Does the leader act out of a close, intimate relationship with God? From this comparison, dialogue and evaluation, it is hoped to be possible to draw a conclusion about what is essentially Christian and what is merely Western or Tanzanian.

Finally, various possible actions promote Christ-like leadership that is culturally appropriate and their likely consequences are considered (:87). Since this is a Christian-ethical analysis and evaluation it is important that all the above aspects are informed by love and a vision of God's kingdom (:88).

2.3 Reflection, Practical Actions and Application in Christian Leadership

As one engages in the analysis, dialogue, evaluation, and reflection of leadership issues by applying Christian norms, values and virtues, kingdom leadership and the biblical use of power as discussed in chapter one, emotions can arise. To express these emotions appropriately, it is essential to have a sound understanding of the context and the situation. Emotions have their place and play an important role in moral reasoning, as Connors and McCormick (1998:175) suggest: "Christian ethics does not entail moral reasoning done in some 'cool', dispassionate or antiseptic manner. It is not (or should not be) ivory-tower theorizing about esoteric questions that have little if any impact on human experience." Ethics has to do with real life experience, which is aroused with passion, dedication and zeal. Emotions have a certain location, they energize for action, and are fashioned in the context of relationships (:189-194). If a situation creates emotions, including anger and rage, it may be an indicator for the critically important beginning of moral reasoning. Passion and commitment lead to practical actions and applications.

From the analysis of the questionnaires, case studies and observations and an evaluation of the cross-cultural dialogue among Westerners and Tanzanians, a Christian-ethical view of leadership may be derived at the end of chapter five. At this point, a number of questions need to be asked, including: What can Westerners learn from Tanzanians and vice versa? Which leadership behaviour needs to change in each society? What are the challenges in cross-cultural partnerships? Which leadership aspects are hindrances in partnerships? Which leadership aspects are fostering partnerships? The answers to these questions are summarized at the end of chapter five. My hope is that this whole process will lead toward a better understanding of the challenges and difficulties sometimes experienced in partnerships and show a way forward to improve relationships and make collaboration more fruitful.

To summarize, in this chapter the methodological research used in this study has been discussed. Before leadership styles can be evaluated, it is essential to understand the context in which leaders operate. To learn more about the leadership context, data are generated through existing literature, interviews, observations, case studies and a group discussion. The main emphasis is on the interviews, observations and case studies supplemented by the literature. Since the interviews play an important part in this research, the interview method was discussed in length. The collected data will reveal information and insights in terms of the importance of a leader's character, theology and culture.

Cultural values play an important role in leadership behaviour. The cultural models by Hofstede and that of Trompenaars and Hampden-Turner, as discussed and compared in this chapter, give insight into which questions to ask in the interviews and how to interpret the data collected. They also provide useful tools for the analysis and interpretation of the social environment outlined in chapters three and four. The following key issues related to leadership have been drawn from the cultural models: Personal information and leadership, character and leadership, relationships and leadership, power and leadership, and conflict and leadership. The information related to these key issues will be presented, compared and interpreted in chapters three and four to identify the major differences and similarities of the two leadership styles. In chapter five, the understanding of the context is expanded through a cross-cultural dialogue in a group discussion. Westerners and Tanzanians assess and discuss the strengths and weaknesses of their leadership styles. Christian-ethical views of leadership need to be discussed, formed and made in community. Through this open dialogue both groups may be able to discover what they can learn from each other. This process and evaluation of leadership styles in the light of the Scriptures may lead to a more global understanding of Christian leadership and, hopefully, to healthier partnerships. To evaluate both leadership styles the biblical norms and values, the vision of kingdom leadership practised by Jesus, and the biblical use of power as discussed in chapter one are applied. The analysis, dialogue, evaluation and reflection of Western and Tanzanian leadership issues will lead to practical actions and application for Christian leadership in chapter five.

As this is an ongoing dialogue, culture is always in transition, and new biblical insights are gained, it is important not to stop here. Kammer (1988:89) argues: "What is required, then, is that we continue our moral reflection after the particular act. We study its consequences; we attempt to learn from its successes and failures so that we can become better partners in dialogue." This dissertation does not claim to come up with a final answer regarding Christian-ethical leadership. It is much more to be understood as part of an existing and ongoing dialogue. It is essential to continue this dialogue as culture and theological understanding changes, people grow and mature personally and spiritually, and gain additional insights. The ultimate goal is that leaders from the West and Tanzania are continually transformed to become more like Christ, practising kingdom leadership.

Chapter 3

The Cultural Contexts, Personal Background and Character of Western, Particularly Germanic and Anglo-Saxon, and Tanzanian Leadership

The first chapter of this dissertation has shown that Christian values and virtues impact a leader's behaviour. Therefore, a leader's character and its formation are important in leadership. Biblical values and virtues and character are influenced by the culture in which one lives. Consequently, Western and Tanzanian leadership may have some aspects that are merely cultural and others that are essentially Christian. Therefore, it is essential to understand the cultural values of each society as discussed in chapter two.

In this chapter the cultural contexts, personal background and character of Western, particularly Germanic and Anglo-Saxon, and Tanzanian leadership are described and compared using data collected from the interviews, participant observations, case studies and existing literature. For the interviews, a questionnaire was used. To present the interviewees' answers, generally the outline of the questionnaire is followed. Occasionally, the order of the answers to the questions has been changed to group the answers together according to themes to provide a logical flow of the argument. First, the answers of the Western respondents are presented and then those of the Tanzanian respondents. How Christian leaders practise biblical values (question 2.12) in their own culture is presented in this chapter. In chapter five, as part of the dialogue, it is presented how Western leaders perceive the practise of biblical values by Tanzanians and vice versa. Before the leadership styles can be evaluated and critiqued from a Christian-ethical perspective, it is essential to understand the context in which leaders operate.

Thus, after the different leadership aspects have been described, they are interpreted and compared, applying the Christian-ethical framework of chapter one and the two cultural value models by Hofstede, Trompenaars and Hampden-Turner, as discussed in chapter two. This will help us to understand why leaders in both societies act the way they do. This description will also enable us to see in which way leadership is influenced by culture, theology, and character and which is dominant. The information from the interviews, observations, case studies and literature presented in this chapter will then be further evaluated in chapter five.

3.1 Cultural Contexts and Leadership

Leadership behaviour, theology and character are culturally influenced. Thus, it is important to have a close look at the cultural context of Western and Tanzanian leadership styles.

3.1.1 Western Context

Because of the constraints of space of this research and since most SIL members in Tanzania come either from Germanic or Anglo-Saxon countries, this study focuses mainly on the Germanic and Anglo-Saxon countries. For the purpose of this research, Germanic countries include Germany, Austria, and the Netherlands[24]. Anglo-Saxon countries include the United States of America, Great Britain, Canada, and Australia.

Western countries are quite diverse. Differences exist among Westerners, such as history, language and cultural values. Germanics tend to be more formal than Anglo-Saxons. Germanic people are more serious and do not smile as much as Anglo-Saxons. "The German language is much more literal than English" (Hall & Hall 1990:50). Anglo-Saxons are not as frank or blunt as Germanics are. The German "consensus decision-making process is often more involved and deliberate than the American, requiring many lateral clearances as well as considerable extensive background research" (:35). In terms of power, "Germans usually prefer that power and position be handled with grace and reserve. Americans in positions of power are often much more ostentatious in their material possessions and in their enthusiasm for publicity about their lavish lifestyles" (:42). It is, therefore, difficult to speak of a 'Western leadership style' as such. Nevertheless, there are enough similarities to warrant this generalised description as is shown in the literature quoted in this and the next chapter as well as in my empirical findings. This is an attempt to describe the common features of the various Western leadership styles. It is usually difficult to make generalizations. Therefore, it is important to bear in mind that these are **tendencies**. Whenever there are significant differences between Western leadership styles, they are pointed out.

Western leadership behaviour, like others, is influenced by culture. My hypothesis is that on a continuum, Germanic and Anglo-Saxon societies tend to be individualistic, assertive, universal, specific, neutral and inner directed. They try to avoid uncertainty as much as possible, have a long-term and sequential time orientation, practise small power distance, and status is usually achieved. These cultural values were discussed at length earlier in chapter two.

3.1.2 Tanzanian Context

Tanzania is a large country and quite diverse from region to region. Major differences exist between Tanzanians, such as language and cultural values.[25] There is a great variety of ethnic groups and leadership styles in Tanzania. It is, therefore, difficult to speak of a single 'Tanzanian leadership style'. Nevertheless, there are enough similarities to warrant a generalised description of

---

[24] According to Hofstede (1997:84), Dutch people are more modest than other Westerners. However, for my empirical research this does not seem to be the case, since it does not affect the data.
[25] The *Ethnologue* (Gordon & Grimes 2005:197) lists 127 living languages in Tanzania.

important tendencies. The Swahili[26] culture serves especially as a kind of over layer or umbrella, which goes across all language groups. This is an attempt to describe the common features of the various Tanzanian leadership styles.

Tanzanian leadership behaviour is influenced by a leader's worldview and culture. Culture in turn is very much influenced by history. Leadership in Tanzania has been strongly influenced by its *traditional, missionary, colonial* and *political* history. This is important to understand, as it influences the Tanzanian leadership style.

The Anglican Tanzanian bishop and theologian Geoffrey Mdimi Mhogolo (1996:v) has observed that many leaders in the Tanzanian Church practise an authoritarian, strong and very top-down leadership style. Some of the reasons for this may lie in the history that has been set by traditions, colonialists and even past missionaries, as Mhogolo points out in his book *Huduma ya Kanisa* – Service of the Church:

> In the Church many ministers see themselves leading as they lead and administer their families; others lead like the German colonialists using the stick, terror and force; others lead like some past missionaries, imitating them as they administered the Church, and other ministers practise a great mixture of various heritages (1996:1).[27]

Traditionally, in Tanzania only a few ethnic groups were ruled by a *king* or a *chief*, whereas the majority of people groups depended on the leadership of the elders, who were very much respected together with some specialists in the village (:2-4). The king was charged with certain responsibilities like fighting war against enemies and being an advisor in difficult court cases. Sometimes if the kings had power over diseases and rain, they were also seen as spiritual kings. If the kings did not fulfil their duties, they could be replaced by the next person in line. As Mhogolo argues, it is interesting to note that it is not the shared leadership model but the "king" tradition that has been carried over and impacts the Church today in many ways:

> Sometimes ministers, especially bishops and catechists or pastors, are kings in their dioceses and parishes. The way they lead and manage demonstrates the heart of a king. They have a few advisors or others do not have any at all. They lead by giving orders only. There is no discussion. There is no debate or reaching a consensus together (1996:4).[28]

---

[26] Swahili is the national language of Tanzania. It is an artificial language, which is a mixture of several Bantu languages, Arabic, German and English. Swahili has served the country well to foster unity among the many different ethnic groups.

[27] All translations in this dissertation from Swahili to English are my own translations and have been proofread by Michael Nchimbi.
Translated from the original Swahili: Katika Kanisa, wahudumu wengi hujikuta wanasimamia kama wanavyosimamia na kutawala familia zao; na wengine hutawala kama wakoloni Wajerumani waliopita, kwa viboko, vitisho na ukali; na wengine kama wamisionari fulani waliopita, wakiwaiga jinsi hao wamisionari walivyokuwa wakitawala Kanisa, na wahudumu wengine wana mchanganyiko mkubwa wa urithi mbalimbali.

[28] Translated from the original Swahili: Wakati mwingine wahudumu, na hasa maaskofu na makasisi au wachungaji ni wafalme katika dayosisi na parishi zao. Jinsi wanavyoongoza na

In traditional African leadership we find both, individual authoritarian leaders like kings and also elders who lead as a group. However, in Tanzania "Owing to *ujamaa*[29] politics, which comprises amongst other things a forced displacement in the whole country, the traditional clan structures only partly function. Many of the young people don't know the traditional structures anymore. The traditional leadership system, where the chieftain discussed with the elders and then came to his decision, exists in only a few places now" (Schubert 2002:4). Ethnic groups are often mixed especially in towns. Traditional structures are still in place mainly in remote areas, such as Malila area in the south or Temi area in the north, where the resettlement has not taken place.

Apart from traditional systems, Tanzanian leadership has also been influenced by *missionaries* and *colonialists* (Mhogolo 1996:10-17). The first missionaries who came to Tanzania faced a very different environment than at home. They had a lot more responsibility and authority than they had in their home countries. During the colonial times, the missionaries and the colonialists were closely related. Hence, there was not much difference in leadership style. Africans were afraid of white people. After the First World War, educated pastors received a lot of responsibilities and authority. People were afraid of bishops, missionaries, all white people and African pastors. According to Mhogolo (:13), it was necessary to be afraid of somebody to express respect. It can be observed that even today, some Tanzanian church leaders lead in a similar way to the first missionaries. They want to be respected not by choice but by necessity. Mhogolo explains this attitude and behaviour:

> African ministers have not realised that how the responsibility of authority was understood by the missionaries had to do with the environment and their understanding together with pressing the Africans to administer them well. Now even though these ministers are Africans they still administer their own people using force, strength, and even punishment (1996:18).[30]

As seen from the discussion above, it can be argued that Tanzanian leadership style has been influenced by several historical factors like traditional kingdoms, family structures, missionaries and colonial governments (Chiwanga 2001:300).

Tanzanian culture is also strongly influenced by many years of *ujamaa*-policy, an African socialism rooted in Christianity and in communal sharing

---

kutawala wanaonyesha moyo wa ufalme. Wana washauri wachache ama pengine hawana kabisa. Hutawala kwa kutoa amri tu. Hakuna kuhojiana. Hakuna kujadiliana na kufikia uamuzi wa pamoja, ...

[29] *Ujamaa* is the Swahili word for familyhood and refers to African socialism.

[30] Translated from the original Swahili: Wahudumu waafrika hawajaona kwamba jinsi madaraka ya mamlaka ilivyoeleweka na wamisionari ilikuwa ni katika mazingira na kuelewa kwao pamoja na kuwabana zaidi waafrika ili wawatawale vyema. Sasa ingawa wahudumu hawa ni waafrika, bado wanawatawala ndugu zao kwa ukali, kwa viboko, hata kutumia mikia ya nge.

(Isichei 1995:340).[31] The influence of this policy can still be felt in all areas of social and political life.[32]

My hypothesis is that on a continuum Tanzanian leaders tend to be collectivist, modest, particular, diffuse, neutral and outer directed. They have weak uncertainty avoidance, short-term and synchronous time orientation, practise large power distance, and status is usually ascribed. These cultural values were discussed at length earlier in chapter two. The tendency of Western and Tanzanian cultural values can be summarized as shown in figure 3.1. My hypothesis concerning Western and Tanzanian leadership tendencies are tested below in chapters three and four.

CULTURAL VALUES OF BOTH GROUPS	
WEST	TANZANIA
Individualistic	Collectivist
Assertive	Modest
Universal	Particular
Specific	Diffuse
Neutral	Neutral
Inner directed	Outer directed

Figure 3.1

It is interesting to note that most values may be different except that people in both societies might be neutral.

3.2 Personal Background and Leadership

A number of factors influence a person's leadership style such as gender, age, nationality and ethnicity, church background, level of education, current occupation and work experience, own leadership role, the experience of the leadership of others and the self-evaluation of one's own leadership. This personal information is essential as people from different genders and age groups may have different perspectives and perceptions of leadership. Their church background may influence their theological understanding of leadership. People's educational level, their current occupation and work experience may

---

[31] The *ujamaa*-policy is presented in the Arusha declaration (TANU 1967), which has been Tanzania's policy on socialism and self-reliance.
[32] *Ujamaa* means familyhood. In Tanzania, it draws in all of the people. This family is a community of shared values and equality (Boon 1998:31). Key to the *ujamaa*-policy is human equality and dignity (TANU 1967; Huddleston 1995:6). The *ujamaa*-concept is also expressed in the Swahili proverb *Umoja ni nguvu* – Unity is strength. The term *umoja* means much more than just unity. The word reflects basically the African worldview of an interdependent community.

impact how they exercise power, conduct meetings, make decisions and solve conflicts. The personal information of the interviewees helps to determine how big the gap between the desired ideal leadership style and the reality is. Thus, what follows in this section is a description of the personal background information of the persons who were interviewed.

The Western and Tanzanian respondents who were part of the research sample represent different *gender* groups (question 1.1). *Western*: male (5)[33]; female (5). *Tanzanian*: male (8); female (2). This provides not only a male but also a female perspective on leadership issues. The female interviewees especially recognise that they are disadvantaged in terms of leadership roles. The *age* (question 1.2) of the respondents ranges as follows. *Western:* one between 20 and 30 years; five between 31 and 40 years; four between 41 and 50 years. *Tanzanian*: two between 20 and 30 years; two between 31 and 40 years; four between 41 and 50 years; two over 50 years. The research showed that younger Tanzanians expect a more participatory leadership approach than older people. The *Western* respondents come from Anglo-Saxon (5) and Germanic (5) countries (question 1.3). In this way a relatively broad spectrum on Western leadership issues is provided. The *Tanzanian* respondents represent a wide variety of different *ethnic groups* such as Ndali, Nyiha, Burunge, Ngoni, Mbugwe, Gogo, Chagga, Zinza, Rangi and Kuria. The respondents come from different *denominational backgrounds* (question 1.4). *Westerners*: Brethren, Free Evangelical Church (originally Catholic), Evangelical Free Church, Baptist Church, Independent Evangelical Church, Presbyterian Church, Pentecostal Assemblies of Canada and the Anglican Church. *Tanzanians*: Anglican Church, Tanzania Assemblies of God, Church of God, Pentecostal Assemblies of God, Roman Catholic Church and Free Pentecostal Church of Tanzania. The respondents' church background influences their theological understanding of leadership since Christian teachings vary. Thus, they have different perspectives on leadership. However, since the respondents represent a great variety of ethnic groups and denominations it is difficult to draw any specific conclusions in reference to these two factors. The main reason for the respondents coming from different backgrounds is to have a relatively balanced spectrum on leadership issues.

In terms of *formal education* (question 1.5) the majority of *Western* respondents have master's degrees. One respondent has a bachelor's degree and one a PhD. The majority of *Tanzanian* respondents have at least completed secondary school in form four or six. Others have earned a certificate, diploma, bachelor's or master's degree. Tanzanian respondents with a higher level of education tend to be more critical and outspoken. They also expect a more participative leadership approach.

The *Western* respondents have had different *occupations* (question 1.6) such as missionary, systems analyst for a software company, Bible school teacher, linguist, translator, translation consultant in training, training coordinator, pastoral ministry, university instructor, personnel supervision, nurse, education secretary and language programs team leader. The *Tanzanian* re-

---

[33] Numbers in parentheses indicate the number of people.

spondents have different occupations such as administrator, researcher, translator, pastors, editor, teacher, nurse and partnership coordinator.

Depending on their age most of them have had *extensive work* and *leadership experience* (question 1.7 & 1.8) in a number of different areas. For the *Westerners* these areas include manager, language project team leader, team captain in various secondary school sports and activities, foreman, construction supervisor, computer project supervisor, church elder, ordained minister, assistant director for personnel, school board member, overseer of training workshops, personnel supervisor, leadership training, the support and professional development of teachers and heads of training institution, and team leader of a multicultural team and several Tanzanian teams. For the *Tanzanians* these areas include church elder, treasurer, chairperson of a school committee, the church youth and Sunday school, pastoral responsibilities, department manager, parish secretary, church area leader, team leader, school principal, head translator and assistant general secretary. The age, educational level and leadership experience may be reflected in the respondents' answers during the interviews. How these different backgrounds influence the respondents' practise of leadership is shown below in relation to their responses.

In terms of the *leadership of others and their assessment of it* (question 1.8) the respondents have had both positive and difficult experiences. A number of *positive* experiences were shared by the *Western* respondents. For example, Leader 4 appreciates that the leadership of the mission organisation is not very directive, giving her a "free hand" in what she can do. She also receives constructive advice if needed and has regular evaluations. Leader 2 says: "It is easiest for me to submit and cooperate with leaders who would provide leadership in a way that was involving me to a certain degree in some of the decision-making processes and who would have more experience and know-how than I had at the time." Others (Leader 3, 7 & Lay Leader 1) have had positive experiences with leaders who "have been well-informed, organised people who had clear goals and were able to lead without treading on other people or offending them ... Good leaders also communicate well with those they are leading" (Lay Leader 1). This kind of leadership is expressed well by Leader 7:

> Another leader of a school in Austria gave me a lot of freedom. She had a clear vision for the school and we had a personal relationship, a friendship. I could understand the vision and also the limitations and guidelines, but was given the freedom and peace to go about my work the way I saw fit.

For some of the Western leaders, the personal relationship seems to be important, as Leader 6 puts it:

> I've always enjoyed leaders who have taken the time to get to know me as an individual. When I worked as a teacher ... it was a very positive experience. The leadership took the time to get to know me and took advantage of the strengths that I had. This allowed me to make a significant contribution to the university.

Having a personal friendship with the leader means that the subordinate feels loved as a person. Leader 5 has observed positive leadership qualities in others such as "confidence, patience, compassion, humility, accepting responsibility, vision-focused, thorough decision-making, prayerful [and] handling stress well".

The *Western* respondents have also experienced some *difficult* aspects in the leadership of others. For Leader 2 it is difficult to accept leaders who have less experience or know-how than him. Other leaders "have either not been fully engaged with their task of leading, or have struggled to put ideas into action, or have not been able to lead others without hurting them in some way" (Lay Leader 1). Leader 3 says:

> It is negative when a person uses leadership to 'rule' over others and uses [her/]his position simply to avoid difficult tasks and assigns them to other people, avoiding jobs that [s/]he doesn't want to do and doing only the easy jobs. A leader who takes credit for everything good and avoids any responsibility or blame when things go wrong loses the respect of all.

Humility and justice are highly valued in the West. Some leaders do not communicate well, as Lay Leader 1 experienced it: "I have had one experience of a pastor in the UK who did not communicate well with the majority of his congregation and left us feeling undervalued and even suspicious of his intentions." Another challenge is when leaders delegate authority and encourage followers to take responsibility, but then they are not loyal to their followers, as Leader 8 shares:

> A headmaster who actively and publicly encourages staff to take a leadership role and have their own ideas and implementation (a good thing) who then publicly derides their decisions and actions because they do not agree with what the headmaster perceived should happen – result a paralysed staff who are not willing to make decisions in case they are 'wrong'.

Such an experience of inconsistent communication and diffuse delegation can be rather frustrating for subordinates because the leader behaves unjustly. Autocratic leadership where the person involved is always right and their way is best can also be a real challenge, as Leader 1 puts it:

> The most negative experience I had was with a person (a pastor in a church where I was working as a custodian) who took all mistakes or differences we had as personal attacks and then would attack back, but not by talking it through, but by not talking and other indirect means. Such situations could go on for weeks or even months – which resulted in severe emotional stress.

This example suggests that Westerners expect that conflicts should be addressed and open and transparent communication take place. They value specificity and assertiveness. Both examples above also indicate that Westerners value power sharing as Jesus did, as we have seen in chapter one.

The *Tanzanian* respondents also shared a number of *positive* experiences. For example, Leader 5 has been commissioned by her church into a special ministry: "My church does very well when they pray for me. ... From time to time they visit me at my office to see if I am doing well."[34] The church cares well and prays for her. Others (Lay Leader 2 & 3) mentioned that if the leaders follow the principles of leadership and know their responsibilities, there are usually no problems. According to the respondents, a number of leaders cooperate well with their followers. Leader 4, for example, speaks of the positive example of a bishop:

> You see the atmosphere when he is together with the people. The way people are happy. They have the freedom to joke. It is not bad joking to despise him but to express their fellowship. When they come to his office they are joyful, they sing and tell their stories – not to waste time but because they share freely with him. They share their thoughts. You can see that the work progresses well in the church.[35]

This example suggests that Tanzanians value loving leaders who are approachable. There are Tanzanian leaders who respect and treat their subordinates justly instead of just giving orders. They make sure that the subordinates know their responsibilities. They accept followers with their weaknesses and try to help them, as Leader 2 says: "They make sure that the worker knows her/his responsibilities. If the worker knows her/his responsibilities s/he can fulfil them with no problems instead of waiting for further instructions by the superior today you do this, tomorrow you do that."[36] Tanzanian leaders are expected to be merciful. At the same time people ought to be faithful. Some Tanzanian leaders let other people handle money (Leader 1). Another positive experience is when leaders ask for forgiveness if they did wrong and they also forgive those who did wrong to them (Leader 7). There are leaders who mentor others to take over and become leaders themselves. Once they take on a leadership role, they recognise their mentor leaders, as Leader 7 observes: "I have seen other leaders even recently from one party in the presidential elections when he spoke in his campaign as he was nominated by his party to become president. In his speech he thanked those who mentored him in politics."[37] Being mentored by other leaders is a great example of

---

[34] Translated from the original Swahili: Kanisa langu walifanya vizuri sana wanaponiombea mimi. ... Na mara kwa mara wanakuja ofisini kwangu kunitembelea kuangalia kama naendelea vizuri.
[35] Translated from the original Swahili: Unaona tu hali anapokuwa na watu. Watu wanavyofurahia. Watu wako huru tu wanataniana. Sio utani ule mbaya wa kumdharau. Lakini utani kwa maana kwamba wako pamoja. Halafu wakiingia ofisini kwake wanafurahi, wanaimba, wanapiga story – si kwa maana ya kupoteza wakati lakini kwa maana wako huru na yeye. Wanaanza kutoa mawazo yao. Lakini unaona kazi inaendelea vizuri katika kanisa.
[36] Translated from the original Swahili: Lakini wanamhakikishia kila mfanyakazi ajue wajibu wake. Yule mfanyakazi akijua wajibu wake anaweza kutekeleza wajibu wake bila shida badala ya kungoja kuambiwa na kiongozi leo unafanya hiki, kesho unafanya hiki.
[37] Translated from the original Swahili: Nimeona viongozi wengine ambao nimegundua kitu kimoja ambacho hata juzi nilikiona nikisema ni mfano pia niliona hata kwa mgombea wa urais mmoja wa chama kimoja hapa nchini. Alipokuwa alijaribu kuzungumza juu ya azma yake ya

sharing power and passing it on. Tanzanian leaders recognise other leaders' leadership as well (Leader 7).

More *difficult* experiences were mentioned by the *Tanzanian* respondents. Some leaders do not recognise other leaders on a different level like the way pastors view teachers (Leader 5). Some leaders are not aware of their responsibilities therefore the outcomes do not match the authority a leader has. They have not been prepared for their leadership role (Leader 2). They try to copy the leadership of others, which is not always a good example (Leader 2). Leaders have difficulties in moving the organisation forward towards its goals since they do not know the vision and mission of the organisation (Leader 2). Others use their authority badly, especially in the area of money, as Leader 3 points out:

> Often I have heard many pastors saying: "This is **my** church." S/he[38] counts the people in her/his church as her/his people. Now even the offering that is given in the church you will find that no report of the income and outcome of all the money is read. So this money given by the Christians is like her/his money.[39] [my emphasis]

Another common problem seems to be that Tanzanian leaders' personal interest or benefits prevail over those of the people or work, as Lay Leader 2 says: "I think a big problem is the personal interest of a person instead of making sure that the work gets done as it is required."[40] Sometimes Tanzanian leaders are not faithful. A number of leaders lead without giving people the necessary freedom, love and respect. These days people expect a more participatory than authoritarian approach (Leader 4). But the leaders are slow to change. Other leaders accept a leadership position without being committed to the responsibility. This is difficult since they are not willing to provide leadership or give direction, as Leader 7 testifies: "I have seen a leader who does not agree with her/his responsibilities. S/he goes to a meeting and does not express her/his opinion even if s/he has one."[41] There are Tanzanian leaders who do not recognise their mistakes or ask for forgiveness (Leader 7). Some leaders accept advice only from other leaders on the same level or above but not

---

kupata kura kwa wananchi, hasa chama chake kilichomchagua kuwa mgombea wa rais wa chama hicho. Hotuba yake alivyozungumza kwanza alishukuru wale waliomlea katika mambo yake ya kisiasa.

[38] Swahili does not make a distinction between male and female in personal pronouns or nouns.

[39] Translated from the original Swahili: Mara nyingi nimesikia wachungaji wengi wakisema hili ni kanisa langu. Anajihesabia kwamba wale watu walioko kanisani ni wake. Ni kama mali yake ya mfukoni. Sasa hata anapokuwa katika uongozi ni kwamba hata zile sadaka zinazotolewa unakuta kanisa halisomewi riporti ya mapato na matumizi ya matoleo yote ya sadaka na zaka. Kwa hiyo ile pesa inayotolewa na wakristo anaifanya ni mali yake.

[40] Translated from the original Swahili: Nafikiri tatizo kubwa ni kwamba mtazamo wa tm binafsi na si mtazamo wa kazi kwamba ifanyike kazi katika utaratibu uliokusudiwa katika lengo lenyewe.

[41] Translated from the original Swahili: Nimewahi kuona kiongozi ambaye anashindwa kuyakubali majukumu yake. Kiongozi anakwenda kwenye kikao hawezi akaonyesha msimamo wake hata kama anao.

below their level (Leader 7). Another challenge is that often leaders do not recognise the leadership of others (Leader 7).

When asked *"What is your evaluation of how you have functioned as a leader?"* all *Western* respondents were self-critical, recognising their strengths and weaknesses, as Leader 8 shares:

> [For instance i]n a committee meeting [I am] ... able to understand the points of view of different members of community and bring them to a common understanding of the educational value of the topic. [However,] ... at the same meeting my frustration at the poor implementation of a policy that has been discussed many times leads to short words and implied dissatisfaction.

People like leaders to be more patient and gentle at times and have a certain desire for harmony. Some Western respondents see themselves more as a motivator (Leader 4), team member (Leader 5) or promoter (Leader 1) than a leader, which influences their leadership style.

In terms of the respondents' self-evaluation as leaders, the responses by the *Tanzanians* were generally positive. As leaders, the Tanzanian respondents have a desire to cooperate (Leader 2, 3, 4, 5, 7 & Lay Leader 2), to listen (Lay Leader 1), to respect others (Leader 3), to lead justly (Lay Leader 2), to help people (Leader 2 & Lay Leader 3) and to be an example (Lay Leader 1). They are faithful in their ministries (Leader 1 & 3). The results of their work and ministry testify to their positive leadership. A few respondents (Leader 1 & 6) are perceived to be strict leaders because they ensure the work is done properly, as Leader 1 states:

> Others say I am a strict pastor. They tell me: "Why are you choosing the same church elders and not others?" And I told them that one day an older man came to me and said: "Why don't you appoint me as an elder?" I said: "Look. You have not made a decision for Jesus. Now how can you be of help to other people?" There is a man who wants to be a church elder but he drinks beer. He smokes and we know it. How can he be an example for others?[42]

This leader wants to be faithful in his ministry. He exercises his power against the church member. Generally, the respondents are willing to provide leadership and to learn from others. However, some of the respondents also recognise their weaknesses. A number of them recognise the importance and

---

[42] Translated from the original Swahili: Wengine wanasema mchungaji mkali. Wengine wameniambia kwamba: "Kwa nini unachagua wazee wa kanisa karibu wale wale na kwa nini hubadilishi wengine?" Na nimewaambia kwamba siku moja nilimwambia mzee mmoja. Mzee aliniambia: "Kwa nini huniteui kuwa mzee wa kanisa?" Nikamwambia: "Angalia. Wewe hujakata shauri kwa Yesu. Sasa utawasaidiaje watu." Kuna mzee mmoja anataka uzee wa kanisa lakini anakunywa pombe. Anavuta sigara na sisi tunajua. Na anaweza je kuwa mfano kwa watu wengine?

are willing to be critiqued by others, as Leader 1 shares: "I have asked three people who tell me truly if I do well or badly without deceiving me."[43]

The above examples suggest that there are good and bad leaders in both societies. *Westerners* expect a high degree of participatory leadership where leaders share their power and delegate. Westerners perceive it as bad leadership if the leader is authoritarian and does not communicate well. Western leaders should be humble and practise justice. Westerners appreciate low power distance. To summarize the personal experiences of the *Tanzanian* respondents, good leaders value and respect the people they work with. They are caring, helpful and forgiving. Tanzanians value leaders who are loving, community oriented and faithful. On the contrary, bad Tanzanian leaders put their personal interest above those they lead. They are selfish, proud and misuse their authority.

The positive and negative leadership behaviour people experience in both societies is reflected in the leaders' character and theology. Some may be good leaders because their character has been shaped by sound biblical teaching, which has been internalised. This indicates how critical virtues, norms and values are for moral character formation, as was discussed in chapter one. It is important that leaders learn from Jesus. Others are bad leaders because of lack of sound biblical teaching, or they are not willing to learn or the Scripture does not have a personal impact in their lives. As a result, the sinful nature of human beings and the negative aspects of cultural values are still dominant in their leadership behaviour. This is further explored in the next section on "Character and Leadership".

3.3 Character and Leadership

As we have seen in chapter one, character and character formation are key to leadership. A leader's acts are based on certain values. A leader's character is formed individually and in community. A leader's character is shaped by the social environment in which s/he lives and by her/his Christian faith. A good Christian leader may be perceived differently by different people.

The interviewees were asked: *"How would you describe a good Christian leader?"* The *Western* respondents expect a good Christian leader ideally to be "[l]oving, encouraging, humble, listening, compassionate, courageous, just, with integrity" (Leader 2), "open to others, innovative and oriented on the model of Christ's leadership role" (Leader 4). S/he has "wisdom, knowledge" (Leader 3), "[a]bility to lead, experience, [is] confident to make decisions, can take charge [and] initiative" (Lay Leader 1). S/he is a "Servant-leader, committed to the vision and goals of [her/]his organisation in the same way as [s/]he is committed to the welfare of those for whom [s/]he is responsible for" (Leader 2). A good Christian leader is one who "[t]akes responsibility for decisions, ... [is a] good communicator, sees and utilizes resources, delegates,

---

[43] Translated from the original Swahili: Niliteua watu kama watatu ambao wanaweza kuniambia ukweli kama ninafanya vizuri au ninafanya vibaya bila kunidanganya na kunipeleka kwenye shimo.

Chapter 3: The Cultural Contexts, Personal Background and Character 101

and ... is a visionary" (Leader 5). S/he is "One who is able to relate to people on a wide variety of levels and demonstrate Christ's love at the same time" (Leader 6). Leader 9 expects a good Christian leader to set a good biblical example. According to Leader 8, s/he "takes the time to understand others' views of a situation and uses that understanding to move a group forward in a stated direction". Leader 7 describes a good Christian leader as one who

> ... ask[s] good questions to understand the bigger picture and never loses the overview of what is going on in her/his work-field. S/he is excited and committed to train others and to see the power in others raised. S/he ... is always aware of their strengths and weaknesses. As soon as s/he can be replaced for the good of the project, it is time to train the ones, who are coming after her/him to really understand their role and the work-field. A good leader is replaceable and is not holding on to her/his power. A good leader keeps the team s/he is leading focused and the way s/he loves will have an impact on the way people treat each other in the team.

The leader's character plays an important role in Western societies as it is also expressed by a number of authors.[44] There is a strong emphasis on character. Leaders must know who they are before they can lead others. The overall character and a person's integrity are considered to be rather important in Western societies (Hersman 1995:181-183). Westerners value honesty, fairness, and care (Lewis 2003:174 & 180).

The majority of *Tanzanian* respondents (Leader 2, 3, 4, 5, 7 & Lay Leader 1, 2, 3) believe that a good Christian leader must be a committed Christian who lives a spiritual life, as Leader 2 says: "A good Christian leader first of all needs to be a Christian."[45] Then, "a good church leader is the one who has been chosen by God"[46]. A good Christian leader practises love (Leader 1, 3, 4, 5, 6 & Lay Leader 2), humility (Leader 4 & 7) and servanthood (Leader 2 & 3), faithfulness (Leader 2, 3, 5 & 7), honesty (Leader 2, 3, 5 & 6), godly wisdom (Leader 3), respect (Leader 3 & 4), mercy (Leader 3), justice (Leader 6) and cooperates with others (Leader 4 & Lay Leader 1, 2, 3). It is interesting to note that more important than anything else for a good Christian leader in Tanzania is to be loving. Leader 5 specifies this love: "S/he loves others. And not only the people of her/his ethnic group or denomination. No. S/he will love everybody."[47] Leader 7 explains what it means for a good Christian leader to be humble:

> It means that s/he agrees to be humble and to subordinate to someone else. ... Humility in the sense that s/he recognises her/his mistakes. If

---

[44] For expected character attributes for Western leaders see also Grün (2001:13-35), Sanders (1994:51-76), De Pree (1989:16), Maxwell (1999) and Stogdill (in Klopfenstein 1989:44).
[45] Translated from the original Swahili: Kiongozi mzuri wa kikristo kwanza lazima awe mkristo.
[46] Translated from the original Swahili: ... kiongozi bora wa kanisa ni yule aliyechaguliwa na Mungu ...
[47] Translated from the original Swahili: Atapenda wengine. Na sio watu wa kabila lake tu au wa dhehebu lake. Hapana. Atatoa upendo kwa ajili ya wote.

s/he is corrected s/he will make changes. If something is explained to her/him, s/he will do it. If s/he is told something s/he will listen. This is a humble leader. S/he will listen to the advice of others.[48]

"In other words, s/he should be one who lives by example rather than by many words" (Leader 3).[49] To have a close relationship and good cooperation with people seems to be important for a good Christian leader in Tanzania, as Lay Leader 2 says: "For a Christian leader s/he is especially expected to be close to those who s/he leads, maybe to visit the sick, to greet them, to have a devotion."[50] A good Christian leader needs "to know her/his responsibilities"[51] (Lay Leader 2). "A leader ought to like her/his leadership responsibility. S/he should agree to lead. S/he should be willing to give directions. ... S/he should be a leader who is willing to solve the problems of the group" (Leader 7).[52] "S/he should have a vision."[53] A good Christian leader "shows the way and goes before so that others follow"[54]. A number of respondents (Leader 3, 4 & 7) pointed out that forgiveness is important for a good Christian leader, as Leader 7 says: "S/he should be willing to forgive others who have done wrong to her/him. And s/he should be willing to ask for forgiveness when s/he does wrong."[55] A few respondents (Leader 5 & Lay Leader 3) point out that "A good Christian leader continues to learn. S/he looks for more education..." (Leader 5).[56] In all the interviews, the importance of listening was pointed out over and over again. This suggests that leaders with a good moral character who value others listen to people. Listening is very important, as Leader 4 says:

> Last year when I was transferred to the main church, the leader there told me: "This is a very difficult place. A lot of noise. No appreciation." He really discouraged me. But I was not afraid. I knew there are people of God here. ... **I listened to them. And they listened to me.** But I did not face any problems at all. Until today we have a good relationship in

---

[48] Translated from the original Swahili: Kwa maana kwamba anakubali kunyenyekea na kukubali kuwa chini ya mtu wa pili. ... Unyenyekevu kwa maana kwamba atagundua makosa yake. Akisahihishwa atasahihishika. Akielekezwa atatekeleza. Akiambiwa atasikia. ... Huyu ni kiongozi wa unyenyekevu. Atasikia mashauri ya watu wengine.
[49] Translated from the original Swahili: Yaani, awe msikilizaji zaidi kuliko kuwa mzungumzaji zaidi.
[50] Translated from the original Swahili: Kwa kiongozi wa kikristo hasa kitu kikubwa kabisa vilevile anapotakiwa awe karibu na wale ambao anawaongoza labda kuwatembelea wagonjwa, kuwasalimia, kupeleka ibada.
[51] Translated from the original Swahili: ...kujua wajibu wake...
[52] Translated from the original Swahili: Kiongozi aipende kazi yake ya uongozi. Akubali kuongoza. Akubali kutoa maelekezo. ... Awe kiongozi tayari kuifanya kazi ya kutatua matatizo ya kundi.
[53] Translated from the original Swahili: Awe na maono.
[54] Translated from the original Swahili: ...kuonyesha njia na kutangulia ili wengine wafuate.
[55] Translated from the original Swahili: Awe tayari kusamehe wanaomkosea. Na yeye awe tayari kuomba radhi anapokosea.
[56] Translated from the original Swahili: Kiongozi mzuri anajiendeleza, anatafuta elimu zaidi...

the congregation. They have helped in a lot of different things in the church."⁵⁷ [my emphasis]

People in Tanzania expect a leader to listen to them.⁵⁸ When a leader in Tanzania listens, people know s/he cares about them. Listening is an important step of building trust in Tanzania. It is important to note that the ideal picture of a good leader is not only given by junior leaders but also senior leaders. The values and virtues of a good Christian leader as expressed by the respondents reflect what is written in the literature.⁵⁹ It is important to keep in mind that this is an ideal picture, which is at least partly practised by some Tanzanian leaders. Tanzanians and Westerners expect a good Christian leader to be loving and humble.

The questions "How would you describe a good Christian leader?" and *"Who do you consider to be a good leader?"* are closely connected because the first describes the ideal picture, whereas the later the actual reality. Therefore, they are grouped together here. Leadership values are often influenced by *heroes* or *heroines* in the society. A number of *Western* respondents (Leader 1, 2 & 7) mentioned their current or previous supervisors, who they consider to be good leaders. Others mentioned church leaders like pastors (Leader 3 & 7) and house group leaders (Lay Leader 1) or mission (Leader 9) and government leaders (Leader 5 & 8). When asked for what reasons they consider these people as good leaders, it is interesting to note that there are a number of common features why the respondents consider these people as good leaders. In summary, in actual practice these leaders listen, care for and love others, are serving and humble, putting others first and setting an example. They are wise, competent, encouraging and courageous. They are godly and praying people recognising their dependence on God. At the same time they are willing to provide leadership and give clear direction using a participatory approach. One respondent (Leader 3) considers his father as a good leader "because of his dedication and hard work on behalf of others".

It is interesting to note that a number of *Tanzanian* respondents (Leader 2, 6 & 7), especially the older ones, consider the first President of Tanzania the late *Mwalimu* Julius Kambarage Nyerere, who is also called the "Father of the Nation", as a good leader. He is seen and very much respected as a hero and outstanding leader.⁶⁰ The respondents would be careful criticising him or

---

⁵⁷ Translated from the original Swahili: Nilipokuja kanisani mwaka jana niliambiwa na mmoja ambaye aliongoza hapa ... : "Bwana, hapa pagumu sana. Makelele mengi. No appreciation." Akanivunja moyo kabisa. Lakini mimi sikuhofu. Nilijua lakini kuna watu wa Mungu hapa. ... Nikawasikiliza. Nao wakanisikiliza. Lakini sikukutana na ugumu wowote kabisa. Tunakuwa na ushirikiano mzuri katika ... ibada ... mpaka sasa ... Wamesaidia sana katika mambo ya kanisa mengi tu.
⁵⁸ Mwombeki (2004:43) has also made this observation.
⁵⁹ According to Mhogolo (1996:45-46), a church leader in Tanzania is expected to live an exemplary Christian life. S/he should be a just person, a listener, somebody who is patient, compassionate and merciful.
⁶⁰ Mmari (1995:177) describes Nyerere as a man with an outstanding personal character of honesty, humility, simplicity and integrity. He was the first African President who gave up his office voluntarily in 1985 and passed his presidency on to his successor (:176).

other leaders out of respect. If they criticise, they would usually say something positive as well. Even though they recognise that he was not successful in everything, particularly in economics, he at least provided clear directions to move the nation from where it was to where it should be (Leader 2). "[Nyerere] was a leader who feared God. And what he did he wanted to do justice for the lowly people. We should not make a difference between rich and poor. ... All the time, he said all people are equal" (Leader 6).[61] "Nyerere was a good leader because he loved the Tanzanians whom he led. He also did not seek his personal interest or benefits. ... He forgave his enemies. ... He shared his thoughts like a leader... He was faithful in the matters in which he had been advised by others... Nyerere lived what he taught" (Leader 7).[62]

After Nyerere, the former president Benjamin William Mkapa was mentioned by a few respondents (Lay Leader 1 & 3), especially by the younger generation. Mkapa is considered to be a good leader because of all the accomplishments during his period of office. "He did not only talk" (Lay Leader 3)[63], "but was a person of actions. ... He fought corruption even though it was difficult" (Lay Leader 1).[64] "[Mkapa] respected his staff" (Lay Leader 3).[65] "He sought advice. Everywhere he received advice and implemented it" (Lay Leader 1).[66]

After these two presidents, a number of church leaders or supervisors were mentioned by the Tanzanian respondents as good leaders because they listen to God (Leader 5). They serve God and watch their spiritual life carefully (Leader 1). "[W]e sit together with them and discuss different plans. Together we decide we are going to do this and this and this" (Leader 3).[67] They listen to people (Leader 3 & 4), respect them (Leader 4), give them wise council and encourage them (Leader 1 & 4). They are willing to help people with their problems (Leader 3 & 7). They are loved by the people (Leader 1). "[They] share their authority with others below them" (Leader 1).[68] They do not make a difference between people (Leader 4). They are faithful in terms of money (Leader 1). "[They] are quick to forgive others" (Leader 4).[69]

---

[61] Translated from the original Swahili: Alikuwa kiongozi aliyemwogopa Mungu. Na kile alichofanya, alipenda kufanya haki kwa wale wadogo. Tusiwe na tofauti sana kati ya matajiri na maskini. ... Alisema kila wakati kwamba binadamu wote ni sawa.

[62] Translated from the original Swahili: Nyerere alikuwa kiongozi mzuri kwa sababu aliwapenda anaowaongoza watanzania. Halafu Nyerere hakuwa na ubinafsi. ... Alisamehe adui zake watu waliompinga. ...Yeye alitoa mawazo yake kama kiongozi. ... Alikuwa na uaminifu katika mambo ambayo alikuwa na shauri na watu wengine. ... Aliishi maisha yake kama mambo anayofundisha.

[63] Translated from the original Swahili: Hajazungumza kwa maneno tu.

[64] Translated from the original Swahili: ... ni mtu wa vitendo ... Amezuia sana swala ya rushwa ingawaje ni vigumu.

[65] Translated from the original Swahili: ... anajali wafanyakazi wake.

[66] Translated from the original Swahili: Yeye alipenda kutafuta ushauri. Kila sehemu anapata ushauri na anakuja kufanyia kazi.

[67] Translated from the original Swahili: ... tunakaa nao, tunajadiliana nao katika mipango mbalimbali. Na tunafikia kwamba uamuzi sasa ni kwamba tufanye hili na hili na hili.

[68] Translated from the original Swahili: Ameacha madaraka kwa watu wa ngazi ya chini.

[69] Translated from the original Swahili: ... alikuwa mwepesi kumsamehe mtu.

Whereas the Western respondents assume that a good Christian leader is a committed Christian, the Tanzanian respondents emphasised this fact. This suggests that they do recognise and realise the importance of the transforming power of the Holy Spirit. If a leader is a truly committed Christian, it must be reflected in her/his leadership behaviour. Whereas the Westerners emphasised the importance of practising Christian values and virtues, the Tanzanians highlighted the importance of listening and taking advice. The examples above indicate that **both groups appreciate the same leadership qualities**, such as listening, loving, caring, serving, humility, putting others first, setting an example, being wise, competent, encouraging and courageous. These are important biblical values and virtues, which reflect Christ-like leadership as discussed in chapter one. Whereas a good Christian leader practises biblical values and virtues, in a bad leader personal power and insecurity prevail.

It is good to know whom people perceive as good leaders. However, the question is *"How does one become a good leader?"* The *Western* respondents believe that one becomes a good leader by learning from a good leader (Leader 2, 4, 6, 9 & Lay Leader 1), "learning from the mistakes of bad leaders" (Leader 4), listening (Leader 4, 7, 8 & Lay Leader 1), experience (Leader 1 & 2), training (Leader 1), "reflecting on situations, responses and results, seeking the council of others" (Leader 8), "reading good books" (Leader 9), "try[ing] to follow the biblical pattern for leadership" (Lay Leader 1), having "discipline in organisation, time management and implementing planning" (Leader 8), and "adopting and living with integrity a good value system" (Leader 2). Leader 7 says: "I think the first step is to be broken and to acknowledge that you are not any better than anybody else. ... [Good leaders] need to know their weaknesses and strengths and ... where [their] ... most fragile areas are." At the same time they are able to experience "God's grace [and] intervention in growing as a person" (Leader 2). To be a good leader it is essential to recognise dependency on God in prayer (Leader 7). It is interesting to note that half of the respondents (Leader 1, 2, 5, 6 & 9) believe that good leadership is a natural and/or spiritual gifting. To become a good leader, it is important to "have the gifts that are required to lead a group of people (management, counselling ... etc.) and the knowledge of the area ... [one] is going to work in" (Leader 7).

As we have seen in chapter one, for good leaders *character formation* both individually and in community, is essential. It is true that a leader's character is already set during early childhood and even before birth. However, good leaders engage in a life-long learning process. The Western respondents recognise that to become a good leader one's character must be changed. It is interesting to note that none of the respondents mentioned solitude and silence as being an important part of moral formation. But there seems to be an emphasis on personal reflection in the West to become a good leader more than being shaped in community.[70]

---

[70] According to Gosling and Mintzberg (2004:46-59), Western leaders are expected to have a reflective, analytical, contextual, cooperative and action-oriented mind-set.

Tanzanian Leader 2 points out the importance of being called by God in order to become a good leader. Then, people need "to give him practical leadership experience"[71] (Leader 2). Secondly, "A person becomes a good leader if s/he lives with God, if s/he humbles her/himself before God and reads the Word of God" (Leader 1).[72] A number of respondents (Leader 1, 3, 7 & Lay Leader 1, 2, 3) said education and ongoing learning are essential to become a good leader. Not only formal education but also learning from another leader is part of it (Leader 3, 7 & Lay Leader 1, 3), as Leader 3 says: "If you want to be a good leader, you sit below a good leader and you will become a good leader because the other leader above you is good."[73] "One becomes a good leader by learning during her/his leadership from her/his personal mistakes and the mistakes of others" (Leader 7).[74] But "a leader needs to put into practice what s/he learns"[75] (Lay Leader 1) and then persevere (Leader 1).

Westerners believe that one becomes a good leader by having a learning attitude, obtaining good values and through self-reflection. Also gifting is important. For Tanzanians to become a good leader it is important to have a calling, education, gain experience in leadership and be mentored well. It seems that for Westerners, character formation is more important than for Tanzanians, who emphasise the ascribed status. As we have seen above, good Christian leaders practice biblical values and Christ-like leadership as discussed in chapter one. This is further explored below.

3.3.1 Christ-Like Leadership

Leaders' character is reflected in their Christ-like leadership. How leaders practice Christian leadership is influenced by their theological understanding and *which Bible persons or passages they consider as key to Christian leadership* (question 2.2). When the *Western* interviewees were asked about which Bible persons or passages they consider as key to Christian leadership the persons mentioned were Moses, Joshua and Nehemiah. The person most often mentioned was Jesus. It is interesting to note that not even one woman was mentioned. Moses is considered to be a good leader because he was "passionate for what he was doing" (Leader 9). He was "willing to listen to God and to others (e.g. his father-in-law) about what to do and how to do it" (Leader 8).

Joshua, although not a "Moses", and initially behind the scenes, "led the people of Israel with faith, courage, obedience and devotion to God's law" (Leader 5). He was very dependent on God (Leader 5).

"Nehemiah was a man of prayer, full of wisdom, able to motivate and delegate" (Leader 5). He was also very dependent on God (Leader 5). He is an

---

[71] Translated from the original Swahili: ... kumpa ujuzi wa kuongoza.
[72] Translated from the original Swahili: Mtu anakuwa kiongozi mzuri akikaa kwa Mungu, akinyenyekeza kwa Mungu na kusoma Neno la Mungu.
[73] Translated from the original Swahili: Ukitaka kuwa kiongozi mzuri ukikaa chini ya kiongozi mzuri ni bado utakuwa kiongozi mzuri kwa sababu ya yule aliye juu yako ni mzuri.
[74] Translated from the original Swahili: Mtu anakuwa kiongozi mzuri kwa kujifunza katika uongozi wake makosa yake yeye binafsi na makosa ya watu wengine.
[75] Translated from the original Swahili: ... anapojifunza anafanya mazoezi ya yale aliyojifunza.

important example for Christian leadership because of "how he prayed, prepared [and] took action" (Leader 9).

Finally, Jesus was mentioned.

Some respondents also mentioned passages from the Bible as key to Christian leadership, such as Philippians 2:1-9, the Sermon on the Mount (Matthew 5-7), 1 Corinthians 12 and 13. These passages keep leaders "humble and keep ... [them] valuing people more than ... their personal agenda" (Leader 1). "Philippians 2 shows the lengths that Christ was willing to go in order to meet those whom he served at their level" (Leader 6). 1 Timothy 3:1-7(13) was also mentioned "because it contains God's instructions for leadership" (Lay Leader 1). "While this passage deals with 'ministerial' roles (elders/deacons), they also apply to men as they lead their household and others" (Leader 3). Leader 3 continues, "I consider Paul's instructions to be the main biblical passages to deal explicitly with the qualifications and characteristics necessary for Christian leaders".

The persons mentioned by the *Tanzanians* most often were Moses, Nehemiah, David, Paul and Jesus. Only male Leader 7 mentioned Abigail because she was only a housewife, but had a lot of wisdom. Moses is considered to be a good leader because "he listened to the voice of God and was obedient to God's calling" (Leader 3)[76]. However, he did not just do what God asked him to do. "When God called Moses, Moses did not leave immediately. He made sure to know from God who called him what he should do. All his questions he had, he asked God who called him this very day" (Leader 7).[77] He was humble and willing to sacrifice his life for others (Leader 3). Moses delegated his responsibilities to others.

"When Nehemiah heard that the wall of Jerusalem was destroyed he cried before God. He prayed with a deep passion to God" (Leader 3).[78] He had a vision. "Nehemiah was the cup-bearer of the king, a person of the king's household. But he agreed to leave his good job" (Leader 7).[79] He also recognised that he as a leader could not accomplish the task alone (Leader 3). He needed the help of others. He not only gave instructions what to do, but he set an example.

"David had his problems like other people. He had his weaknesses. But David's strength was that he recognised his weaknesses. So he humbled himself before God. He asked God for forgiveness. He asked God to help him as his shepherd" (Leader 4).[80] He recognised his dependence on God (Leader 7).

---

[76] Translated from the original Swahili: ... alitii sauti ya Mungu.
[77] Translated from the original Swahili: Pale Mungu alipomwita Musa, Musa hakutoka tu haraka. Alihakikisha kabisa Mungu ananiita nifanye nini. Maswali yake yote aliyokuwa nayo akamwuliza Mungu siku hiyohiyo Mungu anamwita.
[78] Translated from the original Swahili: Nehemia aliposikia ukuta wa Yerusalemu ulipoanguka kule ni kwamba yeye Nehemia alimlia Mungu. Alikuwa na maombi makali mbele za Mungu.
[79] Translated from the original Swahili: Nehemia alikuwa ni mnyweshaji wa mfalme, mtu wa ikulu. Lakini alikubali pia kuacha kazi hiyo nzuri.
[80] Translated from the original Swahili: Daudi alikuwa na matatizo yake kama watu wengine. Alikuwa na upungufu. Lakini nguvu ya Daudi alikuwa ni mtu wa kujua na yeye ni mdhaifu. Kwa hiyo anastahili kunyenyekea mbele za Mungu. Anaomba msamaha mbele za Mungu. Anamwomba Mungu amsaidie mpaka anasema Mungu kwangu ni mchungaji.

He listened to God and to the people. "He expressed his love and respect for those whom he led" (Leader 7).[81] He forgave others and did not get angry when there was a problem (Leader 7).

Paul is admired because of his various teachings (Lay Leader 3). Paul's intention was not to criticise people but to encourage them when he wrote his letters or visited the churches in person (Lay Leader 1 & Leader 3). "He reminded them to be faithful to God even in difficult times, and to persevere" (Leader 3).[82] When Paul planted a church, he handed his leadership over to others and enabled them (Leader 2). He made sure that the work would continue. "After leading for a certain time he put others in place to lead the work" (Leader 2).[83] "The apostle Paul was willing to endure persecution in prison" (Leader 3).[84] "Paul depended on God. ... He was ready even to die for he believed in God because he knew what his responsibility was" (Lay Leader 2).[85]

Finally, Jesus was mentioned. It is interesting to note that the Tanzanian respondents with higher, especially theological education, were in a better position than the others to explain why they consider certain people in the Bible as key to Christian leadership. There is considerable overlap of both groups as can be seen in figure 3.2. Westerners and Tanzanians consider Moses, Nehemiah, Paul and Jesus as key to Christian leadership.

BIBLE PERSONS OR PASSAGES KEY TO CHRISTIAN LEADERSHIP FOR BOTH GROUPS	
WEST	TANZANIA
Moses	Moses
Joshua	Abigail
Nehemiah	Nehemiah
Jesus	David
Philippians 2:1-19	Jesus
Sermon on the mount (Matthew 5-7)	Paul
1 Timothy 3:1-7(13)	

Figure 3.2

---

[81] Translated from the original Swahili: ... alionyesha upendo na kuwaajali wale ambao anawaongoza.
[82] Translated from the original Swahili: Akiwakumbusha kwamba iweni waaminifu hata kama kuna shida na adha wazivumilie.
[83] Translated from the original Swahili: Baada ya kuongoza kwa muda aliweka wengine ili kuongoza ile kazi.
[84] Translated from the original Swahili: ... mtume Paulo huyuhuyu alivumilia mateso gerezani.
[85] Translated from the original Swahili: Paulo alimtegemea Mungu. Alikuwa tayari hata kufa kwa ajili ya kumtegemea Mungu kwa sababu alijua wajibu wake ni nini.

When asked *"What are the features of authentic leadership as modelled by Christ?"* the *Western* respondents said, Jesus set an example since "he was willing to leave his comfort and status in order to show us the way back to God and to open this way by his sacrificial death" (Leader 4). Jesus demonstrated that "Leadership in the kingdom of God is based on a radically different paradigm than worldly leadership" (Leader 2). "He modelled how a 'Christian' leader should lead" (Leader 3). Jesus was "able to take a diverse group of people and enable them to work together. He taught, encouraged, gave responsibility and allowed accountability" (Leader 8). At the same time, "He welcomes those, who are burdened ... The best leader of this universe offers rest. Which kind of rest, the one that comes as a result of humbleness and gentleness" (Leader 7). The features of authentic leadership as modelled by Christ are "love for the people around him" (Leader 1), "Servant-leader" (Leader 2), "[h]umility, service, wisdom, courage, bravery, the 'first into the breech' and one who calls others to follow after him and his example" (Leader 3), "patience, grace, authority" (Leader 8) and "prayerful always, ... empathetic, [and] purpose driven" (Leader 5). Leader 7 mentions the following features:

> Plan in place, readiness to give up rights and to humble himself, readiness to learn, giving himself with a servant heart, transparency, accountability, listening to the needs of people, always focus [and] goal oriented, absolute unity with the father in heaven, no interest in personal profit, all driven by love, people oriented.

"Sometimes he could be harsh, but even this was motivated by his love for his adversaries" (Leader 1). Leader 4 describes Jesus as follows: "He did everything "spirit filled", therefore he never made errors. He was true, no matter whether he talked to a friend or foe, to people he knew well or saw for the first time." He made decisions sometimes for the people, but also helping them to think them through (Leader 9).

The *Tanzanian* respondents said that the following features of authentic leadership were modelled by Christ: "Jesus had a close relationship with God. ... [He f]ollowed the Word of God and prayed" (Leader 1).[86] "Jesus did not sin" (Lay Leader 3). Therefore, "[A leader's] spiritual and physical life should be clean" (Leader 7).[87] "[H]e depended on God every day" (Leader 5).[88] Jesus had "the heart of being willing, faithful and obedient" (Leader 3).[89] Leader 3 says: "Jesus was willing to go to those who are useless. ... [H]e had a special love... He is willing to forgive."[90] "Jesus said love each other. A leader

---

[86] Translated from the original Swahili: Yesu alisimama upande wa Mungu kabisa. ... Simama katika Neno la Mungu na kuwa mwombaji.
[87] Translated from the original Swahili: Maisha yake ya kiroho na kimwili yawe safi.
[88] Translated from the original Swahili: ... alikuwa anamtegemea Mungu siku zote.
[89] Translated from the original Swahili: ... moyo wa utayari na uaminifu wake na utii wake.
[90] Translated from the original Swahili: Yesu alikuwa tayari kwenda hata kwa wasiofaa. ... yeye alikuwa na upendo wa ajabu ... Tena yuko tayari kusamehe.

should love her/his people and love other leaders" (Leader 7).[91] Jesus had "the ability to make decisions" (Leader 2).[92] He not only made decisions, but he also "followed them through. ... Jesus also enabled people to do their work" (Leader 2).[93] Leader 4 says: "I like the example how Jesus cooperates with his disciples. He teaches them by example. He works himself."[94] "[Jesus] was humble ... [and] honest" (Leader 6).[95] "Jesus likes a servant leader who is willing to serve others" (Leader 7).[96] "Another thing is that he respected all people equally" (Leader 5).[97] "Jesus taught unity"[98] (Leader 7), "Practising justice. Helping people"[99] (Lay Leader 2). Finally, his "good fruits were visible" (Lay Leader 3).[100]

Whereas Westerners see Jesus as an example to practise Christian leadership in a very different way than secular leadership, being self-less, sharing responsibility and authority and being accountable, the Tanzanians focused on the spiritual life of Jesus and the love he had for others. Whereas the Westerners focus much more on Jesus himself, the Tanzanian responses reflect how Jesus relates to other people. These different views are probably due to the individualistic value in the West versus the group orientation in Tanzania. As we have seen in chapter one (1.2.2 Leadership and the Vision of the Kingdom of God), it is important to keep both in perspective. Westerners need to learn more from Jesus how he related to people. Tanzanians can learn from Jesus how he exercised his leadership.

"How are these features of Christ-like character expressed in the West and in Tanzania?" Here only the answers of the respondents regarding their own societies are presented. (The Western and Tanzanian view of how these features are perceived by each other will be presented in chapter five as part of the dialogue.) According to the *Western* respondents, these features of Christ-like character are expressed in various ways by Westerners. Regarding the love and compassion for people, Leader 4 shares the following example:

> A German missionary doctor, who is really concerned for the people and compassionate to his patients. He likes to tell jokes, uses easy examples, going to the villages and singing songs about what he his concerned about (AIDS, poor people, encouragement, commitment). In this way, he his also a good motivator to his staff and fellow missionaries.

---

[91] Translated from the original Swahili: Yesu alisema tupendane sisi kwa sisi. Kiongozi apende kundi lake na apende viongozi wengine.
[92] Translated from the original Swahili: ... uwezo wa kufanya uamuzi.
[93] Translated from the original Swahili: ... kuwa na msimamo kwenye maamuzi yake. ... Yesu pia aliwawezesha watu kwenda kufanya kazi.
[94] Translated from the original Swahili: Mimi napenda mfano wa Yesu Kristo anavyoshirikiana na wanafunzi wake. Anawafundisha kwa mifano. Anatenda kazi na yeye mwenyewe.
[95] Translated from the original Swahili: ... yeye alikuwa mnyenyekevu. ... mkweli.
[96] Translated from the original Swahili: Yesu anapenda kiongozi mtumishi kwa maana kiongozi ambaye yuko tayari kuwatumikia wengine.
[97] Translated from the original Swahili: Halafu kitu kingine ni ile kuwaheshimu watu wote sawasawa.
[98] Translated from the original Swahili: Yesu alifundisha umoja.
[99] Translated from the original Swahili: Kutenda haki. Kusaidia watu.
[100] Translated from the original Swahili: Matokeo mazuri yalionekana.

"Some Western pastors ... clearly do not consider themselves 'above' their congregations and therefore show humility" (Lay Leader 1). Leader 5 says, Western leaders express their servant-heart

> ... by the act of being willing to listen to others and seeking what is best for the other. It is being "willing to go the extra mile, willing to do the most mundane task as an example to others, willing to walk in someone else's shoes". [Always being p]rayerful ... can be expressed by praying for others, praying for all circumstances, and looking to the Father for wisdom, guidance, patience and humility. Courage and empathy can be expressed in godly decision-making and with compassion for others.

"Good leaders make you feel important – even crucial – to the work, but not in a way that puts pressure, but in a motivating way" (Leader 1). There is an "increasing use of team-leadership styles in Western management, the focus on ownership and giving people responsibility" (Leader 8). However, Leader 8 warns, "[an] over-emphasis results in no clear leadership and people not prepared to make the 'final decision'". A Western leader "will always try to come to a team decision and not try to force others by manipulating or influence ideas, but s/he will still communicate her/his opinion and insights. S/he will not be respected explicitly more than any other on the team" (Leader 7).

According to the *Tanzanian* respondents, these features of Christ-like character are expressed in various ways by Tanzanian leaders. In terms of humility it was expressed that many Tanzanian leaders like to be served and practise an authoritarian leadership style seeking their own benefits, as Leader 4 observes:

> You see that our leaders like to be served. They like to dictate. They want to speak. Or they want to sit on the chairs. They expect the food to be brought to them. They expect that they be served water. Everything should be brought to them.[101] You have the right to serve me because I'm your pastor. You have to serve me. But I don't have to do that to you because I am your leader and you are not my leader.

It seems that there is a dissonance between admiring humility as a quality in theory, and not necessarily practising it. Tanzanian Christian leaders recognise the importance of humility as a biblical value, but within the society it is not modelled because of the strong cultural influence. Tanzanians may define humility culturally, which is external humility, rather than biblically as internal humility. For example, humility is expressed in giving respect to older people. Respect as an expression of humility can also be observed when people are always more important than work and keeping time. Since Tanzanian leaders are event oriented they are willing to be interrupted by people and listen when they come with their problems in order to help them. Many

---

[101] Translated from the original Swahili: Unakuta viongozi wetu wanapenda kutumikiwa. Wanapenda kudictate. Waseme. Au wanapenda kukaa katika viti. Waletewe chakula. Waletewe maji. Waletewe kila kitu.

Tanzanians always have an open ear to listen to the problems of their followers and try to help them, as Leader 5 puts it:

> If one hears that I am sick or I have a problem, a big problem, s/he will come to my home and talk to me. S/he will visit me. This person will not help me because maybe s/he knows I do not have any money. S/he will come to help me to clear my thoughts. To make sure that I will forget the things that disturb me. Therefore the person wastes her/his time to help me.[102]

This is an expression of their love. But there is also a deep gap between Christians from different denominations, as Lay Leader 2 puts it plainly: "Within different churches, they call themselves Christians but they have a conflict or quarrel. Instead of worshipping they begin telling each other: 'You are a sinner.' 'You are a sinner.' It is like they are blaming each other."[103] I have noticed, that it goes so far that sometimes people from different denominations will not greet each other on the road. The way faithfulness is practised differs. Certain respondents state that some leaders are faithful in their ministries in terms of handling money (Leader 3), but others are not (Leader 5). Leader 6 says: "Unfortunately here in Africa, we Christians are not transparent. What you do publicly is not the same as what you do when you are alone. I only like to show my good side to people so that they can praise me."[104] This has to do with a strong collectivist value among Tanzanians and its shame culture.

In comparing the groups, it is interesting to note that Westerners emphasise compassion, humility and servanthood as important features of Christ-like leadership, which are contrary to Western culture. On the other hand, Tanzanians emphasise a deep fear of God, cultural humility (respect), and helping other people, which are already part of their culture. The implications of this in terms of leadership and partnership are further explored in chapter five.

Servant leadership is a reflection of a Christ-like character. Thus, before the biblical values and Christian virtues (questions 2.7 & 2.11) are presented, the answers regarding *"How do you understand servant leadership? What picture would you use to describe servant leadership?"* are presented. How servant leadership is understood may vary in different societies. The *Western* respondents understand servant leadership as being "authentic, practised like a free Lord and at the same time like a committed servant" (Leader 4). Leader 5

---

[102] Translated from the original Swahili: Mtu akisikia nimeumwa au nina shida, shida kubwa tu, atakuja nyumbani kwangu kuongea na mimi. Atanichukua. Yule mtu atanisaidia sio kwa sababu anajua labda mimi sina fedha au nini. Atanichukua kwa ajili ya kunisaidia, kutengeneza afya yangu ya akili. Kuhakikisha kwamba nimesahau yale ambayo yananisumbua. Kwa hiyo mtu anapoteza muda wake ananisaidia mimi.

[103] Translated from the original Swahili: Kwa upande wa kikristo labda unakuta kati ya kanisa na kanisa wao wanajiita ni wakristo lakini wana mgogoro au ubaguzi fulani. Badala ya kuabudu badala yake wanaanza kugombana kama wao kwa wao: "Wewe una dhambi." "Wewe una dhambi." Kwa hiyo kama wanajihukumu.

[104] Translated from the original Swahili: Bahati mbaya hapa Afrika, sisi wakristo hatuko wazi. Kwa maana kwamba unachofanya mbele ya watu si kile unachofanya ukiwa peke yako. Napenda kuonyesha upande mzuri tu kwa watu, ili watu waweze kunisifia.

describes servant leadership as "the ability to lead a group with not only wisdom and courage, but also humility and patience ... putting others ahead of self". Leader 6 understands servant leadership as "leading by serving. The picture is one of the leader below or behind the people [s/]he leads instead of above or in front of them." Leader 8 says:

> A servant leader is one who is willing to subject personal opinions, ambitions, desires to what is best for the organisation one is leading, without judgement or resentment. A servant leader shows by example in work style, ethics, and relationships what is required, and holds people accountable for achieving it.

A number of Western respondents (Leader 4, 5 & Lay Leader 1) mentioned the picture of Jesus washing the disciples' feet. The other picture is like a "Shepherd caring for his sheep. Waking up early - [s/]he has a lot to do to keep them healthy, bring them to good pastures and keep them well" (Leader 7).[105]

In the West, servant leadership is often pictured with an upside down triangle, as shown in figure 3.3.

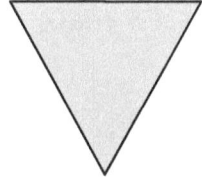

Figure 3.3 (Kessler 2001:20)

According to the above figure, the leader is at the very bottom. Her/his responsibility is to serve others and make them successful. All the credit for success is passed on to the followers. The critical mass of people has the authority to determine the direction in which the organisation is heading. In the extreme case, which I have also seen, the leader is expected to serve but not to lead by exercising authority. In my view, this is not desirable since a leader has authority, which s/he ought to exercise in humility. Within SIL International this can also be a challenge since the organisation has a fairly flat, egalitarian, democratic, grass-root structure as can be seen in the section on "Relationships and Leadership" in chapter four.

The *Tanzanian* respondents understand "Servant leadership as being like Christ"[106] (Lay Leader 3). Servant leadership means serving others like Jesus washed the disciples' feet, in John 13 (Lay Leader 3). Several respondents (Leader 3, 4 & 7) pointed out that servant leadership is by example, as Leader

---

[105] Nouwen (1989:39-45) also compares servant leadership with the task of a shepherd. According to Denny Gunderson (1997), a Protestant theologian from the USA, a servant leader does not control but is obedient, humble, meek, loving, accepting, trusting and willing to receive ministry from a follower such as encouragement, correction or instruction.

[106] Translated from the original Swahili: Uongozi wa utumishi ni kuwa kama Yesu Kristo.

3 says: "Jesus taught people more by actions than by words."[107] A servant leader is "A leader who works with people" (Leader 7).[108] S/he also enables people (Leader 4). Servant leadership is to volunteer wholeheartedly" (Lay Leader 3).[109] A servant leader is somebody who does not seek good payment or benefits but depends on God (Leader 2 & Lay Leader 3). Leader 2 explains: "Servanthood comes from the word 'servant'. ... A tool is often used or a person who is used for the benefit of others or the owner. ... And because we are servants in the church the meaning of servanthood is to be used like a slave [or a tool] serving God."[110] "Servanthood is like a sacrifice of serving God" (Leader 5).[111] "S/he [the leader] is a servant of people. [However, s/he] is still a leader" (Leader 7).[112] Therefore, Leader 7 continues:

> S/he supervises. S/he gives explanations. S/he orders. But s/he should remember that s/he is a servant of those who s/he serves. In other words, s/he should be willing to serve them any time. S/he should be willing to listen to their problems. S/he should be willing to understand the weaknesses of those s/he leads. And s/he should be willing to help them to do better in their areas by teaching and explaining them.[113]

A servant leader "Is a person of people, whom s/he loves and understands"[114] (Leader 7). "A Swahili proverb says 'A leader is a rubbish pit'. ... Therefore, if you are a leader you should be willing to receive blame" (Leader 6).[115] But this should not prevent "A servant leader from practising justice"[116] (Lay Leader 2).

---

[107] Translated from the original Swahili: Yesu alikuwa anawafundisha watu kwa vitendo zaidi kuliko kuwa msemaji tu.

[108] Translated from the original Swahili: Kiongozi ambaye anafanya kazi na watu.

[109] Translated from the original Swahili: Uongozi wa utumishi ni wa kujitolea kwa moyo wako wote.

[110] Translated from the original Swahili: Utumishi linatokana na neno "mtumishi". ... Kutumika mara nyingi ni chombo au mtu anayetumika kwa ajili ya mnufaisha binadamu au mmiliki. ... Na sisi kwa sababu ni watumishi wa kanisa uongozi wa utumishi kwetu maana yake ni kutumika kama mtumwa lakini kumtumikia Mungu.

[111] Translated from the original Swahili: Utumishi ni kama sadaka ya kumtumikia Mungu.

[112] Translated from the original Swahili: Yeye ni mtumishi wa watu. Bado ni kiongozi.

[113] Translated from the original Swahili: Anasimamia. Anatoa maelekezo. Anaagiza. Lakini akumbuke yeye ni mtumishi wa wale anaowatumikia. Kwa maana kwamba yu tayari kuwahudumia wakati wowote. Yu tayari kuwasikiliza watu shida zao. Yu tayari kuwaelewa anaowaongoza mapungufu yao. Na yu tayari kuwasaidia kuwafanya bora katika maeneo mbalimbali kuwafunza, kuwaeleza.

[114] Translated from the original Swahili: Ni mtu wa watu anawapenda na kuwaelewa.

[115] Translated from the original Swahili: Kwenye kiswahili tuna methali inasema "kiongozi ni jalala". ... Kwa hiyo ukiwa kiongozi uwe tayari kupokea lawama.

[116] Translated from the original Swahili: Kiongozi mtumishi ni hivyohivyo atende haki.

Mhogolo proposes the following servant leadership model, which is like a wheel with spokes.

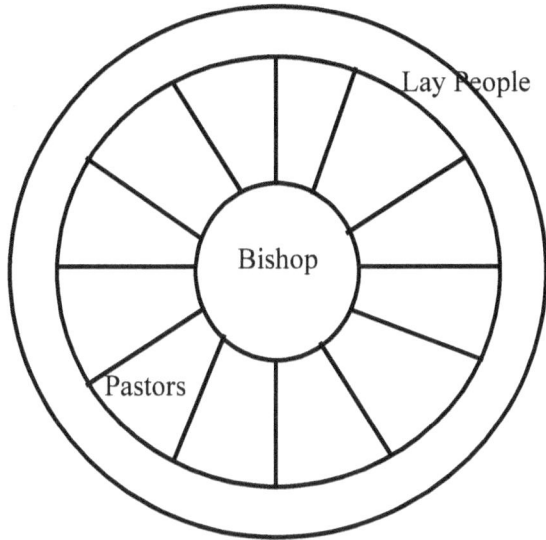

Figure 3.4 (Mhogolo 1996:94)

This leadership model incorporates the need for authority and the importance of community and servanthood. The bishop as the leader is at the centre. He[117] has authority to lead. At the same time he empowers and serves the pastors. He works with the pastors as a team, ministers to them, and empowers them. The pastors are empowered and given authority by the bishop and in turn serve the lay people. This way authority and service move from the inner circle to the outer circle. Thus, the spokes of a wheel are a better symbol for servant leadership than the upside down triangle.

It seems in the West there is a strong emphasis on servanthood where the leader has little authority and the success of the followers is in focus. Tanzanians try to find a balance between leadership and servanthood. They recognise the necessity for a leader to have and exercise authority by providing leadership serving the people by having their welfare in mind. In my view this reflects Christ-like leadership the way it was discussed in chapter one. Jesus was both **leader** and **servant**. The Western model where the leader is at the very bottom does not reflect the value of equality because, in fact, the followers have more power than the leader.

Christ-like leadership has to do with biblical values and virtues. Values and virtues are closely connected. Virtues are lived out values. If one values certain things it is reflected in her/his behaviour. Thus, the responses to the questions *"Which biblical, ethical values related to leadership are important*

---

[117] Mostly I use inclusive language to make a point about gender and the importance of women in society, family, church and leadership. However, most of the leaders in Tanzania are men. Thus, where relevant, I only use "he" if the context of the argument requires it.

to you?" and *"Which Christian virtues or aspects of character do you consider important for leaders to have?"* are presented together in the following chart.

VALUES AND VIRTUES OF BOTH GROUPS		
	WEST	**TANZANIA**
Values	• Love (5) • Humility (7) • Faithfulness (2) • Justice (1) • Mercy (1)	• Love (8) • Humility (5) • Faithfulness (4) • Justice (3) • Mercy (3)
Virtues	• Endurance (2) • Courage (4) • Integrity (4) • Wisdom (3) • Honesty (3) • Peace (3) • Compassion (4) • Forgiveness (2) • Self-discipline (2) • Patience (6) • Listening (2) • To be humble (6) • Loving (3) • Transparent (2)	• Endurance (3) • Prayer (3) • Goodness (2) • Wisdom (3) • Honesty (2) • Godliness (3) • Relationship (2) • Forgiveness (2) • Gentleness (2) • Respect for people (6) • Listening (3) • Passion (3) • Loving (6)

Figure 3.5

It is interesting to note that the interviewees identified the five biblical values of love, humility, faithfulness, justice and mercy as important to leadership. It has been argued in chapter one that these values are core to leadership and partnership. However, I would have expected that justice and faithfulness would have been mentioned more often by the Westerners. At the same time it seems that love is highly valued but may be not as much practised in the West. Tanzanians value faithfulness higher than I expected, but only a few respondents mentioned mercy. During the group discussion the Tanzanian participants indicated that they would like to see more people being faithful and actions being taken if something goes wrong instead of being always merciful without consequences. Both groups value love, humility, faithfulness, justice and mercy. However, the virtue of loving someone, according to the responses, seems to be more important to Tanzanians than to Westerners. Humility and integrity are slightly more valued in the West than in Tanzania. It is interesting to note that so many Western respondents expect a leader to be patient and compassionate. I perceive Tanzanians as being much more patient than Westerners.

Values and virtues influence a leader's behaviour. However, these values and virtues do not exist in a vacuum because human beings live in community which shapes culture.

3.3.2 Christian Leadership and Culture

At the beginning of this chapter, it was noted that leadership behaviour needs to be looked at in context. This section is a further development of how Christian leadership is influenced by culture, which I have argued in chapter two. The interviewees were asked: *"Is leadership influenced by culture?"* The examples below support what the majority (5) of the *Western* respondents said about the influence of culture on leadership. Several (4) expressed the view that leadership is quite often influenced by culture. Only one person did not know if leadership is influenced by culture. The majority (5) of the *Tanzanian* respondents expressed that leadership is quite often influenced by culture. Some (3) believe sometimes and one answered with "yes". Only one person does not think leadership is influenced by culture. When asked, *"In which way is leadership influenced by culture?"*, the *Western* respondents gave a number of answers: "In Tanzania leadership tends to be more hierarchical, top-down, prescriptive than in the West" (Leader 2). Some cultures value some traits like ability more than others such as age and status, as Leader 3 points out:

> I know of people in Tanzania who will not give a younger person (who has more wisdom, knowledge and ability in a certain area) a voice in the discussion simply because they are younger, and how is it possible that a younger person could know more than an elder? Also, I know of a specific example in the States where a younger person's advice was followed simply because he "had a degree", but yet an older man with more practical experience had a better solution.

"If in the West a leader is not addressed respectfully, it will most of the time be overseen as not so important. In Tanzania such an action could lead to serious consequences ..." (Leader 7). Leadership is also influenced by culture "how leaders from different cultures react to people questioning their opinions or asking for the reasons behind their actions. This is acceptable within the British culture, but I think within the Tanzanian culture, it is not so easy to challenge a leader in this way", says Lay Leader 1. Leader 5 says:

> Some cultures prefer a strong leader who is not necessarily accountable to those below her/him. ... The leader is the decision-maker, final authority, no-questions-asked. Other cultures prefer a leader who listens to those below her/him, has compassion for others, and cares about the needs of the whole more than the needs of the leader only.

A good example of how leadership is influenced by culture is how difference in age is perceived in *Tanzania*, as Lay Leader 1 says:

> I am a young person and I have the ability to be a leader. In African culture it is a big thing to respect the big people. But what happens is to be afraid of them. If you are a leader it means that you need to criticise

others in order to help them to change. And for me as a young person, it is very difficult to criticise an older person if s/he has done something wrong. S/he will perceive it as if I am rebuking her/him.[118]

Tanzanian Leader 4 points out how leadership is influenced by culture in terms of exercising authority and humility:

> If I am a leader, it is your responsibility to serve me. I make the decisions. You count me as a semi-god. That means today I am with you. If I become a bishop today, it is as I receive something new. It came into me. I have become a different person. This is the African understanding about a leader. S/he received something from heaven. Now s/he is more intelligent, more powerful, her/his thinking capacity has changed. S/he is perfect. S/he does not do anything wrong. Therefore, anything s/he says or decides is perfect. No discussion. No doubt. No question because the leader has said and the leader has divinely granted wisdom. So the leader is a dictator. S/he is on the king's seat to be served food. When you have become a leader in the African society, people start gathering at your home. They collect maize for you. Those who have cows make sure that your fridge is full of meat. They will bring milk. They will bring water and firewood. The servants bring you young men and girls. This is like an empire. If I come to you, you just sit around. They come to serve you. That is what is happening in the church.[119]

This picture of reality is in stark contrast to the ideal of servant leadership. It also suggests that one's true character may come to the surface once s/he gets into a position of power. Because the church is influenced by culture, it clashes with the teaching of Christ. This also means that it is very difficult to criticise a leader:

> Now in African society when we say that a leader is very respected, it means even if this leader makes a mistake who will criticise her/him?

---

[118] Translated from the original Swahili: Mimi ni kijana naweza kuwa na uwezo kuwa kiongozi. Na utamaduni wa Afrika kitu kikubwa sana wanasema ni kuheshimu watu wakubwa. Lakini kitu ambacho kinafanyika ni kuogopa. Ukiwa kama kiongozi maana yake uko tayari kukosoa na kurekibisha. Na mimi kama kijana ni vigumu sana kumrekibisha mzee hata kama amekosea. Ataona kama nimemtukana.

[119] Translated from the original Swahili: Mimi nikiwa kiongozi mimi ni wajibu wenu nyinyi mnitumikie. Halafu mimi ndiye ninaamua. Nyinyi mnanihesabu kama semi-god. Yaani, leo hii niko pamoja na wewe. Leo hii nikiwa mara moja askofu ni kama kuna kitu fulani kipya kimekuja kwangu. Kimeingia ndani yangu. Nimekuwa mtu tofauti. Hiyo ndiyo African understanding about a leader. Amekuwa kapokea kitu toka mbinguni. Sasa ni kama amekuwa na akili zaidi, more powerful, thinking capacity yake imebadilika. He is perfect. He does not do anything wrong. Kwa hiyo, anything he says and decides is perfect. No discussion. No doubt. No question because the leader has said and the leader has divinely granted wisdom. Kwa hiyo sasa kiongozi anakuwa dictator. Anakuwa kwenye kiti cha mfalme kuhudumiwa chakula. Katika jamii ya kiafrika umeshakuwa kiongozi watu wanakusanya kule nyumbani kwao. Wanakusanya kama debe moja la mahindi. Wanaleta kwenye store yako hapa. Wewe hutakiwi kwenda kufanya kazi. Wale wenye ng'ombe wanahakikisha kuwa utakuwa na ng'ombe wa kuchinja ili fridge yako imejaa. Maziwa wataleta. Maji na kuni wataleta. Watumishi watakuletea vijana wa kiume na wa kike. Kwa hiyo ni empire. Nikija pale kwako wewe, wewe umekaa tu. Wanakuja kukutumika. That is what is happening in the church.

> Who will be the first to say something to this pastor, to this bishop? They will talk below. "The bishop did this. He does this." But who will stand up in a meeting and say: "We have this problem. We hear the bishop ..." Who will address it? First of all, if s/he is told to sit down. If s/he does not sit people will remove her/him. This is where the respect of the bishop comes in (Leader 7).[120]

Another challenge relates to the expectations of the extended family, as Leader 3 says: "One receives some money for a specific ministry. Now s/he may face some problems in the family. Therefore, s/he misuses this money."[121] Sometimes it is difficult for a leader to make a just decision because it may affect one of her/his relatives. There is also quite a bit of group pressure in terms of what other people think.

These examples demonstrate that leadership is strongly influenced by culture. In my view, there is often such a big gap between the ideal leadership picture and the actual practice because the cultural values are more dominant than the biblical. Also in some cases, true biblical transformation has not yet taken place. A cross-cultural dialogue, as discussed in chapter one (1.3 Christian Leadership, the Gospel and Culture), can facilitate such a process.

Before we look at how Western and Tanzanian Christian leaders practise the biblical values of love, justice, mercy, faithfulness and humility (question 2.12), we need to look at the question *"Which biblical values are universal and which are culture specific?"* Basically, the majority of *Western* respondents (9) agreed that they are universal because if a biblical value is defined as a value it is considered good by God's Word, such as love, justice, mercy and so on, and all biblical values are universal. It was argued in chapter one that these values are universal because they are a reflection of God's character. However, it was also said that the application of these values might differ in different cultures according to the cultural context, as Leader 8 puts it:

> Many of the biblical values are universal in their concept but culturally specific in their application. For instance, truth can be seen as important in both cultures, but a leader in the West will sit down and talk with an employee who is not performing and let them know they are not performing. In Tanzania the leader will meet with the staff member but the discussion may be general, the truth is seen as needing to be almost disguised.

Only one Western respondent (Leader 6) believes that biblical values are culture specific.

---

[120] Translated from the original Swahili: Sasa kwenye jamii ya kiafrika kwa mfano utamaduni unaposema tunaheshimu sana, heshimu mtu mkubwa. Maana kwamba hata akikosea huyu kiongozi nani atamkosoa? Nani atakuwa wa kwanza kusema kitu kwa huyu mchunguaji, huyu askofu? Watazungumza kwa chinichini. "Askofu akafanya hivi. Anafanya hivi, jamani." Lakini nani atasimama kwenye mkutano aseme: "Bwana tuna shida hii. Tuna matatizo haya. Tunasikia askofu ..." Nani atadiriki? Kwanza ataambiwa akae chini. Asipokaa wanamtoa watu. Hapa inakuja heshima ya askofu.

[121] Translated from the original Swahili: Watu analetewa kwa mfano fungu la pesa kwa ajili ya kutenda kazi fulani ya Mungu. Sasa anakutana labda na shida ndani ya familia. Sasa anamega ile pesa.

The majority of *Tanzanian* respondents (6) also agreed that they are universal because the law of God is written on the hearts of all people. They are universal in the sense that they must be applied in any society. However, it was also said that these values might be expressed differently in different cultures. A few respondents (3) believe that especially the values of justice, humility and faithfulness are culture specific.

If the biblical values are expressed differently in different cultures, *"How do Western and Tanzanian Christian leaders practise the biblical values of love, justice, mercy, faithfulness and humility in their ministry?"* The responses above have shown that biblical values are expressed in culturally different ways. Here only the answers of the respondents regarding their own societies are presented since this chapter is a self-description of both leadership styles. The Western and Tanzanian view of how they perceive the practice of the biblical values of each other respectively will be presented in chapter five as part of the dialogue between the two groups. It is interesting to note that the *Western* respondents did not give a specific example of how love and mercy are practised by Western leaders in their ministry. This suggests even though love is valued it is not as much practised in reality. It also seems mercy is not much valued and therefore very little practised. In contrast to these two values justice is highly valued and practised. According to Leader 2, "Westerners are used to a high level of justice from their home cultures". Justice in the West is understood to be transparent and specific, as the following example by Leader 8 regarding disciplining a member of staff for professional misconduct demonstrates:

> [There will be a o]ne on one discussion between the head of school and the person involved, depending on the severity of the offence. In cases resulting in dismissal deputies will be present. The situation is laid out, with evidence. The person has the opportunity to discuss with the head, then the discipline is given.

Regarding faithfulness Western leaders do their "jobs in a fully transparent agreed upon way" (Leader 7). "Western Christian leaders sometimes show humility by including themselves as illustrations in their sermons – I'm as bad at this as the next guy" (Lay Leader 1). Western leaders express humility "by the act of [being] willing to listen to others and seeking what is best for the other. [They are] ... willing to go the extra mile, willing to do the most mundane task as an example to others, willing to walk in someone else's shoes" (Leader 5). On the other hand, in the West humility is not necessarily a value a leader must have, as Leader 3 explains: "For example, very few American politicians will ever admit they made a mistake or made the wrong decision. Or they will never admit that they do not know what the best decision in a particular issue is. A political leader must always appear to have everything under control." However, Christians ought to be humble and admit their weaknesses and faults. Christians recognise that God who is in control is the final authority.

Tanzanians express love in the way they receive visitors, as Leader 6 explains: "When a visitor comes at night, it is necessary to give her/him something to eat. Even if there is no food ready, I will look for charcoal, make a fire, and cook some food for her/him. Even if there is no place for her/him to sleep, I will sleep on the floor and offer her/him my bed."[122] A Tanzanian leader employs somebody because of her/his attitude and in order to help her/him and not because of her/his skills (Leader 2). If there is a funeral, Tanzanians leave everything to be with the family of the person who died (Leader 2). Tanzanians feel free to depend on each other (Leader 2). On the other hand, people do not necessarily treat Christians from a different denomination equally because of different theological understandings (Lay Leader 2).

The practice of justice in Tanzania seems to be different than that of love. The practice of justice appears to be a challenging one, since a number of Tanzanian leaders seek their own benefits, which is demonstrated in the following example: "At church we have been blessed with material things. The pastor took everything for himself when it was meant to be shared with everybody. It is obvious that he is trying to improve his own life" (Leader 5).[123]

There are Tanzanian Christian leaders who practise mercy, as Leader 4 testifies: "The bishop ... was quick in forgiving someone. You could have your weakness and he could get really angry. But if you came to his office and told him, 'I have made a mistake', he forgave you and prayed for you. Then he encouraged you. And he said don't do it again."[124]

Tanzanian leaders are faithful in that they consider the Scripture as the inspired and true Word of God and take it seriously (Leader 4). Faithfulness not only relates to the Scripture but also to money. Some leaders are faithful in money matters, as Leader 3 shares:

> At the church he [our pastor] does not touch or handle money. The money stays in the bank. After every Sunday when the offering is collected, on Monday the money goes immediately to the bank. If somebody wants to withdraw money, it is necessary that the congregation know what for. The pastor only receives his salary at the end of the month.[125]

This is in contrast to the other example above, where the pastor used the material things for his personal benefit. However, as it was mentioned above,

---

[122] Translated from the original Swahili: Akifika mgeni hata kama ni usiku, ni lazima kutafuta chakula ili ale. Hata kama kulikuwa hamna chakula, natafuta mkaa, nawasha moto, napika chakula, nampa. Hata kama hana pa kulala mimi nitatandika chini, nitamwachia kitanda.

[123] Translated from the original Swahili: Kwa mfano kama kuna vitu. Tumepata baraka ya vitu kanisani. Halafu mtumishi anachukua vyote wakati ilikuwa kwa ajili ya wote. Sasa inaonekana yeye ni mbinafsi anajali maisha yake.

[124] Translated from the original Swahili: Askofu ... alikuwa mwepesi kumsamehe mtu. Unaweza kuwa ni udhaifu wako kabisa na yeye amekasirika kabisa. Lakini ukiingia ofisini kwake na kumwambia, baba nimekosa, anakusamehe na anakuombea. Halafu anakutia moyo. Na anasema usirudie tena.

[125] Translated from original Swahili: Kwanza pale kanisani yeye hagusi pesa wala hushiki. Pesa zinakaa benki. Na kila Jumapili zaka na sadaka zinapokusanywa Jumatatu lazima ziwe kwa benki. Yule anayetaka kuzichukua ni lazima kanisa lijue kwamba kuna nini kinachofanyika. Na yeye anapewa tu mshahara wake kwa wakati unaofaa.

other leaders are not faithful and transparent in that they act differently in public than at home.

As we have seen above, the ideal of humility and the actual practice sometimes differ. Tanzanian Christians value and expect humility. However, it may not necessarily be applied once one is in a leadership position. Humility is expressed in the way elders and leaders are viewed, as Leader 7 explains:

> For instance, to respect the older people in the African society is very easy, because we in Africa know that the older people are in charge. Every family has their clan elders. ... The elders make the decisions. The elders oversee the life of the society. That means a Christian leader is obedient to leadership. "Remember those who lead you", says the Bible. We are afraid of the respect of those who lead. The respect between us. Therefore the elders, and at church the pastors, are respected because that is how it is known in African society. There is no problem.[126]

This suggests that humility is basically expected from followers but not so much from leaders. As Lay Leader 1 said earlier, it is very difficult to criticise an older person. Therefore, if the older person is a bad leader s/he still needs to be respected because of her/his leadership and age. This is problematic from a Western and Christian perspective. It is difficult to exercise justice in such an environment. Also humility is especially needed in leaders because of abuse of power.

As can be seen from the above discussion a good Christian leader in the West and in Tanzania is expected to have certain character traits. Both groups appreciate the same leadership qualities such as listening, loving and serving. The ideal picture of a good Christian leader is to emulate Jesus as a leader and follow his servant leadership. How this ideal picture matches the reality and actual practice is reflected in who people consider to be a good leader and why, how the features of Christ-like character are expressed and how biblical values and virtues are practised. The actual leadership practice is also reflected in the respondents' experience of the leadership of others and how they have functioned as leaders themselves. Westerners focus on Jesus himself, how he exercised leadership in terms of sharing authority and being accountable. In contrast, Tanzanians emphasise how Jesus related to other people.

Looking at the whole area of character and leadership, it appears that there is a dissonance between the ideal and actual practice in both societies. Whereas biblical values such as love and mercy are a challenge for Western leaders to practise, for Tanzanian leaders, the challenge is justice and faithfulness. Obviously, there is a tension between cultural and biblical values. It

---

[126] Translated from the original Swahili: Kwa mfano kuheshimu wazee katika jamii za kiafrika hiyo ni rahisi sana. Kwa sababu sisi katika eneo la Afrika wazee ndiyo wanajua wanasimamia mambo. Kila familia ina wazee wa ukoo. Kila jamii ina wazee wa kijiji. Wazee wanaamua. Wazee wanasimamia maisha katika jamii. Kwa maana kwamba kiongozi mkristo anakuwa mtii kwa uongozi. "Wakumbukeni wanaowaongoza", Biblia inasema. Tunaogopa ile heshima kwa wale wanaoongoza. Heshima baina yetu. Kwa hiyo wazee na kanisani wachungaji wanaheshimika kwa sababu jamii ya kiafrika ndivyo inavyofahamu. Haina shida.

seems to me that in many areas, the cultural values still dominate. These cultural values gain more influence if a leader is insecure. Then, there is a danger for the leader to abuse her/his personal power neglecting the Christian values. From the data, there is no question about the influence of character on leadership. A leader with a moral character is more likely to practise Christ-like leadership than one with a bad or weak character. Therefore, the worldview of a Christian leader must be transformed to become a biblical worldview.[127] A leader with a good character seems to be more open to act against the negative cultural values, applying biblical teaching in her/his leadership. Thus, spiritual and character formation is absolutely essential in any society to become a good Christian leader. How character formation takes place appears to be different in each society. Whereas Westerners emphasise self-reflection, Tanzanians stress the importance of education, experience and mentoring.

In the next chapter, the leadership features of relationships, power and conflict are considered in both societies.

---

[127] In their book *Disciplining Nations* Miller and Guthrie (2001) stress the importance of developing a biblical worldview since the worldview influences peoples' mindset.

Chapter 4

Relationships, Power and Conflict in Western, Particularly Germanic and Anglo-Saxon, and Tanzanian Leadership

The third chapter has shown that character and theology influence leadership. Leadership is also influenced by the social environment in which leaders live, and its cultural values. A leader's character and theology is shaped and influenced by the social environment. Part of the social environment is how people relate, how they use power, and how they deal with conflict.

In this chapter the Western, particularly Germanic and Anglo-Saxon, and Tanzanian leadership styles are described and compared in terms of relationship, power and conflict based on data collected from the interviews, participant observations, case studies and existing literature. Basically the same way of presenting, comparing and interpreting the information is used as in chapter three. The leadership styles will then be evaluated in chapter five.

4.1 Relationships and Leadership

Leadership has a lot to do with relationships. Leaders lead people. Thus, it is essential to understand how leaders relate to each other and also to their followers and how they perceive relationship versus task. Whereas Westerners tend to be individualistic, Tanzanians live and work in community.

4.1.1 Organisational Structure and Leadership

How relationships among and between leaders and followers are characterized is reflected in the structure and corporate culture of an organisation or church. Therefore, the interviewees were asked to *describe the structure of the organisation or church in which they work* (question 3.1). According to the *Western* respondents, it seems that most Western organisations have a clear structure and hierarchy. However, there is usually some kind of team leadership at the various levels.

Since most of the interviewees work with SIL International and I am most familiar with this organisation, I use it here as an organisational case study. SIL International's structure and corporate culture has been shaped by its history and situational contexts. Because of its origin in the USA and the predominance of members from the USA, along with the representation of members, SIL International is predominantly a Western organisation, even though it is becoming more and more a multicultural organisation. SIL International works in more than seventy countries (Wycliffe International 2004).[128] So the organisational culture of SIL International in each entity var-

---

[128] This includes work among people who live outside their traditional homeland.

ies. Currently there are only very few African leaders in SIL.[129] Thus, not many changes if any have taken place so far. However, some generalizations, which are common to all, can be made.

Individuals are spiritually motivated and are committed to the Great Commission (Matthew 28:16-20). In particular, they have a strong desire to see people having access to the Bible in the language or languages they understand best. Originally, the work of SIL International started in Central and South America (Hefley 1995). In the past, one language team was assigned to one specific language group. Many of the ethnic groups that SIL members served lived in extremely remote places with very little contact with the outside world (Hill & friends 2002:3). Because of the isolated locations and limited technology of the day, communication between the SIL member working in a language allocation and the SIL administration was limited. The SIL member had to be pioneers with plenty of initiative. They needed to know how to work independently. They are described as "hearty individuals, who could function in isolated conditions under difficult conditions" (:3). The language team's responsibility was to learn and analyse the language and the culture, to do literacy work and translate Scripture. The team is usually highly motivated and has a wholehearted, intrinsic and intense emotional commitment to the work being undertaken. This is reflected in long working days. The administration is expected to develop, find and provide the necessary resources to help to complete the product. Once the New Testament was translated, the language team was celebrated as heroes and heroines for their achievement of ten to twenty years of selfless investment and hard work. The translation of a New Testament was emphasised and used to be an important achievement.

Historically, SIL International has a flat, egalitarian, democratic, grass-root structure. Independence, egalitarian democracy and autonomy have been valued. The organisation is heavily influenced by the high value of individualism. The individual is stressed and has quite a bit of autonomy. In practice,

> This means that individuals do not give over any more of their power to leadership than is absolutely necessary to meet goals; they cooperate when it is necessary to accomplish their individual goals. There is suspicion and resistance to decisions coming from the top, and a corresponding respect for the views of those who have grass-roots experience. When group-decision making is necessary, members want to participate in the decisions that affect them, and have difficulty submitting to hierarchical leadership (Hill & friends 2002:5).

This decision-making process requires numerous meetings on all levels. This process takes time. However, I believe in the long run it pays off, since everybody is able to participate and "buy in". Consequently, they own the decision and are committed to it. An additional benefit of this process is creative solutions to problems.

---

[129] The first African SIL branch director is an Ethiopian, who will take office in the year 2007.

Western SIL members tend to be goal, task and work-oriented. Credibility and respect are earned through achievement. To come to work or meetings on time is highly valued. Relationships are valued. However, relationships tend to be built outside of work. As work and recreational time are usually separated, social interactions tend to take place outside work hours (:7). Relationships tend to be instrumental, which can be observed when questions are asked such as: "How can we engage the Church in our work?" instead of asking "How can we engage **with** the Church?" This implies that the purpose of building relationships tends to focus on reaching the organisational ends. Relationships in the West tend to be seen as more instrumental (Trompenaars & Hampden-Turner 2002:131).

As can be seen from the case study above, SIL International's organisational culture can be described as what Trompenaars and Hampden-Turner (:159 & 172-177) call a fulfilment and project-oriented culture. It is certainly more Western than African. Western SIL members are mainly task-oriented and individualistic. In other words, generally the task prevails over the relationship. They receive their value through achievement. Independence is highly valued. Thus, Westerners tend to compete, want to be self-reliant and have a high self-interest for personal growth and fulfilment.

In contrast, the structure of a Tanzanian organisation or church is much more hierarchical than in the West, as the *Tanzanian* respondents described it. For example, Leader 4 explains the organisational structure of the Anglican Church in Tanzania:

> The organisation of the Anglican Church is like a pillar. The bishop is at the top of the pillar. Below him is the pastor, then the catechist, church elders. Last are the lay Christians.[130] Everything from the bottom that they are doing is directed to the head, to the bishop. So the bishop is a very top person. He is very powerful. Anything that is done he has to approve. If he does not agree, you cannot do it.[131]

This strong hierarchy is also reflected in the Catholic Church, which begins with the "Pope, cardinal, bishop, priest, catechists, deacons and other leaders below, [and finally] the Christians"[132] (Lay Leader 2). It seems that in some of the smaller denominations and Pentecostal churches the hierarchy is not as strong, as Leader 1 describes the structure of the Church of God: "[I]n my church the pastor is the leader. S/he has her/his committee of church elders. ... They are the parliament of the church. So the pastor is only the leader. S/he can express her/his thoughts. And they agree or decline."[133] Pentecostal

---

[130] Translated from the original Swahili: Muundo wetu wa kanisa la Anglikana ni kama nguzo. Askofu ni juu ya nguzo. Chini yake ni mchungaji, halafu mkatekisti, wazee wa kanisa. Mwisho kabisa ni wakristo wa kawaida.

[131] Translated from the original Swahili: Chochote kinachotendeka lazima akubali. Asipokubali hamwezi kufanya kitu.

[132] Translated from the original Swahili: Papa, kardinali, askofu, padri, makatekista, mashemasi na viongozi vingine wadogowadogo, wakristo.

[133] Translated from the original Swahili: ... kanisani kwangu mchungaji ndiye kiongozi. Ana baraza lake la wazee wa kanisa. ... Hawa ndiyo bunge la kanisa lile. Kwa hiyo mchungaji ni kiongozi tu. Anaweza kutoa mawazo yake. Wakakubali au wakakataa.

churches usually have a clear organisational structure (Leader 5, 7 & Lay Leader 3). However, it seems that a lot of authority comes from the grass roots, as Leader 7 says: "The largest organ decision-making body is the annual general meeting. All the pastors are delegates and there are two other delegates from each church."[134] In an organisation the leader is usually responsible to a board, as Leader 2 describes: "[T]here is a board of directors... Then comes the general manager. After the general manager there are the department leaders ..."[135]

This hierarchical structure, as described by the Tanzanian respondents, is in contrast to the proposed servant leadership model of a wheel with spokes, where everybody is basically on the same level. In some places, from my experience there may be exceptions to the strong hierarchical structure, as Leader 2 mentioned above at the beginning of the previous chapter, where some leaders give instructions and everybody knows her/his responsibilities. Usually nobody interferes in anybody else's area of responsibility.

When asked, *"What roles exist? How do the various roles interrelate? Who jokes with whom?"* in summary the *Western* respondents said, despite the hierarchy in Western organisations, people can easily joke with each other no matter in which position they are, which is an expression of equality and egalitarian value. Hierarchy in the West is more functional than status driven. The *Tanzanian* respondents said: "When they are at work they respect each other recognising that the other is the superior at work" (Lay Leader 2).[136] "In our leadership everyone knows her/his responsibility in the committee" (Leader 1).[137] Leader 7 says: "I think among the bishops there is good communication. Then between the assistant bishops and the bishop there is good and close communication. Also in the executive committee there is good communication."[138] It seems that whereas communication on the same level is often good, people between different levels do not necessarily communicate, as Leader 5 says: "In my church really they have good levels, but the link, the communication is not very good. For example, from one level to another there is a little problem."[139] The difference between authority levels is also reflected in who can joke with whom. Most respondents (Leader 1, 2, 4, 6, 7, Lay Leader 2 & 3) agree that joking is only appropriate on the same level but not with superiors or subordinates, as Leader 4 puts it: "I as a pastor cannot joke

---

[134] Translated from the original Swahili: Wachungaji wote ni wajumbe na wakilishi wengine wawili kutoka kanisani.
[135] Translated from the original Swahili: ... kuna board of directors ... Baada ya hapo kuna meneja mkuu. Baada ya meneja mkuu kuna wakuu wa idara ...
[136] Translated from the original Swahili: Wanapokuwa kazini unakuta wanaheshimiana kwamba yeye ni mkubwa wangu wa kazi.
[137] Translated from the original Swahili: Sisi uongozi wetu kila mmoja anajua wajibu wake katika baraza.
[138] Translated from the original Swahili: Nafikiri waangalizi wale wana mahusiano mazuri wao kwa wao. Halafu makamwe waangalizi na waangalizi wana mahusiano mazuri na wa karibu. Kwenye kamati kuu sasa hapa kuna uhusiano mzuri.
[139] Translated from the original Swahili: Kanisa langu mimi kweli wana ngazi nzuri lakini link, ile uhusiano sio mzuri sana. Kwa mfano, kutoka ngazi moja kwenda nyingine kuna matatizo kidogo.

with the bishop because he is a very big person. ... Maybe I joke with my fellow pastors because we are on the same level. But I cannot joke with the catechist because I am superior and s/he is subordinate."[140] It seems that joking across authority levels, like in the earlier example above where people joke with the bishop, is an exception, as Leader 6 the school principal says: "I can joke with the teachers, but it is not normal."[141] In the West the power distance is smaller than in Tanzania. This is reflected in the fact that whereas Westerners have no problems with joking between superiors and subordinates, this is hardly possible among Tanzanians. For both groups it is essential to learn how Jesus related to his disciples as master and friend at the same time. As it was discussed in chapter one, Jesus was clearly in authority and at the same time he had a personal relationship with people.

North American Protestant theologian Del Chinchen (2001:166), who lives in Kenya, argues: "African management is structured along the lines of the extended family."[142] As can be seen from the responses above, this is also true for Tanzania, which is very much reflected in the *ujamaa*-policy. The research conducted in a different context by the Germans ethnologist Claude-Hélène Mayer, theologian Christian Boness and social-psychologist Alexander Thomas (2003:77-78) supports this observation:[143] "Until today corporations and companies in Tanzania are formed according to the *ujamaa* model of the extended family."[144] This hierarchical structure in actual practice is in contrast to what has been expressed above by the respondents who desire a more egalitarian and participatory leadership. The question is how a Christ-like character of humility and servanthood, as discussed in chapter one, can be practised appropriately in such a structure. It seems that the values of collectivism and hierarchy are in tension with each other. In collectivist societies the power tends to rest with the group, but not so in Tanzania because of its hierarchical structure.

Below I outline how superiors relate to their subordinates. Thus, I continue presenting the answers to the two questions (questions 3.4 & 3.13), related to what people expect from their employer and leaders. The egalitarian values of *Westerners* are reflected in the responses of *what the respondents expect from their employer* (question 3.4): salary according to performance (4); social security/benefits such as housing and medical (5); employer cares for me like a family member (3); encouragement (7). A number of respondents (6) also ex-

---

[140] Translated from the original Swahili: Mimi kama mchungaji siwezi kumtania askofu kwa sababu ni mtu mkubwa sana. ... Mimi labda ninataniana na wachungaji wenzangu kwa sababu tuko kwenye level moja. Lakini mimi siwezi kumtania katekisti kwa sababu mimi ni mkubwa na yeye ni mdogo.
[141] Translated from the original Swahili: Naweza kuwatania walimu lakini sio kawaida.
[142] See also Chinchen, D. 1995. The patron-client system: A model of indigenous discipleship. *Evangelical Missions Quarterly*. Wheaton: Evangelism and Missions Information Service, October: 164-173.
[143] Mayer, Boness and Thomas (2003) base their research mainly on case studies and interviews.
[144] Translated from the original German: Firmen und Betriebe in Tansania sind bis heute nach dem Modell der Jamaa, der erweiterten Familie, gebildet. Das heißt, die Betriebsleitung steht in einer paternalistischen oder maternalistischen Beziehung zu den Mitarbeitern.

pect clear communication of objectives, goals and responsibilities. These should be shared goals. The respondents also expect "accountability to the institution and to a job description" (Leader 8) and "reasonable expectations" (Leader 7). There should be "an atmosphere in the work environment that promotes completion of the task and the freedom to perform ... [a] job well without unnecessary oversight or interruption from others" (Leader 3). It is interesting to note that the younger respondents expect the employer to care for them like a family member. There seems to be a shift in values among Westerners from generation to generation where the younger people have a stronger desire to be part of a team. However, there is also a clear indication towards a task-orientation, as the respondents expect clear goals and an environment that allows completion of the task.

The family idea in Tanzania described above is also reflected in the responses from the *Tanzanian* respondents: salary according to performance (6); social security/benefits such as housing, medical (5); employer cares for me like a family member (2); encouragement (8). Others expect to be motivated (Lay Leader 1), "to be cared for like a close person"[145] (Lay Leader 1), education (Leader 1), and peaceful (Leader 5) and just environment (Leader 6). According to the answers, first the family value does not seem very high. I expected that more respondents would want the employer to care for them like a family member. But the majority of people have high expectation in terms of social security and benefits, which also reflects some of the family values.

The responses from both groups suggest that there is not much difference in terms of what people expect from their employer. The Western respondents stressed the importance of having a clear understanding of what the objectives, goals and their responsibilities are. Thus, it seems whereas Westerners stress achievement and accountability; for Tanzanians the relationship is more important.

I have observed over the years that a leader in Tanzania is often referred to as a mother or father who cares for and looks after her/his staff. During the farewell celebration when the general secretary of the Bible Society of Tanzania retired, a number of employees said several times: "He was like our father. We welcome the new general secretary into the family of the Bible Society of Tanzania."

Generally, churches and organisations in Tanzania fit best the picture of what Trompenaars and Hampden-Turner (2002:158) call "family"-type organisation, which also reflects the *ujamaa*-philosophy in Tanzania. In such an organisation, the leader is expected to be benign, parental, and caring (Hampden-Turner & Trompenaars 2000:86). The leader of the family-style culture is further described as somebody who "weaves the pattern, sets the tone, models the appropriate posture for the corporation and expects subordinates to be 'on the same wavelength', knowing intuitively what is required; conversely the leader may empathise with the subordinates" (Trompenaars & Hampden-Turner 2002:159). According to the data, this is very true in Tanzania. Trom-

---

[145] Translated from the original Swahili: Kutunza kama mtu wa karibu.

penaars and Hampden-Turner describe the impact if the family culture in an organisation is taken too far:

> Family cultures at their least effective drain the energies and loyalties of subordinates to buoy up the leader, who literally floats on seas of adoration. Leaders get their sense of power and confidence **from** their followers, their charisma fuelled by credulity and by seemingly childlike faith (2002:161). [their emphasis]

These situations can sometimes also be observed in Tanzania, where the leader acts like a king (Mhogolo 1996:4). In diffuse cultures like Tanzania, the hierarchy is maintained through a dependency relationship, as Hampden-Turner and Trompenaars (2000:141-142) put it: "Diffuse relationships have a tendency to maintain hierarchy through reciprocal obligations. Because a powerful superior can always do more for a relatively powerless person than the latter can do for his superior, the powerless person is forever obligated."

According to Hofstede (1997:84), people from East African countries tend to be modest. His (:82) description of people from a modest society is consistent with what can be observed in Tanzania. Tanzanians prefer to have a good working relationship with their direct supervisor. As particularists, Tanzanian employees receive gratification through relationships, especially to the leader. The primary concern of the employees is not the role and function but a goal for the collective to aspire to. Often there is a strong commitment between employer and employee. They like to work with people who cooperate well with one another. Often employees enjoy the security that they will be able to work for the organisation as long as they want to. The leader of an organisation has a holistic responsibility for the employees, which goes beyond the organisation, as Trompenaars and Hampden-Turner explain it:

> The "father" or "elder brother" is influential in **all** situations, whether they have knowledge of the problem or not, whether an event occurs at work, in the canteen or on the way home, and even if someone else present is better qualified. The general happiness and welfare of all employees is regarded as the concern of the family-type corporation, which worries about their housing, the size of their families and whether their wages are sufficient for them to live well (2002:160). [their emphasis]

This is a giving and receiving. Being part of an organisation provides a social context for all members, which gives them meaning and purpose (:63). In turn, the employee tends to be loyal and devoted to the organisation (:91). As communitarians, Tanzanians share the rewards for success as a group.

"What attitudes and actions do followers expect from leaders?" According to the *Western* respondents, Western followers ideally expect the following *attitudes* from their leaders, including: "To be concerned and to care for her/him, to respect her/him in giving her/him the space they need" (Leader 4), humility (Leader 2 & Lay Leader 1), listening and integrity (Leader 2), compassion (Leader 2, 6 & Lay Leader 1), "confident and responsible" (Leader 5), positive (Leader 6), "understanding, vision" (Leader 1), honesty (Leader 9), "authenticity and openness" (Leader 8), "serving, well planned, [and] goal

oriented" (Leader 7). In terms of *actions*, the following is expected by the respondents: "To react to things they told her/him and to change or solve the issue, to be a good example for the followers" (Leader 4), "that they do what they say" (Leader 8), "makes sure that we achieve the goals, give sufficient information" (Leader 7), "help and encouragement" (Leader 1), communication (Leader 5 & Lay Leader 1), clarity (Leader 9), "being loyal to subordinates, treat[ing] subordinates justly and equally" (Leader 2), "making smart and valuable decisions" (Leader 5), "sacrificing and generous" (Leader 6). Meeting these expectations is one way of building trust.

According to the *Tanzanian* respondents, followers ideally expect the following *attitudes* from leaders, including: To be respected and served (Leader 1, 4, 7, Lay Leader 1 & 3), to love (Leader 1, 2, 3 & 4), "to be gentle"[146] (Leader 1, 4 & 5), "to encourage"[147] (Leader 3), to be faithful (Leader 3), "good and generous"[148] (Leader 6). "A leader should not be an oppressor" (Leader 2).[149] "They [followers] expect justice and equality at work"[150] (Leader 5, Lay Leader 2 & 3) and "to recognise that the followers also have a valid contribution to make"[151] (Leader 7). It is interesting to note that ideally people expect equality and some participatory approach. This is often in contrast to the actual practice within the hierarchy, as we have seen above at the beginning of this chapter. In terms of *actions*, the following is expected by the *Tanzanian* respondents from leaders: "A leader should be a good example"[152] (Leader 2 & Lay Leader 1) and "live a good Christian life"[153] (Leader 3 & 4). A leader should listen and cooperate (Leader 4, 7 & Lay Leader 1). S/he should "come to work in time and make an effort at work"[154] (Leader 6 & Lay Leader 3). "You [as a leader] solve their problems. You explain to them your expectations" (Leader 7).[155] Even though people expect to be treated equally and be asked for their opinion, Leader 2 says: "They expect a leader should have the ability to recognise the problems of her/his workers. Even if they do not tell her/him they expect that because s/he is the leader by any means ... s/he should understand [and] recognise their problems and s/he should be able to help."[156] It seems that ideally followers expect to be treated equally. But in reality they want the leader to recognise their problems without telling her/him directly. This contradiction may have to do with a shift in values and different people may have different expectations. In terms of sharing informa-

---

[146] Translated from the original Swahili: Kuonya kwa upole.
[147] Translated from the original Swahili: ... kutia moyo ...
[148] Translated from the original Swahili: ... wema na ukarimu.
[149] Translated from the original Swahili: ... kiongozi asiwe mkandamizaji.
[150] Translated from the original Swahili: Wanategemea haki na usawa katika kazi.
[151] Translated from the original Swahili: ... kuwatambua kwamba nao wana mchango mzuri ...
[152] Translated from the original Swahili: ... kiongozi awe mfano mwema.
[153] Translated from the original Swahili: ... mwenendo mwema wa Kristo ndani ya maisha yao.
[154] Translated from the original Swahili: Kuwahi kazini, bidii ya kazi.
[155] Translated from the original Swahili: Unatatua tatizo lao. Unawaelekeza matarajio yako.
[156] Translated from the original Swahili: Lakini pia wanatarajia kiongozi awe na uwezo kutambua shida za wafanyakazi wake. Hata kama hawatamweleza watatazamia kwamba huyu kwa sababu ni kiongozi kwa njia yoyote utakayotumia ... kiongozi awaelewe, atambue shida zao na aweze kuwasaidia kulingana na shida zao.

tion, it is my observation that subordinates appreciate if information that affects them personally is shared with them early on. However, in reality "It is not uncommon for clergy to have as little notice as one week before a move and not unheard of to be told you are moving by the driver of the lorry who has come for you, your family and all our possessions there and then" (Groves 1998:14).

4.1.2 Trust and Leadership

Trust is the basis of all relationships and thus central to leadership. The importance of building a strong and close relationship should not be underestimated in building trust. Thus, it was important in the interviews to find out *how the interviewees build trust and how they know that they can trust a person* (question 3.5). According to the *Western* respondents, to build trust it is essential "to spend time together, get to know each other, [and] talk at increasingly personal levels to each other" (Leader 2). They also mentioned other trust builders such as: "Being reliable and observing how the other would stick to commitments s/he made" (Leader 2); making "the assumption based on previous experience and a feeling of their character" (Lay Leader 1); "by being trustworthy" (Leader 3); "often it is a result of going through a difficult time together; having good, positive experiences together is also very important" (Leader 5); "trust comes from fulfilled expectations" (Leader 8); "in living a transparent life and in being open - getting to know others" (Leader 7); praying together. For some respondents, one's "past performance is a good indication of future performance" (Leader 3). People can be trusted when "they live what they say they believe" (Leader 7). Some people (Leader 1) also base their judgement about whether they can trust a person or not on intuition. As can be seen from the literature[157], trust in the West is built both on a leader's character and the task. Leaders with a moral character of integrity who keep to their commitments are trustworthy. However, it seems that task and achievement is in the foreground for Westerners in a trusting relationship.

Trust is built in a similar way in Tanzania. According to the *Tanzanian* respondents, building trust takes a lot of time. It is important to get to know the person. The majority of the respondents (7) try to observe how the other person performs. "I will trust any person if s/he truly does what we agreed on" (Leader 7).[158] Is s/he self-motivated (Leader 4)? What one says and does must be consistent: "We observe other people that they are trustworthy by their actions and words" (Leader 3).[159] It is also important to get to know the other on a personal level and to know her/his thinking (Leader 7). Thus, it is essential to be open and transparent. People try to get references from different sources about the person (Lay Leader 2). A person usually can be trusted when s/he

---

[157] See Trompenaars and Hampden-Turner (2002:48), Helander and Nigawila (1996:69), Schroll-Machl (2003:57), Covey (1989:190-199), Dent (1999:199) and Roembke (1998:31 & 102).
[158] Translated from the original Swahili: Nitamwamini mtu yeyote akiwa atakuwa mkweli katika yale mambo tulikubaliana kuyafanya.
[159] Translated from the original Swahili: Tunashuhudia kwa watu wengine kwamba huyu ni mwaminifu ni kwa matendo yake na usemi wake.

has a good history, family and work (Lay Leader 2). A person who truly believes in Christ can be trusted (Leader 3).

It may take a long time to build trust. Thus, it is critical to know *"How is trust breached?"* According to the *Western* respondents, most often trust is breached when a person does not fulfil the other person's expectations in terms of Christian standards or agreements that have been made (Leader 8), as we have seen above. The respondents say other cause for a breach in trust are: "Making important decisions affecting me in a major way without involving me in that decision or at least trying to explain compassionately the necessity of making that decision even if it will be hard for me to live with it" (Leader 2); "by doing something hurtful" (Lay Leader 1); taking advantage of someone (Leader 6); "stealing; not telling the truth" (Leader 9); "if you tell ... [people] something in confidence and they don't keep it private" (Leader 3); "primarily through miscommunication" (Leader 5). Good communication seems to be very critical and important in building trust. Over the years, I and other colleagues have personally observed in many instances that after hearing someone's complaints or opinion, the leader apparently ignores the person's feelings moving on with her/his agenda. In this way people get hurt.

Like in the West, in *Tanzania* most often trust is breached if someone does not do what is expected from her/him, as Leader 2 shares:

> For instance, not working during working hours. The person leaves the office. Maybe s/he is standing outside or is talking to a visitor in the office. Here s/he breaks trust. S/he was trusted to work. ... There is no difference between someone who steals and someone who goes to work without doing any work. Both are thieves. S/he is paid the money for work s/he did not do.[160]

Other reasons mentioned for breaking trust are lying (Leader 5, 7 & Lay Leader 1), not keeping a promise (Leader 5, Lay Leader 1 & 3), stealing or requiring payment that is not justified.

Helander (Helander & Nigawila 1996:69) suggests, in a communitarian society like Tanzania, the locus of trust is in following the group norms. In other words, if one behaves the way s/he is expected to behave, people feel s/he is trustworthy. This leads to a high standard of conformity. The individual is expected to conform to the values of the society. If a person violates these values it means a breach of trust because s/he breaks the set rules. This may result in either excommunication, or if this is not desirable because of the benefit of the group, the conflict is driven underground (:69). In a particularistic society, a person who can be trusted is somebody who honours changing situations (Trompenaars & Hampden-Turner 2002:48). Mutual appraisal is also a very powerful, dynamic and positive tool to develop trust in a collectivist society (Boon 1998:123).

---

[160] Translated from the original Swahili: Kwa mfano ni kutofanya kazi wakati wa kazi. Mtu anaondoka ofisini. Labda anasimama hapo nje ama anaongea na wageni ofisini. Hapa anavunja uaminifu wake. Ameaminiwa kufanya kazi. ... Anayeiba fedha na anayekwenda kazini bila kufanya kazi hakuna tofauti. Wote ni wezi. Maana analipwa fedha ambazo hakufanyia kazi.

4.1.3 Self-Disclosure and Leadership

What kind of information one shares depends on the level of trust. When asked, *"If you have a conversation with somebody, are there certain things you share more easily than others?"* all the Western and Tanzanian respondents said, that the kind of information they share more easily depends on the level of trust and the kind of relationship they have with the other person.

When asked, *"What kind of information do you feel more or less comfortable to disclose?"* the *Western* respondents (Leader 3, 4, 5, 8, 9 & Lay Leader 1) feel more comfortable to disclose specifically work related matters and facts. They also share freely other information including: "Technical information, ... who you know, where to find information, who could help (Leader 4); non-personal issues (Leader 4 & 6); "outcomes of the project, information everybody knows anyway, issues about schooling and housing" (Leader 7); "critical information with a friend; when kids are sick" (Leader 2). One respondent (Leader 1) would also share his faults, weaknesses and mistakes, which in my view is unusual. Other information the respondents feel less comfortable to disclose such as: Personal information (Leader 2, 3, 4, 6 & Lay Leader 1); "relationship to God and things, which I think the other person would be offended by" (Leader 4); "sensitive information pertaining to the organisation" (Leader 2); feelings (Leader 5); "problems at home" (Leader 9); "performance related issues that can be emotive" (Leader 8), "information that would jeopardize the team cooperation or reaching a goal"[161] (Leader 1). One would expect that women might share more freely than men, especially with friends. This is not necessarily the case among the female respondents.

Nevertheless, in terms of self-disclosure and feedback some Westerners are more open than others. The Halls (1990:52) describe Germans as generally more reserved and serious than Americans. Germans tend to keep to themselves. They have strong feelings of privacy and territoriality. Generally, Westerners do not feel very comfortable expressing their needs freely. They prefer to be independent and self-reliant. Germans make a difference in sharing work related information to personal information.[162] Westerners tend to share specific information with others as required or useful. They do not disclose information just for the sake of having a conversation. Specific communication is always more definite and unambiguous (Hampden-Turner & Trompenaars 2000:143).

Like Westerners, the *Tanzanian* respondents (Leader 1, 2, 4, Lay Leader 2 & 3) also feel more comfortable disclosing specifically work related matters. Other information includes: Money that has been received (Leader 1), "normal things that happen every day in life and society"[163] (Leader 2 & Lay Leader 1), information that is relevant for the other person or spiritual things

---

[161] Translated from the original German: Informationen, die die Zusammenarbeit im Team oder das Erreichen eines Zieles gefährden würden ...
[162] Schroll-Machl (2003:57) has observed that in a business context Germans share a lot of information freely.
[163] Translated from the original Swahili: ... mambo yanayohusu jamii, maisha ya jamii ya jumla ...

(Leader 3 & 5), "expertise"[164] (Leader 5), "information that is not confidential"[165] (Leader 7). Sometimes people share only on a need-to-know basis, as Lay Leader 2 says: "If it is very important and s/he needs to know and it is very necessary, I will share it. But if it is not important, I cannot share anything."[166] Only Leader 4 would also share personal things. Other information the respondents feel less comfortable in disclosing is, for example: Confidential information (Leader 1, 2, 3 & Lay Leader 2) and "personal matters... Things that would hurt a person's feelings"[167] (Leader 2), information that could bring harm (Leader 3), "work related issues"[168] (Leader 4), "information that concerns other people"[169] (Leader 5) or information that does not concern the other (Leader 7).

According to my observations, whereas Westerners share information for a certain purpose, Tanzanians are in a constant mood of passing on information. However, it is interesting to observe that Tanzanians often do not inform others about their plans, when they travel or important work related information. This is possibly partly in order to demonstrate power or out of fear that others may misuse the information.

4.1.4 Task, Time and Leadership

The way leaders relate to others can also be seen in terms of how they deal with task versus relationship and also time. To present how Westerners and Tanzanians view task and relationship, the answers to the five questions 3.3, 3.9, 3.10, 3.11 and 3.12 have been grouped together.

The respondents were asked: *"Imagine that you have prepared yourself to go shopping or it has rained for three days and you want to prepare the fields and plant. Visitors come from the neighbourhood. What would you do?"* Most Western (7) and Tanzanian (5) respondents try to find a balance of what they want to accomplish and caring for people. If they want to go shopping or to prepare the fields to plant and visitors come from the neighbourhood, they would visit with them for a short time and then excuse themselves. Only one Western respondent and a few (2) Tanzanian respondents would ask them to come back another time. One Tanzanian would ask a family member to visit with them and leave. Two Western and Tanzanian respondents would make their decision based on who is coming and the importance and urgency of the visit.

During the interviews the respondents were given an example that *"the organisation has been given an assignment to finish by a certain deadline. Unfortunately one of the family members of an employee becomes sick. What*

---

[164] Translated from the original Swahili: ... mambo ya kitaaluma.
[165] Translated from the original Swahili: Mambo ya jumlajumla tu ya siyo ya sirini ...
[166] Translated from the original Swahili: Kama kuna umuhimu sana na anahitajika na ni lazima sana nitamshirikisha. Lakini kama hakuna umuhimu siwezi kumshirikisha kitu chochote.
[167] Translated from the original Swahili: Mambo ya kibinafsi ... Mambo ambayo yanaumiza hisia ya mtu.
[168] Translated from the original Swahili: ... mambo ya kazini.
[169] Translated from the original Swahili: ... mambo yanayohusu watu wengine ...

would you do?" For all the Western and Tanzanian respondents, it is important that the sick family member is in good care. Half (5) of the Western respondents would allow the employee to take care of the family member, taking the risk of not meeting the deadline of the assignment. The other half (5) of the respondents would allow the employee to take care of the basic needs of the sick family member and return as soon as possible to work.

The responses during the interviews reflect a different picture from what Schroll-Machl (2003:51) writes in a very different context: "The management style of German executives is explicitly task oriented. A boss limits his interactions with his employees mainly to business-related themes." The discrepancy between the literature and the answers during the interviews is possibly rooted in the fact that all Western respondents have lived and worked in Tanzania for a number of years. Also because they are Christians and missionaries, people are important to them. Therefore, their values may have changed to a certain degree over time.

The majority (5) of the *Tanzanian* respondents would allow the employee to take care of the basic needs of the sick family member and return as soon as possible to work. Only one person would allow the employee to take an hour to arrange for somebody else to take care of the family member. Others (4) would base their decision of how seriously sick the person is and what the relationship between the employee and the sick person is. If it is a close relative like wife, mother, father or child and the person is seriously sick, then caring for this person certainly prevails over completing a certain task on time.

According to the responses to both questions above, it seems *Tanzanians* feel a tension between relationships versus task. Tanzanians try to keep a good relationship and care for the other. At the same time they want to accomplish what needs to be done. The relationship prevails over the task. This suggests a high value of group orientation. Whereas Westerners tend to be task-oriented, Tanzanians are more people-oriented. Therefore, it is important for both groups to learn from Jesus. Jesus was very relational. But at the same time he focused on what he needed to accomplish.

When asked, *"How are tasks and goals achieved?"*, the majority (5) of the *Western* respondents believe it depends on the task and on the personality of the people, because some people achieve more alone and others more in groups. It is interesting to note that only one person believes that people ideally achieve alone and assume personal responsibility, whereas some respondents (4) believe that people ideally achieve in groups, which assume joint responsibility. These answers indicate that there may be a gap between a desired value and a practised value in reality, because in the suggested answer it says "ideally". According to my observations, in reality many Westerners tend to achieve alone and thus assume personal responsibility for what they are doing. However, in recent years the importance of teamwork has been emphasised in the West.

All *Tanzanian* respondents believe that people ideally achieve in groups, which assume joint responsibility. This clearly suggests that collectivism is highly valued in Tanzania. As collectivists, Tanzanians share the rewards of success as a group, as well as assuming joint responsibility (Hampden-Turner

& Trompenaars 2000:71). Thus, a Tanzanian leader does not manage individual people but groups (Hofstede 1997:65).

How people view task and time is related to their level of uncertainty avoidance. This is reflected in the answers to the question: *"If you have a contract with someone and the circumstances change what would you do?"* The responses by the *Westerners* were rather mixed: Keep the contract (2); adjust the contract to the circumstances (2); try to change the circumstances in order to keep the contract (2); ignore the contract in light of changing situations (1); depending on the circumstances (3). According to my personal observations, Western leaders have strong uncertainty avoidance. It is interesting to note that according to Hofstede (1997:113), Germanic countries tend to have higher uncertainty avoidance than Anglo-Saxon countries. A real exception seems to be Great Britain with rather low uncertainty avoidance. Generally, they try to keep an agreement and stick to the rules even though the answers of the respondents were quite mixed. Westerners experience discomfort when the environment seems "out of control" or changeable (Trompenaars & Hampden-Turner 2002:155). Western leaders expect the other person to keep the agreement and play by the agreed upon rules. They would rather keep the contract or change the circumstances than adjust the contract if the circumstances change. The contract is usually seen as something definite (:40).

Tanzanians try to avoid uncertainty if possible, as the answers suggest. The majority (7) of the respondents would adjust the contract to the circumstances. A few (2) would try to change the circumstances in order to keep the contract. Only one person would ignore the contract in light of the changing situation. One person said it would be necessary to finish the contract and then change it if possible. I would have expected that more people would ignore the contract and do whatever is necessary and appropriate. My personal experience is that people would not necessarily keep close to a contract, which is consistent with what Lay Leader 3 says: "Tanzanians have a law but we do not follow it. A person can do something different even if you have agreed".[170] However, it seems that this is currently changing in Tanzania. More and more people consider it as important to have contracts as legal documents. The answers suggest that there is a value shift taking place.

In Tanzania uncertainty is a normal feature of life. People are event-oriented rather than time-oriented. So each day is accepted as it comes. People can never be sure if there will be enough rain so that the harvest is sufficient. Somebody can never know if the bus is going to break down and not reach the destination on time. It seems that Tanzanians are better able to deal well with ambiguous situations than Westerners, as the following encounter demonstrates. Because of the realities Tanzanians face each day, in practice their uncertainty avoidance is weak. However, if they had a choice they would probably desire stronger uncertainty avoidance. Thus, it seems that as on a continuum Tanzanians are probably somewhere in between leaning towards slightly stronger uncertainty avoidance.

---

[170] Translated from the original Swahili: Watanzania wana sheria lakini hatufuatilii. Mtu anaweza kuamua kugeuza tu hata kama mmekubaliana.

A few years ago my Tanzanian colleague and I were invited to teach a one week course on "Language and Scripture Use" in the town of Tabora. In order to plan each lesson well, I needed to have a lot of detailed information. How many lessons? How long is each lesson? When are the lessons scheduled during the day? How many students will attend? What is their level of education and English proficiency? After intensive communication with the person in charge of the course, I had some indication of what to expect. However, it was still not completely satisfactory for me. My Tanzanian colleague did not seem to worry too much about these details. It seemed he had a much more relaxed attitude than I. When we arrived in Tabora, we had to adjust to a different schedule than we were first given, which I found slightly challenging. One morning it started to rain heavily while I was teaching. Because of the tin roof, it was so noisy that I had to stop teaching for thirty minutes. Again I had to adjust my teaching schedule because of this unforeseen interruption. The Tanzanians had much less problems with this than I had. It seems that because Tanzanians tend to be outer-directed, they are able to adapt to a changing environment more easily then Westerners (Hampden-Turner & Trompenaars 2000:250-251). People from outer-directed cultures like Tanzanians tend to have a flexible attitude, are willing to compromise and keep the peace (Trompenaars & Hampden-Turner 2002:155).

It is interesting to note *what people would do if they have an appointment and a visitor comes to see them unexpectedly* (question 3.12). The majority (5) of *Western* respondents said they would keep their appointment when a visitor comes to see them unexpectedly. Some (3) would be late for the appointment. A few (2) would base their decision on how important the visitor and the person with whom they have the appointment are. I would have expected the number of people keeping the appointment much higher.[171] I have personally noticed that in the past, I was extremely time oriented and punctual. Having lived and worked in Tanzania for many years, this has changed. The same may be the case with some of the respondents.

Regarding time Westerners tend to have a *long-term* and *sequential time orientation*. In Western societies, task prevails over relationships. Western leaders plan their daily schedule very carefully, as Trompenaars and Hampden-Turner (2002:125) point out: "Sequential people tend to schedule very tightly, with thin divisions between time slots. It is rude to be even a few minutes late because the whole day's schedule of events is affected." Westerners plan months and years ahead. They do not like to be interrupted during work. Western leaders tend to separate work and leisure time, as relationships tend to be built outside of work. They keep business matters and private issues separate. Many save money over a period of time to implement plans.

The responses of the Tanzanians were surprisingly different from the Westerners. The majority (8) of the *Tanzanian* respondents would keep the appointment. Only one would either be late for the appointment or spend time with the visitor and not keep the appointment. These responses are in stark

---

[171] Schroll-Machl (2003:119-120) has observed that Germans are extremely inflexible in terms of time.

contrast to the information in the literature[172] and what Lay Leader 3 says: "We Tanzanians are not time-oriented".[173] The Tanzanian participants during the group discussion also pointed out that this is an ideal. Most of the respondents have worked with Westerners for many years. Thus, they may have been influenced by Western values. However, I have also noticed that in urban centres, people are slowly becoming more time oriented. On the other hand, since change happens a lot slower in villages, a rural person would most likely respond very differently and be either late or not keep the appointment.

Tanzanians tend to be *synchronous time-oriented*. This means they are event-oriented rather than time-oriented. Time is a sequence of events (Mbiti 1974:21). Time is produced or created by events (:24). Whenever a certain event happens, attention is paid to it without there being concern about the future or what is next. These events are then easily remembered. By remembering events, time is created.[174] This is demonstrated in what Trompenaars and Hampden-Turner (2002:133) write about synchronic cultures like Tanzania: "Synchronic cultures carry their pasts through the present into the future and will refuse to consider changing unless convinced that their heritage is safe."

From the empirical data, it seems that Westerners try to learn from and adopt to Tanzanian culture to be more event and people oriented, whereas Tanzanians see the value of keeping time and commitments.

4.2 Power and Leadership

Power is core to leadership. This can be seen throughout history. Leaders usually occupy positions of power and authority. First of all, it is important to know how people understand power. When asked *"What is power?"*, in summary, the *Western* respondents define power as follows: Power is the authority to make decisions on behalf of other people and/or things and the means to see these decisions through, even against the will or consent of those involved. It is the ability and opportunity to make things happen. Power is the authority and the ability to control circumstances and people.[175]

In summary, all the *Tanzanian* respondents agreed that power is the freedom of making a decision that was authorized within a scope of limitations, which someone else cannot oppose and it is the ability to do something within a certain time.

---

[172] See Mayer, Boness and Thomas (2003:143-148).
[173] Translated from the original Swahili: Sisi watanzania hatuendi sana na muda.
[174] This past-orientation in Tanzania is also reflected in the language use of Swahili in terms of time. Swahili has basically two words that express time: *zamani* and *sasa*. *Zamani* refers to the past that goes way back. *Sasa* describes the present, which is also taken a little bit into the future (Mbiti 1974:28). There is no Swahili word for future other than *wakati ujao*.
[175] Webster's Third New International Dictionary defines power as "the capability of action or of producing an effect. Power is control, authority, jurisdiction, command, dominion, sway. Power indicates possession of the ability to wield coercive force, permissive authority or substantial influence" (in Helander & Nigawila 1996:129). Klopfenstein (1989:51) distinguishes between power and authority: "While **power** is the leader's **capacity** to control, **authority** is the leader's **right** to exert power" [my emphasis].

With reference to *whether power is a good or a bad thing* (question 4.2) the *Western* respondents believe power is a good thing because it "is a very essential thing, as long as it is performed to bring change and reformation and to help those people under the power or influenced by that power to move towards the goal, which they can identify with or know it is 'a good way' for us (our community, organisation, church, country)" (Leader 4). It is good to empower people to do the right things. The respondents also believe "power is bad or evil if it is used to manipulate and to drive people or if the people under that power or influenced by it feel in bondage and perceive 'those up there' are exercising power for their own sake" (Leader 4). A few respondents believe that power is neither good nor bad. Leader 2 says, "It is the character of the person in power that will normally determine whether it is used for good or bad".

Similarly, all *Tanzanian* respondents believe power is good, especially if it is used well, because it enables a person to act. "One person should be the leader who has the power and s/he will have the last word, which is then followed by the people" (Lay Leader 1).[176] Power enables the leader to provide order, supervision and direction (Leader 5 & 7). "Power is not something you have been given to oppress people" (Leader 3).[177] A few respondents (3) raised their concern that power can be a bad thing if it is used badly, unjustly and against the expectations of the followers, which can be painful (Leader 2, 3 & 6).[178] Generally, both groups consider power to be a good thing if used well. The responses of both groups indicate that their experience has not always been positive. My personal observation is that Westerners tend to be more suspicious of power than Tanzanians.

When asked *"What gives a person power?"*, according to the *Western* respondents, it is position (Leader 1, 2, 3, 5, 7, 8, 9 & Lay Leader 1), personality (Leader 1, 5, 8), character (Leader 1, 2, 7 & 8), friends, relationships and communication skills (Leader 1 & 7), knowledge (Leader 2), experience, abilities

---

[176] Translated from the original Swahili: Mtu mmoja awe kiongozi ambaye ana mamlaka na atakuwa na neno la mwisho na watu wanakubali kufuata.

[177] Translated from the original Swahili: Mamlaka si kitu ambacho umepewa kuwakandamiza watu.

[178] Power and authority play a fundamental role in the Tanzanian sphere, which is also reflected in the language. There are several words in Swahili, which are associated with power: *uwezo, nguvu, mamlaka, utawala,* and *amri* (Taasisi ya Uchunguzi wa Kiswahili 1996:591). *Uwezo* is the ability and strength one has to accomplish something. A person has control over her/himself or somebody else (Johnson 1939:530). In one sense *nguvu* can be the physical power and energy to act or speak (:338). It can have a positive connotation but can also mean a force against somebody's will. On the other hand, *nguvu* is also related to spiritual power (Mayer *et al* 2003:139). Whereas *uwezo* and *nguvu* are somehow personalized, *mamlaka, utawala,* and *amri* are used in the public political domain. *Mamlaka* is the ability, authority and power over things or people, which a person has received because of her/his position (Taasisi ya Uchunguzi wa Kiswahili 1981:151). *Utawala* is the area of authority, which is exercised by a person who has been appointed to a position of power (Mayer *et al* 2003:139). *Utawala* is often used in the area of management and administration, which is clearly defined. *Amri* is commanding an order (Taasisi ya Uchunguzi wa Kiswahili 1981:7). The order is expected to be followed obediently. The different meaning and use of these various words for power in Swahili reflect the significance of power in Tanzanian society.

and age (Lay Leader 1), resources, education, intellect and wisdom (Leader 3), violence and war (Leader 2), God, and "the willingness of others to accept that power and follow its current" (Leader 4).[179]

The main sources of power in the West indicate a tendency towards an *achieved* status. However, there are also power sources, which refer to an *ascribed* status, such as contacts, friends and relationships, personality and character and age.

The *Tanzanian* respondents mentioned very different sources of power. Some of the main sources are achieved and others ascribed. *Achieved* sources of power in Tanzania are trust and honesty (Leader 2, 4, 5 & Lay Leader 2), performance and ability (Lay Leader 1, 2 & Leader 1, 2, 7), treating people equally (Leader 2), force (Lay Leader 2 & Leader 6), wisdom, deceitfulness, seeking advice from others and common sense (Lay Leader 2). *Ascribed* sources of power are being elected (Leader 3, 4, 6 & Lay Leader 2), education (Leader 3, 4 & Lay Leader 2), people and relationships (Leader 4, 5, 7, Lay Leader 2 & 3), cooperative agreement (Leader 1), being appointed and calling (Leader 3), and inheritance (Lay Leader 2). Whereas status is usually achieved in the West, the data above indicate that in Tanzania, it is achieved as well as ascribed. In Tanzania, age plays a very important factor. According to my observations, Tanzanian leaders are almost always in the forties-and-above age bracket. If a person has reached a certain age, s/he is entitled to be promoted not necessarily so much because of her/his skills and accomplishments but because of her/his age. In ascribed-oriented cultures like Tanzania older people are well respected, as Trompenaars and Hampden-Turner (2002:109) explain: "Older people are held to be important **so that** they will be nourished and sustained by other's respect" [their emphasis].

"What kinds of people have more power than others?" There are certain people in the West and in Tanzania who have more power than others. According to the *Western* respondents, these include people with "outgoing personalities" (Leader 7), "charisma and the ability to lead naturally [and] people with a 'calling' who are determined to live it out" (Leader 4), and "those who enjoy leading, making decisions etc. and signal their readiness to take on a certain office, together with making an impression on others that they could do a decent job, which will enhance their chances to come to this position of power" (Leader 2). They also said, others include "experienced, able, older people in positions where they have influence over others" (Lay Leader 1), "those whom God has gifted more and those who have learned to manipulate the system to get what they want" (Leader 3), "those who are able to gain the submission of others" (Leader 6), "excellent communicators" (Leader 5), "people who are high up in the hierarchy, people with strong personalities, aggressive people" (Leader 1), and "leaders who lead people who do not have very much background in education" (Leader 9). Also "elected

---

[179] These sources of power have also been observed by the researchers Hersman (1995:62, 85 & 110), Hofstede (1997:39) and the Halls (1990:41). The Halls (:42) observe, "in the United States, power is reflected in the location, furnishings, and style of offices. ... Germans usually prefer that power and position be handled with grace and reserve".

leaders will have more power than others due to their position" (Leader 5). The exception seems to be in Australia, where group authority is definitely preferred over leader authority. Australians have little respect for position, title and education. The quality of the person is the key (Hersman 1995:158). In Canada leaders try to keep a low-key profile (Lewis 2003:175).

Most societies have some kind of hierarchy. Power distance has to do with the system of status, role and prestige in a society. The higher a person's status is the more prestige, power and authority s/he has. In Western societies power, status, role and prestige do not necessarily go together (Hofstede 1997:39). In fact, people prefer if they do not. For instance, Western leaders have no great problem riding to work by bicycle or helping to wash the dishes after a work event. If a Tanzanian has reached a certain position s/he would not necessarily do this. Westerners also do not observe a very formal dress code, whereas in Tanzania the dress code is very important. Whereas Westerners tend to achieve status, Tanzanians ascribe it.

The *Tanzanian* respondents said, those people who are in a high position, the educated, adults and older people, and have been in a certain place for a long time especially have more power than others. There are also people who have more power than others, including: "Those who cooperate and relate well to others, godly people, who have organised their governing body well" [180] (Lay Leader 3); who have been chosen by many people (Lay Leader 2); who have been called by God (Leader 3); who like their work and are trustworthy (Leader 3); who act justly and morally (Leader 2); "who deal with the evil and disobedient people in the society" [181]; who support the lower people; wealthy people; witches; traditional leaders and rain makers (Leader 2); men (Leader 5 & 6). The respondents presented quite different views. It is interesting to note that followers who are also young consider achieved power more relevant, whereas the older leaders focus more on the ascribed status. Also, it was the women who pointed out that men have more power than women.

According to the information from the interviews and my own observations over the years, each group within Tanzanian society is positioned according to their status, role, and prestige as can be seen in figure 4.1.

---

[180] Translated from the original Swahili: Wale wanaoshirikisha wenzao ... Wale ambao wanamshirikisha Mungu sana. Wale ambao wameweka serikali zao vizuri.
[181] Translated from the original Swahili: ... anayepambana na maovu na maasi katika jamii ...

Chapter 4: Relationships, Power and Conflict in Western Leadership

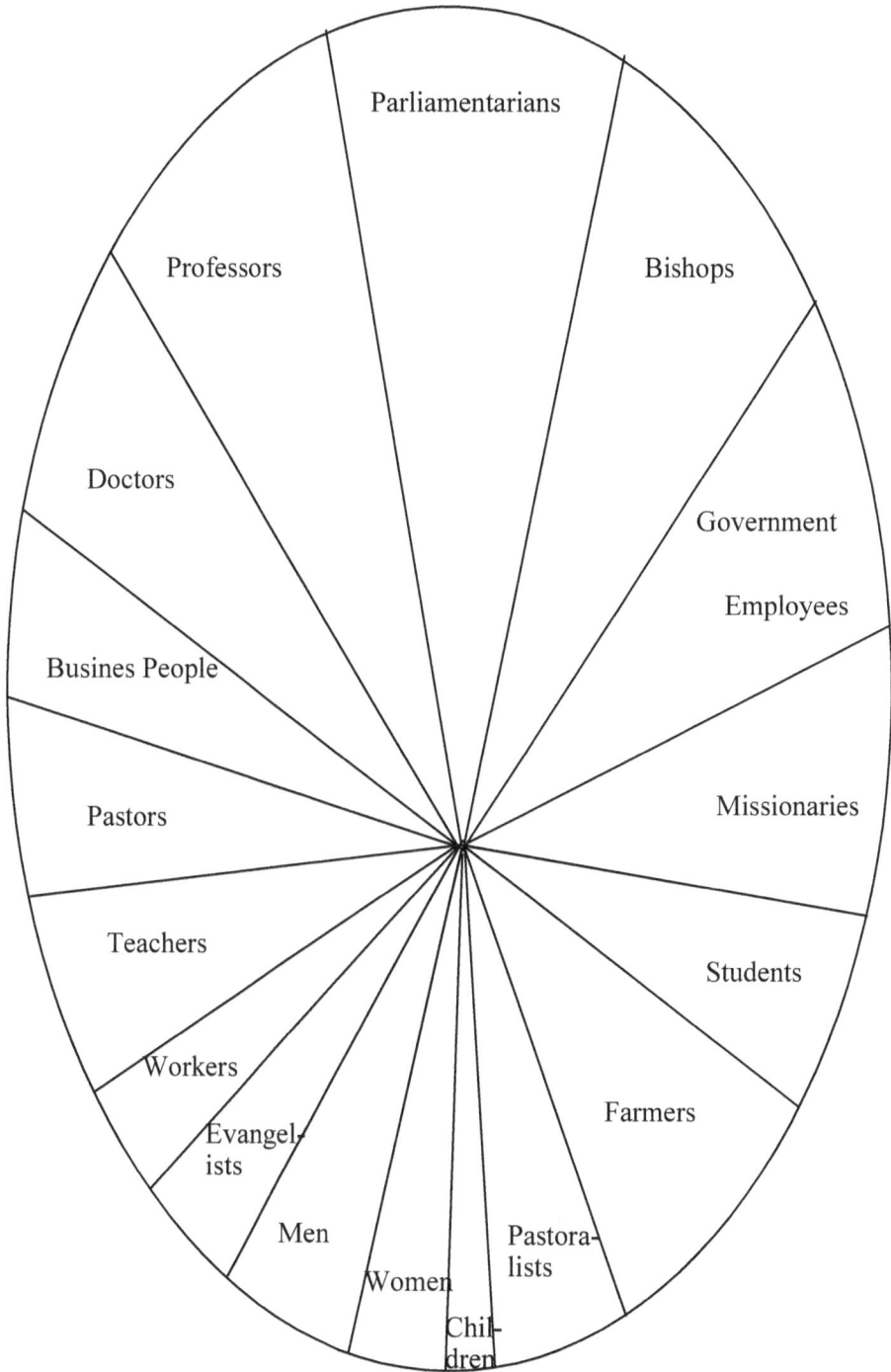

Figure 4.1 (adapted from Müller 2003)

Groups in the above figure 4.1 that are positioned high in the ellipse have high prestige. Prestige is like honour. Prestige is the product of a person's status and role. The amount of circumference space taken indicates the status level of a group. According to my observations over the years, parliamentarians, professors and bishops have a high status and prestige within Tanzanian society. Philip Groves (1998:14), an Anglican theologian who taught church leaders for a number of years in Tanzania, points out how much power a bishop has. He is the ultimate holder of the truth in his diocese. The bishop is in charge of discipline and governs. Doctors, small business people, pastors, government employees and missionaries also carry a high status in comparison, but less prestige. Teachers, students, farmers and evangelists have a lower status and also low prestige. However, farmers still have a higher status in comparison to the other professions within the position range. The groups with the lowest status and prestige in Tanzania are definitely pastoralists, women and children. They have very little influence within the society. Because of its culture and history, generally, the power distance in Tanzania is rather large.[182]

I have noticed that people with a certain status and prestige in Tanzania are entitled to a number of privileges, such as a parking place, tea and food brought to the office, a large office, a good sized house and a car and driver (Hofstede 1997:38). These are important status symbols. These status symbols are in contrast to an expected leaders' character of humility and servanthood as discussed in chapter one. Tanzanians do not necessarily seem to have a problem with this tension because they define humility and servanthood, differently. According to the group discussion participants, Tanzanians define humility as respecting and valuing other people without necessarily putting themselves below their own position. They also define themselves as **being** in relation to the other, whereas Westerners define themselves often in what they **do**. Therefore, they perceive status symbols differently than Westerners.

People of a higher status in Tanzania are also usually accompanied when they attend meetings. A few years ago, a particular meeting was scheduled. During the preparations of the meeting it was agreed that each organisation would attend the meeting with no more than two delegates. One of the leaders arrived at the meeting together with three other delegates. This was a clear statement of his status and power he carried. Nobody ever questioned why this organisation was represented by four delegates instead of two like the others. Questioning this organisation may have caused a confrontation, which Tanzanians try to avoid if at all possible. People may also have recognised that this organisation has more power than the others. "Unaccompanied people in communitarian cultures are assumed to lack status" (Trompenaars & Hampden-Turner 2002:60).

Peoples' behaviour may change when they become leaders. Mhogolo explains how a person's behaviour changes when s/he becomes a leader:

---

[182] There are a few ethnic groups like the Datooga and Massai that have an egalitarian structure. It is interesting to note that these ethnic groups are not Bantu but Nilotic.

> If somebody is appointed as a bishop or political leader, he does not cultivate his field or plot anymore himself. There are people who will do it for him. Once he is in a leadership position, he is not supposed to do these things himself but to be served by others. This concept is very strong in our culture. When I became bishop I still had a plot, which I cultivated. People told me I ought not to be doing this. But I continued to cultivate my plot to set an example (2004).

This example demonstrates how strongly the attitude towards activity and work is linked to the idea of status and power (Maletzke 1996:149). If a person has reached a higher status s/he is expected to let other people do certain activities who have not reached the same status. However, it also shows how the gospel can overturn culture.

Who has more power than someone else can also be expressed in the use of *titles*. Thus, the question about using titles (question 4.14) is placed here rather than later. When asked, *"Do you always introduce someone using their title?"*, the *Western* respondents' answered: quite often (2), sometimes (7), not often (1). In achieving cultures like the West, status is attributed to those who have accomplished something. Their authority is justified by experience, skill and knowledge. In Western societies status is achieved through accomplishments. In some societies like Germany, the Netherlands, Austria and Great Britain, the use of titles is more important than in Australia and the USA (Lewis 2003:167, 181, 192, 210, 221). Germanics tend to be more formal than Anglo-Saxons. But even though if the first impression may be that Anglo-Saxons are quite informal, for instance using first name instead of surname, in formal settings they also emphasis formalities such as titles. However, generally titles are not as important in the West as they might be in other parts of the world. They are mostly used when relevant to the competence somebody brings to the task (Trompenaars & Hampden-Turner 2002:118).

Titles and privileges are connected. Superiors in the West do not necessarily have specific privileges because of their position. Status symbols like an excessively expensive car or a huge house are suspect. In fact, "leaders may enhance their informal status by renouncing formal symbols: the minister taking the streetcar to work" (Hofstede 1997:39).

Titles play an important role in *Tanzania,* as is reflected in the respondents' answers to whether they always introduce someone using their title: yes (3), quite often (3), sometimes (1), not often (3). Some of the younger people (Lay Leader 1 & 2) and Christians (Leader 3 & 5) from small churches would not use titles as much as others. This suggests that younger people desire a value change towards more equality. Some of the smaller churches do not emphasis power structures as much as the main stream churches.

In Tanzania titles are certainly more important than in the West, which also reflects a larger power distance. According to Hofstede (1997:26), power distance in East Africa is large in comparison with the other fifty countries and two regions.[183] The status of a person ascribed by the organisation is more important than what s/he has achieved. A leader's authority is usually not challenged. A person's title must reflect her/his status. Therefore, it is important to say not just that you are a manager, but a manager of finance, personnel, marketing and so on. Titles are very important and always used if possible, as they clarify a person's status. Titles confer status and respect. Often people are only addressed by their titles like *mwalimu* – teacher or *mchungaji* – pastor rather than by their names, even in a close personal relationship. Bishops often are not just addressed as *Askofu* – Bishop but *Baba Askofu* – Father Bishop or *Mhashamu Askofu* – Honourable Bishop. If people are called by their names, it is usually the surname not the first name. Formal respect and deference are very important. In a work situation, this very fact demonstrates that subordinates and superiors consider each other as existentially unequal (:35). This can also be seen the way people greet each other. A highly respected person is greeted by not only shaking hands but also supporting the right lower arm with the left hand while shaking hands.[184]

However, it is interesting that Nyerere, because of his *ujamaa* policy and his desire to introduce the value of equality in the society, did not like to be addressed using honourable titles, as Mwansasu observes:

> Nyerere's humility is shown in his distaste for, and personal discouragement of, such grandiose and ostentatious words as Bwana (Sir, Mr), Mheshimiwa (Honourable), Mtukufu (His Majesty, His Lordship, Most Respectful), Mkombozi (Redeemer, Saviour) as titles for formal or official address. Instead he succeeded in popularising Ndugu (comrade) as a title for formal address to be applied to all Tanzanians (in Mmari 1995:178).

Nyerere's behaviour was certainly contradictory to the Tanzanian culture and not everybody agreed with him. However, it was an attempt to promote equality within the society. It was partly successful when people started to call each other *ndugu* – fellow. But because of the strong cultural values, it was not possible to overcome the large power distance so that everybody would be fully equal.

Space and *time* are important indicators how power is communicated (Hall & Hall 1990:10 & 21). The Halls observe how space communicates power in the USA and Germany:

> A corner office suite in the United States is conventionally occupied by the 'brass', and a private office in any location has more status than a

---

[183] The countries and regions in which the research was conducted are: Malaysia, Guatemala, Panama, Philippines, Mexico, Venezuela, Arab countries, Equador, Indonesia, India, West Africa, Yugoslavia, Singapore, Brazil, France, Hong Kong, Colombia, Salvador, Turkey, Belgium, East Africa, Peru, Thailand, Chile, Portugal, Uruguay, Greece, South Korea, Iran, Taiwan, Spain, Pakistan, Japan, Italy, Argentina, South Africa, Jamaica, USA, Canada, Netherlands, Australia, Costa Rica, Germany FR, Great Britain, Switzerland, Finland, Norway, Sweden, Ireland (Republic of), New Zealand, Denmark, Israel, Austria.

[184] This is in contrast to the expectation that everybody should be treated equally as we have seen above.

desk in the open without walls. In both German and American business, the top floors are reserved for high-ranking officials and executives (1990:10).

They further observe how time communicates power:

> Waiting time, for example, carries strong messages which work on the part of the brain that mobilizes the emotions (the limbic systems). In the U.S. only those people with very high status can keep others waiting and get away with it. In general those individuals are the very ones who know enough of human relations to avoid "insults of time" whenever possible. It is the petty bureaucrat who likes to throw his weight around, the bully who takes pleasure in putting people down, or the insecure executive with an inflated ego who keeps visitors waiting. (1990:21).

In Germany such behaviour is considered rude, regardless of somebody's title (Schroll-Machl 2003:126). It is clear that if leaders in the West let others wait unnecessarily, they are abusing their power.

In *Tanzania* the size and design of a person's office is a great indicator of her/his status. Leaders of higher status usually have their office either on the top floor or at the end of the hallway. The larger the office and the desk are, the higher one's status and level of power are. Prominent people often have a big enough office to accommodate not only a desk but also chairs and a table to receive visitors and to have meetings.

Leadership in Tanzania is honoured by the right to sit at the high place. When I visit a church, I am usually requested to sit at the very front on a special chair. That way I am honoured not only as a visitor but also as a missionary, who has a certain status within the society. On several occasions, I tried to sit with the ordinary church members. This was not acceptable as I was frequently requested to sit in the front. If I had not followed the request, I would have insulted people. Similar behaviour can also be observed in other situations.[185] In meetings or functions people of higher rank usually sit at a special table, which is called the "high table". Not everybody agrees with this expressed behaviour of honour, as Groves observes:

> Many bishops try to resist being the peak of the triangle. For example, they may not accept the position of the guest of honour at a service where they are not officiating and they may sit in an ordinary pew, but the people feel awkward and even insulted by such behaviour and try to pass honour on to their bishop in a way which is hard to resist (1998:14).

Some Tanzanian leaders try to set a biblical example. This is really difficult and challenging for them because the cultural values are so strong.

The use of *time* in Tanzania also indicates how much power one has. As part of my responsibilities, I have visited church leaders such as bishops, general secretaries and chairpersons from time to time. Since many of these leaders have a busy schedule, I usually arrange an appointment ahead of time. On several occasions I had to wait one or even two hours to see a bishop even

---

[185] Also see Groves (1998:14).

though I was on time and nobody else was in his office. First I was a bit irritated and wondered why I had to wait such a long time for no obvious reasons, at least to me. Later I learned that prominent people communicate their power and status to others by letting them wait (Hampden-Turner & Trompenaars 2000:311).

4.2.1 Women and Leadership

Power distance can also be seen in how women are perceived as leaders. When asked, *"In your context, how are women perceived as leaders in terms of their status and role?"*, generally, most *Western* respondents (Leader 1, 2, 4, 5, 6, 7, 8 & Lay Leader 1) said that they perceive women and men equally as leaders with the same or even greater leadership capabilities than men. Female Leader 4 points out: "It depends on the personality of the women. I have no problems being accepted by younger and older colleagues, by Tanzanian and Western staff, and by male and female personnel." Male Leader 2 observes:

> Women in ... [our organisation] are increasingly taking over leadership positions to the point that it makes you wonder what happened to the men. I believe that they are generally well accepted by the membership. Although this might be a generalization, I personally believe that women in leadership often function better in such a role as their feminine strengths such as communicating well, socializing well, being better in contact with their own vulnerability often makes them more compassionate, better listening leaders.

However, a number of respondents (Leader 3, 7, 9 & Lay Leader 1), especially female, pointed out that some Westerners still have problems with women in leadership. This can be seen in the way women are sometimes treated by men, as female Leader 4 testifies: "Some years ago I had a newly married colleague who was here with his wife for one year. He had difficulties accepting my leadership, even though I was older, had more experience and was the appointed leader."

One may assume that the level of *gender egalitarianism* is high in the West. In recent years worldwide cross-cultural leadership research was conducted, which is known as the GLOBE study.[186] The GLOBE study looked particularly at the category of gender egalitarianism. It is interesting that the result is quite different from what one might expect. The value of gender egalitarianism is the highest in Germanic and Anglo-Saxon countries. However, when it comes to the actual practice of gender egalitarianism, the Germanic countries are reported at the lower end of all countries (House *et al* 2004:375-376). The Anglo-Saxon societies are somewhere in the middle in terms of gender egalitarianism (:376). More and more women in the West are in leadership roles. However, women in leadership positions have to prove themselves by building credibility and may be regarded with wariness by their

---

[186] The GLOBE study is a cross-cultural research program on leadership that has been conducted in 62 countries around the world.

male peers (Hall & Hall 1990:67 & 165). As a result women may not have access to the same crucial power networks as men do. So they need to build their own networks.

The *Tanzanian* respondents recognise that it is very difficult for a woman to be a leader because of the culture. "According to our culture and tradition, people have seen that a woman cannot be a leader. And it is only because of our culture and tradition that a woman is a person to be married. And she is a person who is like a weak thing that has no strength" (Leader 3).[187] Leader 4 says: "[Women] don't think well. Tough issues they cannot hold their mind. They need soft things like cooking and washing children. But for the big issues, put the men aside and they can do it." This is also echoed by female Leader 5 saying: "I am surprised the Church of God has many pastors who are women. But even at the top leadership they still put men."[188] Women leaders face a tremendous challenge in Tanzania, as female Leader 6 points out: "African male leaders like to be at the top. When a woman rises high, people ask questions. How did she make it there? Maybe she used a means that is not good to get the position."[189] Leader 6 goes on to say: "Often if a woman is a leader not everybody regards her as a leader. He thinks it is only a woman. And often men do not like to be led by a woman."[190] However, women are somewhat recognised as leaders in the family, as Leader 2 explains: "In our context women are often recognised as leaders in the family. There are very few who have risen above the family position to be a top leader."[191] However, there are more and more women moving into leadership positions, as Leader 2 continues:

> There are still women who are accepted as leaders. The good thing is about women who become leaders is that they truly have a leadership profile. It is not like the men who can become leaders because they are men. But the women do not get it because of being women. They get it because they have the ability to lead.[192]

---

[187] Translated from the original Swahili: Kutokana na mila na desturi zetu ni kwamba watu wameona kwamba mwanamke hawezi kuwa kiongozi. Na ni kwa sababu tu ya mila na desturi kwamba mwanamke yeye ni mtu wa kuolewa. Na ni mtu ambaye labda ni kama chombo dhaifu ambacho kisichona nguvu.

[188] Translated from the original Swahili: Nashangaa kabisa Kanisa la Mungu lina wachungaji wengi ambao ni wanawake. Lakini hata katika uongozi wa juu bado wanaweka wanaume.

[189] Translated from the original Swahili: Viongozi wa Afrika wanaume wanapenda kuwa juu. Mwanamke anapopanda sana watu wanajiuliza maswali. Amefikaje kule? Labda amepita kwenye njia ambazo sio nzuri ili apate cheo.

[190] Translated from the original Swahili: Mara nyingi kiongozi kama mwanamke si kila mtu atamwona ni kiongozi. Anaona ni mwanamke tu. Na mara nyingi wanaume hawapendi kuongozwa na mwanamke.

[191] Translated from the original Swahili: Katika mazingira yetu wanawake wanatambulika viongozi mara nyingi katika familia. Wako wachache sana wamevuka kiwango cha familia kuwa kiongozi juu.

[192] Translated from the original Swahili: Bado akina mama wanakubaliwa kama viongozi. Uzuri sasa akina mama wanaojitekeza kuwa viongozi ni kwamba kweli wana sifa za uongozi. Siyo kama wanaume wanaweza kupata tu kwa sababu ni wanaume. Lakini akina mama hawapati kwa sababu ya kuwa akina mama. Wanapata kwa sababu wana uwezo wa kuongoza.

It seems that women can be accepted as leaders "If they have the ability to do the work"[193], as female Leader 6 says.

Generally, women are more accepted as leaders in the West than they are in Tanzania. It took many years in Western societies to see this change happening. It can also be observed that it is slowly changing in Tanzania as well. But there is still a long way to go, especially in the Church.

4.2.2 Use of Power and Leadership

Power distance and how power is used is also reflected *how leaders relate to their subordinates* (question 4.7). Some (4) *Western* respondents observed that leaders relate in a friendly way as friends and peers to their subordinates. The majority (5) of respondents said that leaders relate in a friendly manner, but keep some distance. One respondent thinks that it depends on the leader's personality. It is interesting to note that both Austrian respondents said that leaders relate in a friendly way as friends and peers to their subordinates. Also the German and Dutch respondents said that leaders relate in a friendly manner, but keeping some distance. There seems to be a tendency in Germanic countries to keep a social distance between superior and subordinates.

The answers of the Western respondents give a slightly different picture when compared with the literature, which may have to do with the difference between business and Christian context. Generally, Western leaders are expected to exercise their power in humility.[194] In other words, Western leaders should not demonstrate their power over their subordinates by looking down on them. They should not feel the leader's power. Western leaders need to treat their subordinates with an attitude of humility to show them their appreciation. Americans consider too much power and authority unwise or even dangerous (Hall & Hall 1990:148). Western countries and organisations with small power distance tend to be *egalitarian*. Members of these societies are more or less treated as equals. A person can have a relationship with somebody else independent of the other's status (Hofstede 1997:33). There is little formal respect and deference. In a work situation, this very fact demonstrates that subordinates and superiors consider each other as existentially equal (:36). This is also well reflected in SIL's leadership and follower ethos, for example:

> All members of SIL are considered to have equal right to opinions, resources, and vote. To give preference to those in positions of leadership is inconsistent with this egalitarian value. Calling people by their first names rather than by titles is evidence of this equality. Leaders in SIL gain little by trying to exercise authoritative power, but are more successful when they lead by example and through persuasion. Challenging leaders is not necessarily a sign of disrespect; open dialogue is considered to be healthy (Hill & friends 2002:6).

---

[193] Translated from the original Swahili: Kama wana uwezo wa kufanya kazi.
[194] See also Grün (2001:92).

As we have seen above, within this egalitarian environment power distance between the leader and the staff is fairly small. In a Western organisation with a fairly small power distance where subordinates and superiors consider each other as existentially equal the organisational structure has mainly to do with the distribution of different roles. In fact, these roles may be changed at any time. So it can easily happen that someone who today is my subordinate may tomorrow be my boss (Hofstede 1997:36). Trompenaars and Hampden-Turner (2002:63) point out that "Authority originates in an individual's skill at performing tasks, and an individual's knowledge is used to make the organisational instrument work effectively". Hierarchy and equality seem to be contradictory. However, they are not mutually exclusive. Whereas hierarchy provides connection, equality makes hierarchy responsive and responsible (De Pree 1989:145). In some Western countries hierarchy plays a more important role than in others as the Halls (1990:61) observe: "German lines of authority must be followed religiously. Key people must be informed about all developments, and any major decision involving new projects or significant amounts of money must go to the top for approval." This is also reflected in the relationship between superior and subordinates. In Germany, Austria and Great Britain, there is a clear social distance between the employee and the boss (Schroll-Machl 2003:136-139; Lewis 2003:180 & 210).

The majority (7) of *Tanzanian* respondents observed that leaders relate to their subordinates in a friendly manner, but keep some distance. One person said that leaders relate with social distance but politely. A few (2) observed that leaders relate to their subordinates with social distance according to their position. It was not surprising that all respondents consider some social distance as normal and important.

Leaders in Tanzania are expected to be always accessible and friendly but distant (Mayer *et al* 2003:36-37). Whereas the leadership style in the West is participatory and egalitarian, in Tanzania it is *paternalistic* (:37). Some leaders use the language of command instead of asking and advising (Mwombeki 2004:69). However, people do not like to be commanded or ordered. More and more people appreciate a team approach with good and open communication where their opinion is valued.

Westerners expect participative leadership, which is reflected in the answers of the Western respondents to the question: *"As a subordinate I expect to be consulted and my opinion to be seriously considered and incorporated, to be consulted and my opinion to be considered, to be consulted but the boss makes the final decision, or to be told what to do."* One Western respondent expects to be consulted and her opinion to be seriously considered and incorporated. The majority (8) of respondents said that they expect to be consulted and their opinion to be considered. This is very high, but does not surprise me. It reflects how Westerners view leadership. As subordinates they expect to have a certain amount of authority, which also reflects the small power distance. Only one respondent expects to be consulted but the boss makes the final decision.

Western leaders sometimes face a dilemma. In one sense the leader is expected to be strong and visionary. According to the GLOBE study, visionary leadership is endorsed significantly in the Anglo-Saxon countries (House *et al* 2004:334). On the other hand, there is a commitment to consensus and egalitarianism within Western societies. Participative management is fairly common and somewhat expected in the West.[195]

The *Tanzanian* respondents expect to be at least consulted. Some (4) respondents expect to be consulted and their opinion to be seriously considered and incorporated. A few (2) respondents expect to be consulted and their opinion to be considered. Some (4) respondents expect to be consulted but the boss makes the final decision. It is interesting to note that the respondents (Leader 3, 6, 7 & Lay Leader 2) with a higher level of education expect that their opinion is not only considered but also incorporated. According to my observations, the expectations of the Tanzanians go somewhat against their experience and also cultural values. During the group discussion the Tanzanian participants clearly said that the boss is expected to lead and give direction. The Tanzanian leader is trusted and has the credibility to lead when s/he comes from within the community and understands the context. If a leader asks the subordinates about their opinion, it decreases her/his authority.

There seems to be a slow shift in people's attitude towards leadership in Tanzania. Earlier, leaders were in principle never questioned, as the earlier example in chapter three about criticising leaders also indicates. When the leader said something, it was done. A great deal of trust was placed in leaders. This is now starting to crumble. More and more young and educated people question leaders today. Not everybody would submit anymore unconditionally to a leader. Leader 2 says: "The parishes do not accept every pastor anymore with an authoritarian leadership style. How can it be that the pastor has all the power and authority to make decisions even though s/he is paid by the parish?" If they are dissatisfied with leaders who do not fulfil their responsibilities people will voice it (Mwombeki 2004:10). Sometimes they voice it openly and publicly. Other times it is demonstrated through their behaviour. They will not cooperate with the pastor. If s/he calls a meeting, they do not attend. The offering goes down. Church attendance decreases.[196]

This shift in attitude and behaviour may have to do with the increasing level of education, and the awareness and understanding of democracy through which Tanzanians have gained more self-confidence. Therefore, these days they are more willing to question certain leadership behaviour than years ago. According to Mwombeki (:11), people expect leaders to be faithful and responsible. They should be knowledgeable about how to move forward. They should be able to communicate their thoughts in a way it is understood and agreeable. It is sad, but needs to be recognised that more than 150 years of

---

[195] De Pree (1989:25-29) outlines a number of participative premises, which arise from the heart and out of a personal philosophy about people:
Respect people.
Understand that what we believe precedes policy and practice.
Agree on the rights of work.
Understand the respective role and relationship of contractual agreements and covenants.
Understand that relationships count more than structure.
[196] This observation has also been made by Mwombeki (2004:10-11).

church presence did not have this effect.[197] "The main reason is", George Kinoti (2003:2), a Kenyan Christian leader and Professor of Zoology writes, "that we in East Africa failed to apply the gospel to the whole life, limiting it to spiritual life only. We read the scriptures selectively, placing emphasis on those that talked about salvation and neglecting those that talked about justice, peace and material wellbeing." Also the early missionaries and colonialists set an example of authoritarian leadership, which has had a strong impact for many decades. "To many African nationalists, Christianity was identified with Western imperialism and the Church as an agent of slavery, racialism and colonial domination. ... A return to tradition became the cry of the day: African traditional values, ways of life and religion!" (Adeyemo 1993:3). Only in recent years church leaders have been trained specifically regarding leadership issues and seminars are conducted in the churches.

The question is: Is the expectation by Westerners and Tanzanians to be consulted valid from a biblical point of view? Jesus certainly did not always consult his disciples. However, the point here is that people move away from a "blind" obedience towards a mindful and active submission.

How authority and accountability are exercised (question 4.6) has a lot to do with the valid use and abuse of power. Thus, this question is grouped together with questions 4.9, 4.10, 4.11 and 4.12. When asked, *"How are authority and accountability exercised?"*, the *Western* respondents said, in the West there is usually a clear system of authority and accountability. The scope of authority is clearly defined "through open discussion and consent of all parties involved [and] exercised in a clear job description" (Leader 4). People are usually held accountable from bottom up "through regular control of books, achievements, defining new goals together" (Leader 4), "through regular reporting and an annual interview with one's supervisor" (Leader 2). Within a team the team members hold each other accountable (Lay Leader 1). The level of accountability is demonstrated by how people take responsibility for certain decisions and mistakes (Leader 5). It seems to be the exception where "manipulating that system to one's own advantage is common and even rewarded in some cases" (Leader 6). Most Westerners expect that the lines of authority and responsibility are respected and followed.[198]

The *Tanzanian* respondents observed two different issues regarding authority and accountability. The majority (7) said that in many places authority and accountability are not exercised well. "If a person has already become a leader with authority, s/he does not listen any more to people below her/him" (Lay Leader 3).[199] Often authority and accountability do not go together: "If a person has been given authority, often s/he forgets her/his accountability" (Leader 5).[200] There are others with authority who seek their own personal benefits in-

---

[197] Ludwig Krapf came as the first missionary to East Africa in 1844 (Anderson 1977:1).
[198] The same observations have been made by the Halls (1990:159) and Schroll-Machl (2003:76) in their research.
[199] Translated from the original Swahili: Mtu ameshakuwa mkubwa na mamlaka mtu wa chini hawezi kusikilizwa.
[200] Translated from the original Swahili: Mtu akishapewa mamlaka mara nyingi anasahau wajibu wake.

stead of those who gave them the authority (Lay Leader 2). It is as if people do not consider that their authority means they should be held accountable at the same time, as Leader 4 puts it: "Here in Tanzania authority is not measured against accountability. But my authority guides everything and is even above my accountability. I cannot be held accountable because I am above it."[201] However, a few (3) of the Tanzanian respondents believe there are also other leaders who exercise authority and accountability as it should be. Authority is what leaders oversee. Tanzanian leaders do their best according to their abilities. Leader 2 points out: "If you are a leader of a certain group, you are accountable to them. If you are not accountable your authority decreases. If you are accountable, your authority stays and increases. But first good performance of this authority is necessary."[202]

According to Mhogolo (1996:5-8), traditionally, in the family there is usually a clear line of authority. As we have seen above, within Tanzanian organisations and churches, there is a strong hierarchical system with clear lines of authority. However, the accountability system seems to be weak in some places. As we have seen earlier in chapter three, a leader usually cannot be criticised. Therefore, it is a challenge to hold them accountable. This is also reflected in the abuse of power, as the respondents indicate below.

The way authority and accountability are exercised can also be seen in the positive and negative use of power. Thus, the answers to these questions (4.9, 4.10, 4.11 & 4.12) are presented here. There are a number of situations where *power was exercised positively* (question 4.9) by *Western* leaders as the following example from the interviews demonstrates. "When ... [two leaders in our entity] worked together very closely I had the impression that things were thought through very well and that they were leading well. Their honesty, listening and transparency gave a feeling of being cared for well" (Leader 7). Westerners experience power positively when leaders consult with their followers and incorporate their opinion.

The *Tanzanian* respondents mentioned a number of positive situations, especially in the area of cooperation and joint decision-making, as the following instance shows:

> Since we have started translation in our office, all the plans that were prepared by the leadership in authority they have often shared with us. We have been sitting together. They have received our opinions. They have listened to our advice. We have done the work. And we have been successful (Leader 3).[203]

---

[201] Translated from the original Swahili: Hapa kwetu mamlaka yetu haipimwi na wajibu wako. Ila mamlaka yangu ndiyo yanayoongoza kila kitu na yako juu hata ya wajibu wangu. Siwezi kupimwa na wajibu kwa sababu niko juu ya wajibu.
[202] Translated from the original Swahili: Ukiwa kiongozi wa jamii fulani wajibu wako ni huu. Usipofanya wajibu wako mamlaka yako inaondoka. Ukifanya wajibu wako mamlaka yako inabaki na kuzidi. Lakini kwanza lazima kuwa na utekelezaji wa nafasi ile ya mamlaka uliyopewa.
[203] Translated from the original Swahili: Nichukulie hapa ofisini kwetu ni kwamba tangu tumeanza kutafsiri ile mipango yote ambayo iliyopangwa na uongozi wa juu kama wenye mamlaka mara nyingi ni kwamba wametushirikisha. Tumekaa nao. Wamepokea maoni yetu. Wamesikia ushauri wetu. Tumetenda kazi. Tukafanikiwa.

In one company, employees have been well informed about what their responsibilities are and nobody else would interfere (Leader 2). According to my observations and those of other Tanzanian leaders in the group discussion, this seems to be the exception. Very often people do not have a job description.

However, the *abuse of power* in both societies seems to be a concern for the respondents. Despite the positive examples of power exercised positively, the abuse of power in the West also seems to be a concern for the *Western* respondents. When asked, *"How often is the abuse of power an issue in the West?"* they replied: very often (3), quite often (4), sometimes (1), don't know (2). The *Tanzanian* interviewees were asked to give their perspective on power abuse in the West. The responses were as follows: very often (2), quite often (1), sometimes (3), not often (3), don't know (1).

When asked, *"How often is the abuse of power an issue in Tanzania?"* the *Western* respondents perceive the abuse of power in Tanzania as follows: very often (5), quite often (2), not often (1), don't know (2). The *Tanzanians* replied: very often (1), quite often (6), sometimes (3).

Generally, the perception is that the abuse of power is more an issue in Tanzania than in the West. How much power is abused in a country can be seen in the level of corruption. The respondents' perception is consistent with public statistics such as the corruption perceptions index published by the German-based *Transparency International*.[204] Western countries are certainly not perceived as being without corruption, but are considered less corrupt than Tanzania. This does not give Westerners permission when they come to work in Tanzania to have a different kind of accountability than Tanzanians. Tanzanian Leader 1 expects the same kind of accountability for Westerners as for Tanzanians:

> The problem of Westerners is when they come here as missionaries, I have seen that they do not want others to know things. For instance, like the missionary ... no doubt she receives a lot of money for church activities. She alone knows how much came in, how much has been used and she writes the report. But is there anyone else who understands? It is necessary to have a person who understands as well.[205]

Westerners may be accountable to their home constituents and because of the high trust level they may think there is no need for accountability between

---

[204] The index (Transparency International 2005:8) "defines corruption as the abuse of public office for private gain" and measures "the degree to which corruption is perceived to exist among public officials and politicians". The corruption perceptions index 2005 ranks 159 countries based on 16 different polls and surveys from 10 independent institutions (:9-10). According to the corruption perceptions index, the Western countries, including Australia, Austria, Netherlands, United Kingdom, Canada, Germany and the USA, belong to the least corrupt countries in the world, ranking between nine and 17, where as Tanzania is at place 88.

[205] Translated from the original Swahili: Na shida ya wazungu wanapokuja kuwa wamissionari hapa ambaye nimeona hawataki watu wengine wajue. Kwa mfano kama mmissionari ... lazima anapata pesa nyingi kwa ajili ya shughuli ya kanisa. Yeye mwenyewe anajua ngapi zimeingia, ngapi zimetumika na anaandika riporti. Lakini je, kuna mtu mwingine anaelewa? Lazima kuwa na mtu ambaye anaelewa pia.

them and Tanzanians. But how can the home constituents necessarily know that the missionary's report is true. Tanzanians would like to see Westerners being more transparent in what they are doing.

According to the *Western* respondents, the *abuse of power* occurs (question 4.12) in the West in a number of ways such as "abuse of children, corruption" (Leader 2), "benefit[ing] her/himself or a specific group of people rather than the whole" (Leader 5), "in the use of school property for personal use [like] vehicles [and] computers" (Leader 8), "by taking advantage of the privileges in a job like cell phone calls [and] airplane tickets" (Leader 7), "laying people off because some investor wants to restructure a company for maximizing their profit" (Leader 2), "when a church leader makes followers of him or herself, rather than of Jesus" (Lay Leader 1), and "male-female relationships at work" (Leader 9). The respondents further said, power is also abused "if someone is not fit for the job or someone else wants the position, by … [making] the unwanted person … feel the opposition, get depressed and unhappy with the situation and quit the job" (Leader 4). Some Western leaders misuse their power by manipulating people, as Leader 3 shares: "For example, some pastors use their position to manipulate people into giving money. Just watch almost any show by faith healers today. If you want to be blessed, send in money to God (his address is the same as my address) and God is bound by his Word to bless you."

According to the *Tanzanian* respondents, power is abused, "For instance, [when] people employ others giving them preference because of family, because of the clan, to help the people from their village or people from the same ethnic group" (Leader 2).[206] Leader 2 also shares the following example:

> We had a bishop who asked some donors to build a university in his region. But he wanted them to build the university in his village. These donors said: "If you want us to build in your village, we will not come. He insisted that they build it there. And they said: "We are not coming." Later they moved. They went to another region. So the people did not get anything.[207]

"Other people use church money in a way they should not. They use it for their own benefit and not for the benefit of the church" (Leader 3).[208] People abuse their power for their own benefit, as Leader 4 says:

> If a person like the principal or a department leader or … district commissioner, hospital leader or doctor gets an office, the person uses this

---

[206] Translated from the original Swahili: Kwa mfano watu wanaajiri watu kwa kupendelea kwa sababu ya undugu, kwa sababu ya ukoo, kwa sababu ya kutaka kuwafanyia vizuri watu wa kijijini kwenu au watu wa kabila lenu.
[207] Translated from the original Swahili: Tulikuwa na askofu mmoja alikuwa ameombwa wafadhili wameomba kujenga chuo kikuu cha falsafa katika mkoa wake. Lakini yeye akataka wapeleke wakajenge chuo hiki kijijini kwao. Wale wafadhili wakasema: "Kama unataka kupeleka kijijini kwako sisi hatuendi." Akalazimisha wapeleke. Na wenyewe wakasema: "Hatuendi." Badaye wakahama. Wakaenda mkoa mwingine. Kwa hiyo watu wamekosa.
[208] Translated from the original Swahili: Lakini watu wengine ni kwamba wanatumia pesa za kanisa visivyo. Wanatumia kwa manufaa yao na si manufaa ya kanisa.

office for her/his own benefit. So s/he does not do her/his work the way it should be done, but s/he regards it as an opportunity. So the result is that the normal people have a problem. You have a certain thing to do and if the office is efficient, it should take only one day. ... But you will be send around so that you give some money. If you are sick, at the hospital you will be sent around. The doctor will not be serious. S/he waits until you give some money. If you give money, it is done immediately.[209]

Other examples of power abuse were mentioned such as "teachers beating students or students damaging property, lying, hiding problems, making decisions that are inconsistent with the law" (Leader 5)[210], "loans are not distributed to the affected people" (Lay Leader 2)[211], or organisations are privatised or sold without informing the employees (Leader 6). The answers from the interviews suggest that people have more negative than positive experiences of power. Leader 2 says power is abused "because it is impacted by the tradition and culture".[212] It may be easier to abuse power in Tanzania since status is ascribed and not achieved, as in the West. Thus, the impact of culture seems to be stronger than that of the gospel. During the group discussion the Tanzanians also pointed out that the abuse of power has also to do with the fact that leaders are insecure. Once they reach their position they are afraid of losing it again. So they do everything they can to strengthen their position of power.

4.2.3 Meetings and Leadership

Power is often used and expressed in *meetings*. Meetings are a good place to observe how power is exercised. To understand how power is distributed and used in meetings it is necessary to look at the different roles and tasks of the chairperson and the delegates. The questions *"What authority do delegates have in a meeting? In which way are delegates empowered?"* are closely connected to the other two questions *"What is the role of the chairperson in a meeting?"* and *"What is the task of a representative before, during and after a meeting?"*. Hence, the responses to these questions are grouped together.

---

[209] Translated from the original Swahili: Mtu akipata ofisi kama mkuu wa chuo au mkuu wa idara au ... mkuu wa wilaya, mkuu wa hospitali au mganga, mtu anatumia ile ofisi yake kwa faida yake mwenyewe. Kwa hiyo hafanyi jinsi kazi yake inavyomwongoza ila anaanglia ile kama opportunity. Kwa hiyo matokeo yake ni wale watu wa kawaida wanapata shida. Unakuta unaweza ukawa na jambo ambalo kama ofisi iko efficient inaweza kuchukua siku moja tu. ... Lakini utakuwa na mizunguko mingi ili mradi wanataka utoe pesa. Ukiwa unaumwa hospitalini watakuzungusha. Daktari atakuwa haiko serious. Anasubiri utoe fedha. Ukitoa fedha haraka sana.
[210] Translated from the original Swahili: Waalimu kuwapiga wanafunzi au wanafunzi kuchoma mali. Kusema uwongo au kuficha matatizo. Kuasi amri ya viongozi kinyume cha sheria.
[211] Translated from the original Swahili: Mikopo inakuja lakini haifikii walengwa ambao wamekusudi wa kupata ule mkopo.
[212] Translated from the original Swahili: Kwa sababu inaathiriwa na mila na desturi ...

The *Western* respondents agree that the role of the chairperson (question 4.13) is basically "Preparing materials for the meeting, leading the meeting, seeing that everybody has an opportunity to contribute, summarizing, [and] leading towards a decision without dominating the outcome" (Leader 2). The chairperson "needs to open, regulate and close the meeting" (Leader 4) and "to ensure that the meeting accomplishes what the attendees have set out to do" (Leader 6). It is important that s/he is "objective, and withholds from comments as much as possible" (Leader 9). "The chairperson does not necessarily have more power than the other members" (Leader 7). After the meeting, it is her/his responsibility "to hold ... [delegates] accountable for the implementation of board ... decisions" (Leader 8).[213]

The role of the chairperson in *Tanzania* is similar to in the West. "The chairperson leads the meeting in such a way that the agenda is discussed well and people are given the opportunity to share their thoughts and to connect them with those of their colleagues so that they reach an answer or agreement together. So the chairperson is not a talker. S/he is an enabler" (Leader 4).[214] However, the chairperson has more power than in the West. Since s/he gives permission to those who speak it is not always an open discussion, as Lay Leader 2 observes: "When questions are asked s/he [the chairperson] chooses the one who s/he wants to answer. ... Therefore there is not complete freedom."[215] After the discussion "Then s/he should help to come to a decision" (Leader 7).[216] This can be by consensus or by vote. "If there is a vote s/he should also vote. If there is a disagreement her/his vote should help to make the decision as advised" (Leader 7).[217] However, the chairperson has a lot of power because sometimes "In a meeting s/he makes the final decision"[218] (Lay Leader 1). If a decision has been made "Another responsibility of the chairperson is to ensure that the secretary writes in the minutes what was decided by the delegates"[219] (Leader 3).[220]

I have seen all three options of a consensus, vote or the chairperson having the final word to arrive at a decision in meetings in Tanzania. But it seems that the preference is to come to a consensus. However, it needs to be recog-

---

[213] Dale (1986:128) confirms that the chairperson in the West is mainly responsible for the process of a meeting.
[214] Translated from the original Swahili: Mwenyekiti katika kikao yeye anaongoza kikao kwa maana ya kwamba agenda zilizopo zinazungumzwa vizuri na kuwapa nafasi watu wote kutoa mawazo yao na kuunganisha hoja na wenzao kwa pamoja na mwenyewe kuweza kufikia jibu au makubaliano kwa pamoja. Kwa hiyo mwenyekiti si msemaji. Yeye ni mwezeshaji.
[215] Translated from the original Swahili: Katika maswali sasa yeye anamchagua anayetaka kujibu swali. ... Kwa hiyo uhuru kamili haupo.
[216] Translated from the original Swahili: Halafu asaidie maamuzi kufanyika.
[217] Translated from the original Swahili: Kama ni kura inapigwa na yeye apige kura. Kama wamefungana kura yake isaidie kufanya maamuzi inavyoshauriwa.
[218] Translated from the original Swahili: Kwenye kikao ana maamumizi ya mwisho.
[219] Translated from the original Swahili: Kazi nyingine ni kwamba lazima ahakikishe kwamba mhutasari, yaani mwandishi kama katibu anaandika mhutasari inayolingana na yale yaliyoamuliwa na wajumbe.
[220] These responsibilities of a chairperson are also described by Mhogolgo (1996:73-75) and Mwombeki (2004:74-84).

nised that the word of the chairperson has a lot of weight. When the chairperson summarizes the discussion and incorporates her/his own opinion usually nobody will say anything against it.

"What is the task of a representative before, during and after a meeting?" According to the *Western* respondents, Westerners tend to come to meetings to share information, discuss issues, to seek agreement and make decisions. The respondents said that the task of a representative *before* a meeting is to be well prepared and informed in advance of the meeting by reading reports and minutes and gathering opinions of those they are representing so that they come to the meetings with questions, queries and ideas. According to the respondents, *during* a meeting delegates in the West are expected to participate actively, listen to others and consider their opinion compared with overall goals. Sometimes the task of the delegates depends on the nature of the meeting and also on the agendas of the delegates. "Some delegates collect information only. Others are sent in an effort to effect some kind of change" (Leader 6). They "are empowered through open lines of communication with the executive body of the organisation. Only if all necessary information is shared are delegates empowered meaningfully to contribute to the decision-making process" (Leader 2). Representatives should "voice the views, opinions and desires of ... [their] constituents for the most part. [They are] ... also expected to give input of [their] ... own personal position" (Leader 3). "Delegates are empowered in that their constituents have sent ... [them] to be their delegate[s] and they are speaking on behalf of the constituents" (Leader 3). Delegates need to "be willing to answer questions about work completed and take on work that is assigned" (Leader 8). *After* the meeting, according to the respondents, delegates should read the minutes and take note of what they should follow up, consider and change. Delegates must keep confidentiality if this is requested. They would give a report to the constituents after the meeting. Delegates are expected to support decisions made, to follow up and implement them after the meeting.

In *Tanzania* the task of a delegate before, during and after a meeting is basically the same as in the West. The respondents agree that *during* a meeting, delegates are mainly empowered by their constituencies: "Those who elect to represent them give them the authority" (Leader 2).[221] The other option is "by the constitution or guideline of the church" (Leader 4).[222] "A delegate should listen well, ask questions and contribute issues" (Leader 5).[223] "*After* a meeting "S/he has the task to report the decisions of the meeting to the people who sent her/him" (Leader 2).[224] However, "S/he should not tell it everybody. S/he will tell those who sent her/him" [225] (Leader 7). Often the information is not

---

[221] Translated from the original Swahili: Wale waliowachagua kuwakilisha wale ndiyo wanawapa mamlaka.
[222] Translated from the original Swahili: ... kwa njia ya katiba au kanuni za kanisa.
[223] Translated from the original Swahili: Mjumbe anatakiwa kusikiliza vizuri, kuuliza maswali na kuchangia hoja.
[224] Translated from the original Swahili: Baada ya kikao ana kazi ya kupeleka kutoa tafsiri ya maamuzi ya kikao kwa watu waliomtuma.
[225] Translated from the original Swahili: Asimwambie kila mtu. Waliomtuma atawaambia.

filtered down. Subsequently, sometimes there is little communication, implementation or change in different parts of the Church.

I have observed that often at a meeting delegates are bound by the wishes of those who sent them. This can go so far that delegates are not able to make a decision at the meeting before having consulted with their office or superiors. Consequently, no decisions or actions are taken at the meeting other than information sharing. In reality meetings are sometimes used as a rubber stamp, as Mhogolo points out:

> Despite the good intention of participative leadership, many leaders like bishops, pastors, catechists and others use committees or synods to move their own agendas forward. They use the committee as a rubber stamp only. The committee members have no freedom to share their opinion and if they express it, it will be put down and devalued. From the outside it looks like the church is led by the committee, but from the inside the committee does not work at all. Maybe the committee is there to say 'Yes, yes only' if they approve a good decision. Such leadership makes its actions ridiculous, especially if the decision was already decided by the superiors (1996:70-71).[226]

How a meeting is conducted certainly depends on the chairperson, her/his leadership style and character. It can be argued that Western delegates are often truly empowered by their constituents and have authority to speak and make decisions on behalf of them, whereas Tanzanian delegates may be overruled, often by their leaders in authority.

4.2.4 Decision-Making and Leadership

Decisions are often made in meetings. The decision-making process can be quite different in different societies. Thus, in any kind of collaboration it is essential to understand how decisions are made. So the interviewees were asked: *"How are decisions made? What process is followed?"* The Western respondents described the decision-making process as follows. Decisions are made "In a (mostly) democratic fashion for the most part" (Leader 3). "The topic is presented. Often the church elders have done some pre-processing, which is shared" (Leader 1). "People are given the opportunity to ask specific questions. Other people can jump in and give information. Then when all the 'facts' are present, usually someone speaks up for a particular decision. Others may object and advocate a different decision" (Leader 3). "A participatory

---

[226] Translated from the original Swahili: Pamoja na nia njema ya kuwa na uongozi wa pamoja, viongozi wengi, wakiwemo maaskofu, makasisi, wachungaji, makatekisti na wengine, hutumia kamati au sinodi kupitishia mambo yao tu. Wanatumia kamati kama muhuri tu. Wanakamati hawana uhuru wowote wa kutoa mawazo, na kama wakitoa, mawazo yao hupuuzwa na kutothaminiwa. Kwa nje, inaonekana kanisa linaongozwa na kamati, lakini kwa ndani, kamati hazifanyi kazi kabisa, labda kazi ya kamati ni kusema, 'Ndiyo ndiyo tu' wakipitisha maamuzi mazuri, uongozi huwa unapuuzia utekelezaji wake, hasa maamuzi yaliyokwisha kuamuriwa na wakubwa.

approach is used to tap all the available creativity" (Leader 5).[227] "A motion is proposed and voted on. ... Depending on the issue, voting is conducted by secret ballot" (Lay Leader 1).[228] Sometimes a "conclusion with consensus" (Leader 5) is desired.

According to Hersman's (1995:85) and Halls' (1990:59, 170) research, it seems that Anglo-Saxon societies like Britain and the USA have a much more top-down decision-making process than Germanic societies. In the USA, at work the boss makes the decision without necessarily consulting their subordinates. According to the research done by Hofstede (1997:94), Trompenaars and Hampden-Turner (2002:61), and Lewis (2003:124), note that as individualists, Western leaders tend to be lone decision-makers at the top rather than group discussion leaders. However, it seems that there may be a shift in Western societies moving towards a more participative decision-making behaviour, as the Halls (1990:160) observe: "[T]here is a small but growing trend toward information-based organizations which emphasize shared information and decentralized control." It appears that there is a gap between Anglo-Saxon and Germanic countries. This may have to do with some major historical and political changes from autocratic to democratic systems in Germanic societies. There is a strong rejection against authoritarian leadership because of the negative experience during the *Third Reich* with Adolf Hitler as a dictator. Until this day, the German word *Führer*, which means guide, carries a very strong negative connotation. Thus, Germans highly value consensus (Schroll-Machl 2003:96) and participative leadership. Subordinates clearly expect to be engaged and consulted in any decision-making process. Since Westerners are achievement-oriented, the decision-making process should be clear and straightforward without wasting time, in order to result in action.[229] Once a decision has been made as an oral contract, as part of the minutes of a meeting or as a formalised, written, legal document, ethically a person from a Western society usually sticks to the decision (Lewis 2003:125; Hall & Hall 1990:35). People who disagree with the decision are expected to agree to disagree, but go along with the decision being made. A decision is not re-discussed unless there are valid reasons to revisit it. In decision-oriented societies like in the West, it is expected that decisions have a binding and lasting quality (Hesselgrave 1991:614).

Individuals in Western societies with a *small power distance* expect to participate and have a say in the decision-making process. Westerners as individualists will frequently ask for a vote to come to a decision because "This gives victory to the majority of individuals present and the minority are expected to yield peacefully, not to remain silent but to offer no more than verbal dissent to the will of the majority" (Hampden-Turner & Trompenaars 2000:95). To process and to make a decision in an individualistic society is typically fast and incisive (:96). In an achievement-oriented culture like West-

---

[227] This description of the discussion process is in agreement with Douglas (in Helander & Niwagila 1996:69).
[228] Also see Lewis (2003:124-130).
[229] This is especially true of Germans, as Schroll-Machl (2003:55) observes.

ern countries, decisions can only be challenged on technical and functional grounds (Trompenaars & Hampden-Turner 2002:119).

In *Tanzania* there are basically two ways in which decisions are made, as Leader 7 says: "There is the decision by consensus and there is the decision by vote and the majority counts."[230] Leader 7 describes the decision-making process as follows:

> The decision is made after the contributions of the delegates are summarized. It is possible to vote, but during the discussion you observe which points that are presented are agreed to by others. Even if there are those which are opposed by many. The result is that the chairperson needs to look at which discussion point has been agreed by many. You present these again. You make a proposal: "There are three different thoughts. Some have said this. Others have said this. Now which one do you think should be decided? Is it this one?" You give them permission. They talk. "As I hear it, many delegates prefer this. Is this true?" "Yes, it's true." So you observe the direction of the meeting. The decision can be made as many delegates focus on one point.[231]

If no clear consensus is reached a vote can be taken: "Many decisions are made by voting" (Leader 6).[232] It was expressed by a few respondents that "there is also a place where the leader has a voice to make a decision" (Leader 3).[233] "A leader has a certain authority. S/he can decide as a leader using her/his common sense but following the constitution and work guidelines" (Leader 2).[234] It can be observed that often a leader makes a lone decision without consulting others. However, if a discussion takes place, Mayer, Boness and Thomas describe the process as follows:

> The chairperson (Sw. *mwenyekiti*), who is usually also the leader asks the participants to express their opinions after he has presented the agenda item. How the participants express their opinions is very different from what Western leaders are used to: Every participant connects to the chairperson's proposal or the previous speaker, takes it up and praises it, and possibly adds another aspect. The statements are defi-

---

[230] Translated from the original Swahili: Kwa hiyo kuna maamuzi ya kauli moja kwa wengi na kuna maamuzi kwa kupiga kura na kuhesabu walio wengi.

[231] Translated from the original Swahili: Maamuzi yanafanyika baada ya kujumuisha michango ya watu wajumbe. Inaweza kupigwa kura lakini unaangalia katika mazungumzo na hoja zinazotolewa zipi zinaungwa mkono na wengine. Hata kama kuna zile zinatolewa zipi zinapingwa na wengi. Matokeo yake ni kile anatakiwa mwenyekiti sasa kuangalia ni hoja ipi ambayo wengi wameunga mkono. Uitoe tena upya. Ufanye mhutasi: "Jamani, kuna mawazo ya aina tatu. Wengine wamesema hivi. Wengine wamesema hivi. Sasa lipi mnadhani ni jambo la kuamulia? Ni hili?" Unawaruhusu. Wanasema pale. "Jamani, ninaposikiliza wajumbe wengi wanapendelea hivi. Ndivyo kweli?" "Ndiyo kweli." Kwa hiyo unaangalia mwelekeo wa mkutano. Maamuzi yanaweza kutolewa kwa wengi kutetea hoja fulani kwa wajumbe.

[232] Translated from the original Swahili: Maamuzi mengi yanafanyika kwa kupiga kura.

[233] Translated from the original Swahili: Lakini kuna mahali kiongozi vilevile ana sauti ya kutoa maamuzi.

[234] Translated from the original Swahili: Kuna mamlaka aliyonayo kama kiongozi. Anaweza kuamua yeye kama kiongozi kwa busara zake lakini kwa kuzingatia kanuni na miongozo yake ya kazi.

nitely not in competition or very different from each other. That way the participants move towards a common understanding. Everybody feels comfortable with this collective opinion (2003:99-100).[235]

This discussion process ensures that the harmonic atmosphere is protected. I have personally observed this process in many different meetings in Tanzania over and over again. There is a strong desire to achieve a consensus in a collectivist society like Tanzania, as can be seen in the role of the chairperson and delegates during meetings. Sometimes voting may be appropriate. Voting is certainly not the first choice, as Trompenaars and Hampden-Turner (2002:61) point out: "The communitarian society will intuitively refrain from voting because this will not show respect to the individuals who are against a majority decision. It prefers to deliberate until consensus is reached. The final result takes longer to achieve, but will be much more stable." To process and to make a decision in a collectivist society like Tanzania takes usually more time than expected (:60; Hampden-Turner & Trompenaars 2000:97). Tanzanians do not like to be pushed towards a decision. In fact, as particularists they get suspicious when hurried (Trompenaars & Hampden-Turner 2002:40-41). They need a considerable amount of time to build a personal relationship first and grow close to their partner. However, if this time is used well in the beginning it will be saved in the avoidance of trouble in the future.

As the chairperson of a forum in Tanzania, I faced several instances where a person did not respect a decision made in a meeting. The decision was either discussed again or just handled in a different manner than expected or not followed through. I also observed situations where decisions were made in a meeting but not reflected in the minutes. Once a decision has been made as an oral contract, as part of the minutes of a meeting or as a formalised, written, legal document, the particularist views the contract as a rough guideline or approximation (:40). A decision is not necessarily binding (Mayer *et al* 2003:84). Often it can just be an appeal to engage the issue. This can be difficult in a partnership when Westerners expect an agreement to be kept. It may be perceived as not being honest.

If a decision is made by a superior in Tanzania it is usually not questioned. Subordinates obey the decision made by their boss. If a decision is challenged, this is only done by people with higher authority (Trompenaars & Hampden-Turner 2002:119). It is expected that the superior takes full responsibility for the consequences of a decision that has been made (Mayer *et al* 2003:70). This can have the result that sometimes nobody has the courage to make a decision. Generally, subordinates do not have the authority to make even

---

[235] Translated from the original German: Der Vorsitzende (sw. mwenyekiti), der im Allgemeinen auch der Leiter ist, ruft die einzelnen Teilnehmer zur Stellungnahme auf, nachdem er die zu beschließenden Angelegenheiten angesprochen hat. Die Art der Stellungnahme der Teilnehmer unterscheidet sich bedeutend von der Art, die westliche Führungskräfte von Meetings kennen: Jeder gefragte Teilnehmer knüpft an den Vorschlag des Vorsitzenden oder des Vorredners an, nimmt ihn wägend und lobend auf und ergänzt möglicherweise noch einen Aspekt. Auf keinen Fall sind die Statements konkurrent oder grob abweichend. So bewegen sich die Teilnehmer auf eine gemeinsam getragene Auffassung hin. Alle fühlen sich in dieser kollektiven Meinung aufgehoben.

relatively small decisions, since authority is usually not delegated downwards (:70). Decisions tend to be made at the top.

In comparison, the major difference in the decision-making process in the West and in Tanzania is that in the West decisions are mainly made by the delegates with the chairperson being neutral. In an individualistic culture like the West, a representative has the authority and can make a decision on the spot, whereas in Tanzania usually only the top leader has the authority to make a decision. In Tanzania the chairperson has more influence in leading towards a decision. Whereas in the West decisions are often made by voting, in Tanzania the preference is reaching consensus. In the West the outcome of a meeting is more important than the process, which is the case in Tanzania. When a decision is made it is usually binding in the West, whereas in Tanzania it can be overruled subsequently by the leader.

4.3 Conflict and Leadership

Leaders spend a good amount of their time dealing with conflicts.[236] Leadership behaviour can be observed well in how leaders deal with conflict. The interviewees were asked: *"If somebody expresses a different opinion in a meeting, what do you think is the best way of dealing with it?"* The majority of *Western* respondents (Leader 2, 5, 6 8, 9 & Lay Leader 1) pointed out that first of all it is important to listen, "genuinely seeking to understand what the other is thinking and feeling, inviting input from others on it in a non-challenging way, trying to find a compromise if possible, if not possible go with the majority" (Leader 2). "Do not comment on it before the person has finished speaking. Consider the different opinion carefully!" (Leader 9). "Oftentimes though, ulterior motives lie behind the opinion and it becomes necessary to take the individual aside (as a leader) and discipline them" (Leader 6). "If there is no resolution and the decision cannot be postponed to another day, the leader will make the decision" (Leader 7).

If a conflict arises in individualistic cultures like the West, it is addressed directly between the two parties. Talking to a third person about a conflict would be seen as talking behind somebody's back and insulting. An apology can be appropriate. But a disagreement can also lead to the termination of a relationship. Hofstede (1997:58) points out that for a Westerner "speaking one's mind is a virtue. Telling the truth about how one feels is the characteristic of a sincere and honest person. Confrontation can be salutary, a clash of opinions is believed to lead to higher truth". This is a classic characteristic for a specific, assertive society. Specific cultures tend to separate the person from the issue discussed. Only if the two parties are not able to resolve the conflict is a third party involved as mediator.

In *Tanzania* the best way of dealing with conflict is "First of all, as the chairperson or leader you need to evaluate whether the opinion is part of the

---

[236] It is said, "Average persons spend an estimated 30 percent of our time dealing with some kind of conflict" (Dale 1986:159).

agenda or not" (Lay Leader 1).[237] If it is within the agenda, it needs to be discussed "To allow the person to share her/his thoughts and to allow other delegates to explain their concerns regarding her/his thoughts" (Leader 7).[238] "If a person has a different opinion, the delegates will have listened to it. And if this opinion will make more sense s/he will be supported. If there is support they will vote" (Leader 2).[239] The other option is that the person with a different opinion needs to submit to the majority, which happens quite frequently, as Leader 3 says:

> Now often a decision is made by the majority because many decide – a Swahili proverb says, "many should be given". If one person does not want to agree with many people we will not agree with her/his decision. We agree with the decision of many. So I will tell her/him: "Many have decided this which is good. Now we ask you to change your heart and join the majority. But if you do not want to, we will leave you."[240]

Dealing with conflict in Tanzania is a rather challenging and difficult issue.[241] Tanzanians are generally *non-confrontational*. An important contributing key factor is that Tanzanian society is a shame-oriented culture. A direct confrontation would mean that a person may not only "lose face" but also loses her/his dignity. Collectivist societies like Tanzania have a strong need for harmony, as Hofstede points out:

> In a situation of intense and continuous social contact, the maintenance of *harmony* with one's social environment becomes a key virtue which extends to other spheres beyond the family. In most collectivist cultures, direct confrontation of another person is considered rude and undesirable. The word 'no' is seldom used, because saying no *is* a confrontation, 'you may be right' or 'we will think about it' are examples of polite ways of turning down a request (1997:58). [his emphasis]

Any potential conflict is avoided in Tanzania since it threatens the harmony of the group (Mayer *et al* 2003:39).

"How do you restore peace after a disagreement or conflict?" According to the *Western* respondents, to restore peace it is important to talk things through, apologize and forgive one another and pray together to be reconciled.

---

[237] Translated from the original Swahili: Kwanza kama mwenyekiti au kiongozi inatakiwa upime yale mawazo yako ndani. Yanahusiana na miniti au agenda zile zinazoongelea au iko nje.
[238] Translated from the original Swahili: Kumruhusu mtu atoe mawazo yake na kuruhusu wajumbe wengine watoe hoja zao juu ya mawazo yake.
[239] Translated from the original Swahili: Mtu akileta maoni tofauti wajumbe watakuwa wamesikia maoni yake. Na kama haya maoni yatakuwa na busara zaidi ataungwa mkono. Akiungwa mkono basi watapiga kura.
[240] Translated from the original Swahili: Sasa maamuzi mara nyingi ni ya wengi kwa sababu wengi wanapoamua – waswahili wanasema wengi wape. Mtu mmoja yeye hataki kukubaliana na watu wengine ni kwamba sasa hapo hatutasimama katika maamuzi wake. Tunasimama katika maamuzi ya wengi. Kwa hiyo yule tu nitamwambia kabisa: "Bwana, maamuzi watu wengi wameamua jambo hili ni jema. Sasa wewe mtu mmoja tunaomba urejeshe moyo wako ujiunge na wengi. Lakini kama hutaki tutakuacha."
[241] See also Mwombeki (2004:67-73) and Mayer, Boness and Thomas (2003:19-20 & 35) on how Tanzanians deal with conflict.

This is usually done between the two people involved if they desire it (Leader 5). If one has a different opinion sometimes it is necessary to submit and go with the majority (Leader 4). "In difficult conflict situations, which may affect more people the pastor may intervene and even preach about it" (Leader 1). "If agreement cannot be reached [among Westerners, it is also possible to] agree to disagree with the concept or idea, not the person" (Leader 8).

According to the majority of *Tanzanian* respondents (6), the best way to restore peace is by talking about it within the group and sincerely forgiving one another. To discuss the issue openly is the ideal first step to restoring peace after a disagreement or conflict. This is not always possible, especially when the power distance is great. A mediator can help to overcome the power distance and maintain a certain level of harmony so that people do not lose face.[242] Secondly, it is essential that people sincerely forgive one another (Leader 4). Sometimes it is difficult to know whether reconciliation has taken place, as Lay Leader 3 says: "I have a lot of doubts because people can say 'I have forgiven you'. But s/he has not forgiven you, even in the church. ... People say, 'I have forgiven her/him, but you cannot know if it is true'."[243] To know that forgiveness and reconciliation has truly taken place, it is good to state it publicly either at church or by some other means, as the following example demonstrates: "There was a pastor ... who did wrong to all his Pentecostal fellow Christians. He announced in the radio 'I have forgiven my colleagues'. He asked many people for forgiveness through the radio. That was a good example" (Lay Leader 3).[244] This suggests in a collectivist society like Tanzania, reconciliation should take place in public. Tanzanians also deal with conflicts by making jokes (Lay Leader 1) or one just has to submit to the group (Leader 1), which demonstrates a strong desire for harmony and consensus. Modest cultures like Tanzania prefer to resolve conflicts by compromise and negotiations.

Whereas Westerners mainly deal with conflict on an individual basis and want to see justice, for Tanzanians reconciliation is a group process to rebuild relationships, harmony and community.

How people deal with conflict and restore peace leads consequently to the question: *"Are harmony and consensus ultimate goals?"* For the majority of the *Western* respondents, harmony and consensus are either quite often (3) or sometimes (4) ultimate goals. A few (2) believe it is not often the ultimate goal. Only one person believes that harmony and consensus are never ultimate goals. For the majority of *Tanzanian* respondents, harmony and consensus are either always (4) or quite often (5) ultimate goals. Only one person believes, it is only sometimes the ultimate goal. The strong desire for harmony and con-

---

[242] Mayer, Boness and Thomas (2003:27 & 39-40) also describe how Tanzanians use a mediator in conflict situations.
[243] Translated from the original Swahili: Nina kuwa na wasiwasi sana kwa sababu watu wanaweza kusema "mimi nimekusamehe". Lakini kumbe hajakusamehe hata makanisani. ... Watu wanasema "nimemsamehe" lakini huwezi kujua kama ni kweli.
[244] Translated from the original Swahili: Kuna mchungaji ... alikosana na wenzake wote wapentekoste. Alitangaza kwenye vyombo vya habari kwamba "mimi nimewasamehe wenzangu". Aliomba msamaha kwa watu wengi kwa njia ya redio. Ilikuwa mfano mzuri.

sensus in the West is much higher than I expected. This may have to do with some of the theological teaching that Christians ought to live together in harmony and love. Thus, the responses may reflect more an ideal picture than the reality. However, it is also possible that the Western respondents have been influenced by living in Tanzania. According to the Western responses, Germanics have a stronger desire for harmony than Anglo-Saxons. My own observations are different. In my view, the desire for harmony has not only to do with culture but also with personality. According to my observations and Schroll-Machl (2003:173), Germans are more confrontational: "Germans are often seen as being very confrontational and completely unafraid of conflict: Germans address mistakes, express criticism, name and analyze problems and difficulties, and clearly state their opinions in arguments." However, the desire for harmony and consensus among Tanzanians is still higher than in the West.

"Do you agree that aggression and emotions should not be shown?" Some (4) *Westerners* said that quite often it is not appropriate to show aggression and emotions. The majority (5) said that sometimes it is appropriate to show aggression and emotions. Only one person believes it is appropriate to show aggression and emotions. This question is challenging since some of the respondents would deal with aggression differently than with emotions. Showing aggression is usually inappropriate, whereas showing anger or emotions can be very appropriate.

The majority of *Tanzanian* respondents (5) said that it is never appropriate to show aggression or emotions. One said, quite often it is not appropriate to show aggression or emotions. A few (3) said that sometimes it is appropriate to show aggression or emotions. One person did not know the answer.

However, there may be occasions *when aggression and emotions may be ventilated at proper times and places* (question 5.5). The following answers were given by the *Westerners*: yes (6), quite often (3), sometimes (1). It seems there are certainly occasions when aggression and emotions may be appropriately ventilated.

It is interesting to note that in most Western societies, anger expressed publicly is unacceptable, and is considered inappropriate and embarrassing. Germany seems to be an exception, where anger simply shows a person's strong disagreement (Hersman 1995:185). Some Westerners may show their feelings of annoyance and hurt openly, especially when they are disappointed (Schroll-Machl 2003:58).

The following answers were given by the *Tanzanians*: yes (3), sometimes (1), not often (4), no (2).

No negative emotions should be expressed, as Mayer, Boness and Thomas (2003:91) point out: "In Tanzania it is not acceptable to express negative emotions in front of others, such as fury, anger, arrogance, or mockery."[245] The tone of voice tends to be self-controlled and shows respect. Often people

---

[245] Translated from the original German: Es gilt in Tansania als ungehörig, negativen Emotionen vor anderen freien Lauf zu lassen und beispielsweise Wut, Ärger, Arroganz oder Verhöhnung auszudrücken.

speak with a low voice. Emotions of temper, frustrations and anger are not necessarily shown (:15 & 23). Emotions are very much controlled. If they are expressed then only indirectly (:39). In this way, the atmosphere continues to be harmonic and without conflict, at least on the surface.

According to Hofstede (1997:84), Western countries tend to be *assertive*, whereas Tanzania is more *modest*. Thus, characteristics of a Western leader are assertiveness, decisiveness and aggressiveness (:94). Hofstede's description of people from an assertive society is partly consistent with what is presented in the literature and what can be observed in Western countries. According to my empirical findings, it seems that most Western countries are moderately assertive, positioned somewhere in the middle. There might be a shift in Western societies to become more modest. Since Tanzania is a collectivist society people tend to be more modest than assertive in comparison to Westerners. People and harmonic relationships play an important role.

However, a slightly different picture was presented when the respondents were asked: *"If you have a different opinion, is it important for you to keep face and be willing to submit for a certain purpose?"* The following answers were given by the *Western* respondents: always (1), quite often (4), sometimes (5). The answers suggest that the Germanic respondents are more willing than the Anglo-Saxons to express a different opinion. The *Tanzanian* respondents gave the following answers: always (2), quite often (1), not often (5), never (2). Especially the Tanzanian respondents who have a higher level of education expect to express their opinion. As we have seen above in the previous subsection on "Power and Leadership", these are also the ones who expect that their opinion is seriously considered and incorporated. Because of the strong group orientation in Tanzania, harmony and consensus are highly valued. Thus, to express a different opinion Tanzanians need to find an appropriate way in which to do it, so that harmony and good relations are sustained. This also means that people with more education and a sound biblical understanding of servant leadership expect the level of power distance to decrease.

Conflict has a lot to do with the way leaders *communicate*. Often conflict is caused by miscommunication. Thus, the interviewees were asked: *"What form should a leader's communication take?"* It is interesting to note that only one *Western* respondent expects a leader's communication to be direct, to the point, purposeful in relating and precise. The majority (7) of the respondents expect a leader's communication to be transparent and providing background information. Few (2) said, a good leader has various methods of communicating with others and always uses the one which is most appropriate to the situation. So Western leaders should communicate clearly and give enough information.

Different communication styles can cause conflict. Communication is a great indicator of whether societies are more affective than neutral. Western leaders communicate predominantly verbally on paper, through film and conversation (Trompenaars & Hampden-Turner 2002:74). They prefer written communication and agreements (Rodrigues 2001:326). The communication tends to be direct, precise, blunt, definitive and transparent (Trompenaars &

Chapter 4: Relationships, Power and Conflict in Western Leadership

Hampden-Turner 2002:100). Especially German leaders are well known for being very explicit and direct. According to Schroll-Machl (2003:47), "Professionally Germans communicate primarily objectively and stay on the task level". They are goal-oriented people who support their discussion contributions and arguments with facts (:48). This clear and straightforward communication style is considered to be the most honest, straightforward, authentic and a credible mode of conduct (:166). The Western communication pattern can be seen in figure 4.2 below.

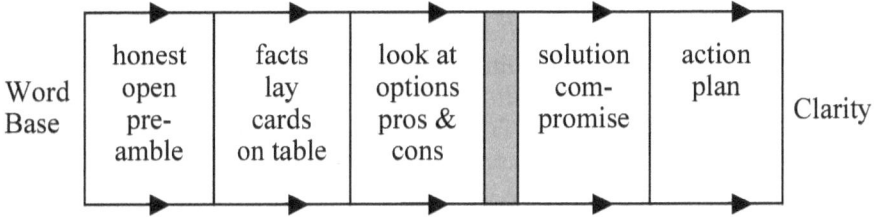

Figure 4.2 (adapted from Lewis 2003:99-102)

Leaders in the West look for facts and logic. They may ask a few questions for clarification. As soon as they think they have a clear picture, they prepare for debate and discussion. David Hesselgrave (1991:457), a North American Protestant missiologist, writes: "When it comes to communication, in full accord with our bias toward individualism, we Westerners expect open channels of communication in every direction…" The conversation can move quickly back and forth between two or more people. This style of verbal communication is shown in figure 4.3:

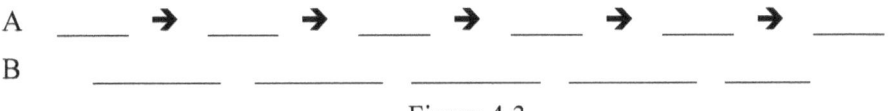

Figure 4.3

It can be observed that Western leaders tend to start talking before the other person has finished her/his sentence.

Some Western communication is *non-verbal*. In terms of non-verbal communication, in most European countries **handshaking** is quite common, while in the United States it is not. Westerners usually have close **eye contact** when they talk to each other. Interest is confirmed through eye contact (Trompenaars & Hampden-Turner 2002:76). Lack of eye contact suggests that the person is either not telling the truth, hiding something, is disrespectful or lacks self-confidence. On the other hand, if the eye contact is too long and intensive, it can be intimidating especially between men and women. Westerners like to have enough **personal space** around them. In a conversation, they usually sit opposite each other so that each person can see the other well. North Americans who are sitting in a large room feel most comfortable if the personal distance is about 5.5 feet (Maletzke 1996:62).

The majority (5) of *Tanzanian* respondents expect a leader's communication to be transparent and provide background information. Some (3) expect elaborative communication, giving examples. A few (2) expect direct, to the point, purposeful, and precise communication. Even though Tanzanian communication in reality tends to be more diffuse and indirect than that of Westerners, Tanzanians seem to appreciate a more direct and clear communication.

According to my observations, Tanzanian leaders prefer spoken communication and agreements. If a letter is written to someone in Tanzania, it is good either to deliver the letter personally and explain the content of it, or at least follow up the letter by phone. Communication among Tanzanians is more circular than linear. Since it is a diffuse and shame-oriented culture, people take much more time to get to the point and beat around the bush. "Diffuse communication styles are indirect – drop hints, and let the other interpret your full meaning" (Hampden-Turner & Trompenaars 2000:155). The other person is expected to be able to decode and interpret the message (:155). Sometimes this communication style can be perceived by Westerners as being evasive, slippery and full of euphemisms.

Tanzanians approach an issue from the general perspective towards the specifics. The general tendency is to look at relationships and connections before considering all the separate pieces. This has also to do with avoiding loss of face. The Tanzanian communication pattern can be seen in figure 4.4 below.

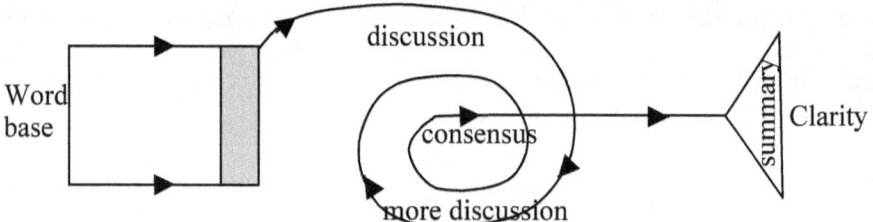

Figure 4.4 (adapted from Lewis 2003:99-102)

As we have seen above in the section on decision-making, a Tanzanian listens, confirms what the previous speakers said, and connects to it by adding another thought. Slowly the argument is shaped and reaches a consensus with which the whole group is comfortable. This discussion process allows for a continued harmonic atmosphere. It may well be possible that during the conversation there are times of silence when people think and reflect what has been said.

In a conversation or discussion, it is not polite to interrupt. In fact, a Tanzanian gives the other person time to finish her/his sentence and possibly waits a little while to digest what the other has been saying before s/he responds. This style of verbal communication is shown in figure 4.5.

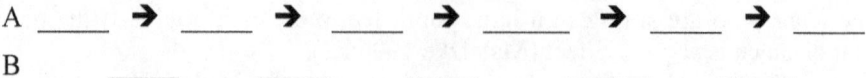

Figure 4.5

One waits until the other has finished the sentence. It is a sign of respect for the other person to take time to process the information without talking yourself.

Non-verbal communication is an important part in any society. It is essential to understand the non-verbal clues. If these are not understood, it can potentially lead to a communication breakdown in a partnership. In terms of non-verbal communication, in Tanzania **handshaking** as part of the greeting is very important and a must. To show somebody respect s/he is greeted by not only shaking hands but also supporting the right lower arm with the left hand while shaking hands.

Tanzanians usually do not have close **eye contact** when they talk to each other. Interest is confirmed through eye contact. In fact, they may stand or sit next to each other while talking, rather than opposite one another. Close eye contact, even between the same gender, can be intimidating.

If a person raises her/his **eyebrows** it may be an expression of agreement. I still remember when I asked one of my boys, who have so far spent most of their life in Tanzania, a question. After not having heard a response to my question, I asked him again. His reply was simply: "But Dad, I already told you." It took me a while until I realised that he said "yes" by lifting his eyebrows.

When a person visits at another's home and leaves, s/he must be **accompanied** to the next crossroad. If this is not done the host basically communicates the message to the visitor that s/he is not welcome again. At an office it is polite to take the person at least to the exit door or gate.

Non-verbal communication is a big part of Tanzanian's communication. Not understanding the non-verbal communication and being able to "read between the lines" can cause a tremendous amount of conflict. Thus, in cross-cultural collaboration, it is extremely important for Westerners to be able to understand the non-verbal communication of Tanzanian leaders and vice versa, since they can be significant indicators. The message of the body language may be very different from the spoken words.

The results of this research demonstrate that culture is interwoven in all aspects of leadership. From the empirical data and the literature, it becomes clear that there are major differences between the two leadership styles. These differences are mainly rooted in the different cultural values of the two societies.

Western organisations tend to be egalitarian. In contrast, Tanzanian organisations are more hierarchical. This impacts how leaders relate to their subordinates and vice versa. In practice, Western leaders exercise a more participatory leadership approach than Tanzanians.

As individualists Westerners are very much task oriented, whereas Tanzanians are strongly people oriented. This is reflected in the fact that Westerners expect clear goals and delegated responsibilities. Whereas Westerners are satisfied when these goals are achieved, Tanzanians stress the relationships. Tanzanian subordinates expect their leaders to understand their problems and help to solve them. Whereas Westerners focus on the end result, Tanzanians emphasise the process.

Whereas Westerners are time oriented, Tanzanians are event oriented. Both groups feel a tension between being people oriented versus time and task orientation. Whereas Tanzanians feel the tension between having good relationships and at the same time being more task and time oriented, Westerners would like to be more people oriented.

Tanzanians practise a large power distance with a strong hierarchy, whereas Westerners are much more egalitarian. For instance, in Tanzania committee decisions can be overruled by the leader. In the West delegates are truly empowered.

In the West status tends to be achieved. Traditionally, in Tanzania status is ascribed. However, it seems that there is a slow value shift taking place in Tanzania. These days status is not only ascribed but sometimes also achieved. This can be seen in the way women can earn respect through their achievements and therefore become leaders.

Generally, both groups consider power as good if used well. However, it seems to be easier to abuse power in Tanzania because status tends to be ascribed. In addition, the abuse of power increases when leaders are insecure.

As a collectivist society and because of their desire for harmony and consensus, Tanzanians are more modest than Westerners. The Western directness and assertiveness can easily create conflict. Whereas Westerners do conflict resolution on an individual basis, Tanzanians use a group process to restore relationships and harmony. This is also reflected in the different communication styles of the two groups.

Despite all these differences, it is also interesting to note that both groups try to avoid uncertainty as much as possible if they can. For Tanzanians this is much more difficult as they live in an environment where many things cannot be controlled and are unpredictable. However, they are better able to deal with uncertainty than Westerners.

Now that the two different leadership styles have been described and compared, we have a basis from which Westerners and Tanzanians can enter into a cross-cultural dialogue. Chapter five discusses how they view, perceive and assess each other's leadership and what they can learn from each other. In chapter five the information from chapters one, two, three and four is brought together. The two leadership styles are evaluated in light of the Bible, biblical norms and values, Christ-like character, kingdom leadership and the valid use of power. In a learning community, it is essential to ask the question what can Westerners learn from Tanzanian leaders and vice versa. Finally, the two leadership styles and their impact on partnerships in terms of challenges and hindrances are considered. I will also suggest ways in which to foster cross-cultural partnerships as a way forward into the future.

Chapter 5

A Christian-Ethical Dialogue and Evaluation of Western and Tanzanian Leadership Styles and their Impact on Cross-Cultural Partnerships

In the previous two chapters, the main features of Western and Tanzanian leadership have been described and compared. We have seen that Western and Tanzanian leadership is influenced by the leader's character, theology and culture. The ideal picture of a good Christian leader is similar in both societies. We have seen that there is a stark contrast between the ideal, expectations, theory and the actual practice. It appears that in many places the cultural values are more dominant than the biblical values. Westerners are faced with the challenge of moving towards a more Christian leadership style, especially in terms of practising love and mercy. Tanzanian leaders are challenged to be more just and faithful.

We have also seen that the major differences between the two leadership styles are cultural. This is reflected in the way leaders practise their relationships, exercise power and deal with conflict.

The main purpose of this last chapter is to identify what is merely Western or Tanzanian and what is essentially Christian in terms of leadership. How do the differences in leadership affect cross-cultural partnerships? What can leaders from different backgrounds in a cross-cultural setting learn from each other? What leadership behaviour needs to change in each society? In which ways can kingdom leadership be appropriately contextualized? From this dialogue, a composite picture of Christian leadership style may be drawn. The similarities and differences may help all the parties to see more clearly how the different leadership styles affect cross-cultural partnerships, so that practical steps can be taken to foster healthier collaboration.

In what follows, first, Westerners and Tanzanians enter into a cross-cultural dialogue. From the responses during the interviews, Tanzanians present their view of Western leadership and vice versa. They assess each other's strengths and weaknesses. Furthermore, as a group they discuss their views of each other's leadership style and how they understand Christian leadership. The results of this discussion are presented below. Second, the two leadership styles are evaluated, the cultural contexts taken into consideration, applying the biblical values and virtues and kingdom leadership as discussed in chapter one. Third, through this dialogue the cultural chains can be unlocked and we will be able to discover what is merely Western or Tanzanian and what essentially Christian. The discussion of what both groups can learn from each other may result in a better understanding of what Christian leadership can look like. Finally, we will look at how the differences of the two leadership styles affect cross-cultural relationships and how they can be overcome to foster collaboration so that partnerships become healthier and more fruitful.

5.1 A Dialogue about Western and Tanzanian Leadership Styles

As we have seen earlier in chapters three and four, there are similarities and differences between Western and Tanzanian leadership. To see these similarities and differences more clearly, a cross-cultural dialogue is helpful. Both groups' understanding of Christian leadership is culturally biased. Through a dialogue, it can be identified which leadership aspects are merely Western and which are Tanzanian and what is essentially Christian. Each group may have some biblical understanding and practice from which a synthesis can be drawn. This will lead to a better understanding of Christian-ethical leadership. To facilitate such a dialogue, a group discussion was conducted, as explained in chapter two as part of the methodology.

5.1.1 Differences between Western and Tanzanian Leadership

The interviewees were asked: *"Do you think there are any differences in Western and Tanzanian leadership styles?"* The majority of *Westerners* believe that there are differences in the two leadership styles, as their answers indicate: yes (4), quite often (5), no (1). Leader 6 believes "that different styles of leadership exist but that they are all practised within Tanzanian and Western contexts by different individuals". Thus, he does not think there are specific differences between Western and Tanzanian leadership. The *Tanzanians* responded to this question as follows: yes (2), quite often (4), sometimes (3), not often (1). It is interesting to note that the responses by the Tanzanians were more differentiated than the Westerners. The clear response by the Westerners did not surprise me. But, I would have expected that Tanzanians see more differences. Maybe it is because the Tanzanian respondents see only a small window of Western leadership, whereas the Westerners are fully emerged in the Tanzanian culture and thus experience the differences more strongly.

"What are these differences?" The *Western* respondents pointed out the following differences. "The ... [Western] leaders I know would prefer a more *egalitarian* style, whereas African leaders more often refer to a more *hierarchical* style of leadership" (Leader 1) [my emphasis]. The egalitarian and hierarchical values are reflected in the behaviour that, whereas "Westerners ask for volunteers for committees, [Tanzanians] assign people to committees without asking first" (Lay Leader 1). The difference between *ascribed* and *achieved* leadership was pointed out by several respondents (Leader 7, 8 & 9). Leader 7 describes well how these different values are reflected in the leadership behaviour: "A Tanzanian leader is seen as the holder of the power and energy in a certain system, s/he is powerful, has to be respected and s/he is looked up to. A Western leader is seen as a capable, well informed and educated expert, who has insights and can help to ensure a project reaches its goals" (Leader 7). "Western leaders tend to want the highest quality people around them; Tanzanian leaders prefer their friends and family" (Leader 5). Westerners also *plan* differently than Tanzanians, as Leader 4 observes: "We

are together as a committee to prepare for a big meeting. I would like to see a timetable and plan of the meeting developing. My Tanzanian co-members use a lot of time talking about life, family, what has happened and our organisation." What Leader 4 experienced is also echoed by Leader 8: "Western leadership tends to be *time* and *product* focused, Tanzanian tends to be *relationship* focused (the point of the meeting is to get together to share ideas, not necessarily come to conclusions)" [my emphasis]. Leader 3 mentioned the *democratic process* in the West versus *consensus building* in Tanzania, and *formal* discussion style in Tanzania versus *informal* discussion style in the West. Lay Leader 1 says, whereas "Westerners [practise] *private* church discipline, [Tanzanians] exercise *public* church discipline" [my emphasis]. This suggests a difference of individualism versus collectivism.

The *Tanzanian* respondents mentioned the following differences of the two leadership styles. "If the wife is ill, Africans would like to care for her all the time. Westerners would give her in someone else's care so that he can continue to work" (Leader 1).[246] "Many African leaders have a relation with the employees. But Western leaders relate to their work" (Leader 2).[247] This suggests that whereas Tanzanians are *people oriented*, Westerners are *task oriented*. As we have seen in chapter four, Leader 7 points out the difference between *hierarchy* and *egalitarian* values, when he says: "Western leadership does not very much respect position. Position is something normal. But in our context position is important."[248] These different values are reflected in the following example, as Leader 7 continues:

> Many Western leaders have a different relation with their workers. They do not keep her/him very distant. ... You cannot know who is of lower rank and who is of higher rank. But we [Tanzanians] make a difference. In some churches, the pastor eats alone and the bishop eats alone. You cannot mix them. I have seen in some houses where house workers eat together with the missionary at the same table.[249]

Another difference is that "Western leaders have a plan for the whole year. But for us Africans it is possible that we even do not have a work plan for the day" (Leader 3).[250] This means that Westerners have a different *time orienta-*

---

[246] Translated from the original Swahili: Kwa waafrika mke anapokuwa mgonjwa wangependa wamtunze wakati wote. Wazungu wangependa kumkabidhi mtu mwingine ili yeye aendelee na kazi.

[247] Translated from the original Swahili: Viongozi wa kiafrika walio wengi wana uhusiano na wafanyakazi. Lakini viongozi wa kimagharibi wanahusiana na kazi.

[248] Translated from the original Swahili: Uongozi wa kizungu hawajali sana cheo. Cheo kwao ni kitu cha kawaida. Lakini katika mazingira yetu cheo ni muhimu.

[249] Translated from the original Swahili: Viongozi wengi wa kimagharibi uhusiano wao na wafanyakazi wao wa chini ni tofauti. Mfanyakazi hawamwoni hawamweki mbali sana. ... Huwezi kujua nani mdogo na nani mkubwa. Lakini kwetu hapa tofauti ipo. Katika kanisa lingine mchungaji anakula peke yake na askofu peke yake. Huwezi kuwachanganya. Nimeona katika nyumba zingine watumishi wa ndani wanakula pamoja na mmissionari kwenye meza.

[250] Translated from the original Swahili: Wenzetu wazungu katika uongozi ni kwamba kiongozi anakuwa na utaratibu wa kazi ndani ya mwaka tena. Lakini kwa sisi waafrika inawezekana hata taratibu za kutenda kazi kwa siku hatunazo bado.

tion than Tanzanians, as Leader 3 continues: "Westerners respect time more than we [Tanzanians] do."[251] As we have seen in the previous chapter four, whereas Westerners have a long-term and sequential time orientation, Tanzanians are event oriented. Even though Tanzanians may not plan a lot, it seems that Tanzanian Christian leaders have a strong *commitment* to their ministry, as Leader 3 observes: "If you look at [Tanzanian] church workers, their whole life is only ministry oriented. To the point when s/he forgets the family. Then the family becomes a problem. S/he continues to go and evangelize and preach. So s/he does not respect the family. But you, our [Western] colleagues, give the family priority".[252]

During the group discussion, the Westerners pointed out that this perception of the Tanzanians has to do with the fact that Westerners are time and task oriented. They separate task and family. Because it is very stressful to live and work in a foreign culture, Westerners finish their work on time and retreat back to their families as their comfort zone, whereas Tanzanians are comfortable in the wider community. Over the years I have noticed that Tanzanians invest a lot of their time in ministry, make many sacrifices and the family has a lower priority. According to the Tanzanian participants in the group discussion, people may have different motivations to do so. Some may be truly spiritually motivated. But others also do it out of personal interest. They may hope to gain more prestige and get material benefit. I have also observed that the new generation of missionaries gives a higher priority to the family than the earlier missionaries. People realise that the family is part of the ministry. That does not necessarily mean they are less committed to their ministry, which the following example demonstrates. Somehow Tanzanian Leader 3 contradicts himself saying: "You [Westerners] are faithful looking after a project. You work hard, but we Africans we are only a few who are faithful."[253] I find it strange that Tanzanians have such a commitment to their ministry and at the same time they are not faithful in a certain project. Most likely it has something to do with the question of ownership. One is committed and responsible for what s/he owns. But the Tanzanian participants also said frankly during the group discussion that unfortunately many Tanzanians are motivated by economic considerations or seeking personal benefits, as Leader 2 says: "It's all business these days – all about money. If they attend a workshop, you have to give people money. It's not easy to involve people in something without paying them money. If you see they are doing evangelistic business – the motivation is money!"

---

[251] Translated from the original Swahili: Ni kwamba wenzetu nyinyi katika uongozi mnajali muda zaidi kuliko sisi.

[252] Translated from the original Swahili: Hata ukiangalia watumishi kwa upande wa kanisa kuna wengine yaani maisha yake yote yameelekea kwenye huduma tu. Amesahau mpaka familia. Sasa familia inapata shida. Yeye anaendelea kwenda na uinjilisti na kuhubiri. Kwa hiyo hajali hata familia. Lakini wenzetu nyinyi ni kwamba familia vilevile mmempa kipao mbele kwa nafasi yake.

[253] Translated from the original Swahili: Vilevile mmekuwa waaminifu katika kutunza miradi, kama ni kitu chochote ni kwamba mnajitahidi sana kutenda ile kazi lakini sisi waafrika ni wachache tu ambao ni waaminifu katika hilo.

A number of Tanzanian respondents also pointed out the difference in *communication*. "You [Westerners] are used to calling a spade a spade. We go around.[254] You [Westerners] go straight to the point, we [Tanzanians] don't. You don't care what people say. We do. ... They [Tanzanians] are afraid to tell the truth because they do not want to hurt the other" (Leader 6).[255] Saying one thing and meaning something else also happens with agreements: "Tanzanians have a law but we do not follow it. A person can do something different even if you have agreed" (Lay Leader 3).[256] According to Trompenaars and Hampden-Turner (2002:48 & 101), this is a reflection of particularism and diffuseness. Even though the intention of the indirect communication style sometimes may be good, in my view more often it has negative effects. The respondents really appreciate and value the benefits of direct communication as practised by Westerners. Tanzanian Lay Leader 2 believes another difference in leadership style is that Tanzanians are more open and share more easily their plans and money matters than Westerners. This observation is in contrast to the earlier example in which church leaders use church offerings for their own personal benefits. It is also in contrast with the direct and open communication of Westerners. What Lay Leader 2 refers to is that when money is donated, Westerners tend not to be as transparent about its use as Tanzanians. This is true from my observations. I think Westerners may be more careful not to create jealousy and raise unnecessary expectations. It may also have to do with the different values of individualism versus collectivism.

The following chart is a synthesis of the differences between the two leadership styles derived from the data in chapters three, four and five.

---

[254] Translated from the original Swahili: Sisi tunazunguka hivi.
[255] Translated from the original Swahili: Sisi tunajali. ... Wanaogopa kusema ukweli, kwa sababu ya kuogopa kumwumiza mtu.
[256] Translated from the original Swahili: Watanzania wana sheria lakini hatufuatilii. Mtu anaweza kuamua kugeuza tu hata kama mmekubaliana.

LEADERSHIP DIFFERENCES OF THE TWO GROUPS	
WEST	TANZANIA
Egalitarian	Hierarchical
Achieved status	Ascribed status
Task and time oriented	People and event oriented
Long-term oriented	Short-term oriented
Democratic process	Consensus building
Informal discussion style	Formal discussion style
Private church discipline	Public church discipline
Division of work and leisure time	Holistic life style
Faithful	Unfaithful
Direct communication	Indirect communication
Not transparent with money issues but with travel intentions and plans	Transparent with money issues but not with travel intentions and plans

Figure 5.1

In this summary it is interesting to note that most differences refer to cultural values. Only a few Christian values and virtues such as transparency and faithfulness, which were only mentioned by Tanzanians, refer to a leader's character.

5.1.2 Christ-like Leadership in the West and in Tanzania

Some differences and similarities were also mentioned when the two questions from the questionnaire about character and the practice of biblical values were asked: *"How are these features of Christ-like character expressed in the West and in Tanzania? How do Western and Tanzanian Christian leaders practise the biblical values of love, justice, mercy, faithfulness and humility in their ministry? Comment on any similarities and differences."* These two questions are closely connected. Thus, I treat them together. First, the Tanzanian view of Western leadership is presented and then, in turn, Westerners comment on their experience of Tanzanian leadership.

During the interviews, a number of *Tanzanian* respondents (Leader 1, 3, 4, Lay Leader 1 & 2) said that there are similarities between the two leadership styles because "both European countries and Tanzania have taken many things from the Bible" (Leader 1).[257] In fact, there should not be much differ-

---

[257] Translated from the original Swahili: Nchi za Ulaya na nchi ya Tanzania zote zimechukua mambo mengi kutoka Biblia.

ence "because we all live under the Word of God" (Leader 3).[258] However, there are some differences in practice because of different cultures (Leader 1, 2, 3, 5 & Lay Leader 1). "Sometimes it is difficult to differentiate between Christian and Western [leadership]" (Leader 2).[259] However, Tanzanians perceive Westerners has having little *love*, as Leader 1 observes:

> Christian love is translated with helping each other if you have a problem. Culturally this is different for Westerners. Africans consider this as love if a visitor can come at any time without any notice and stay over night. This is different for a Westerner until you tell her/him. For this reason others say: "This Westerner is a very bad person. If you go to her/him you cannot stay over night." But this is your culture.[260]

Because of their individualism, Westerners are very independent and often expect the same from others. Consequently they are perceived as unloving. Leader 2 also expresses helping each other as an expression of love:

> Western leadership, as I perceive it, you very much respect the capability of doing a job than helping a person in her/his work. That means Western leadership wants a person to do the work alone. S/he should have the ability to do the work. Whereas African leadership can give a person work with the purpose of helping her/him without considering her/his working abilities. If you trust her/him you help her/him.[261]

This basically means for Westerners work is more important than the person, which Tanzanians perceive as a lack of love. But it does not mean that Westerners do not practise love at all, as Leader 5 observes:

> Others give. They share with the poor. S/he does not buy nice things for her/his home but uses the money for the poor. Instead s/he gives the money to educate children at school who are not her/his own without even knowing them. S/he treats people who are sick. Or just think, s/he comes from a good home, a good country and comes to Tanzania where there is dust and all the rest and illnesses. S/he sacrifices her/his life for other people.[262]

---

[258] Translated from the original Swahili: ... kwa sababu wote tunaishi chini ya Neno la Mungu ...
[259] Translated from the original Swahili: Wakati mwingine kutenganisha kati ya ukristo na umagharibi ni vigumu.
[260] Translated from the original Swahili: Upendo wa kikristo unatafsiriwa kama njia ya kusaidiana ukiwa na shida. Kiutamaduni ni tofauti kwa wazungu. ... Kwa waafrika hii wanaona ni upendo kwamba mgeni anaweza kuja wakati wowote bila taarifa yoyote na kulala. Kwa mzungu ni tofauti. Ni mpaka umwambie. Kwa maana hiyo wale wengine wanasema: "Huyu yule mzungu mbaya sana. Ukienda kwake huwezi kulala?" Lakini kumbe ni kiutamaduni wenu.
[261] Translated from the original Swahili: Uongozi wa kimagharibi una kwa mtazamo wangu mimi kwamba unajali sana uwezo wa kutenda kazi kuliko kufikiri mtu kama mtu kutaka kumsaidia katika kazi. Yaani uongozi wa magharibi unataka mtu afanye kazi mwenyewe. Awe na uwezo kufanya kazi. Wakati wa uongozi wa kiafrika anaweza kumweka mtu katika kazi kwa maana tu anataka kumsaidia bila kujali uwezo wa kazi kama ukimwamini unamsaidia.
[262] Translated from the original Swahili: Wengine ni watoaji. Wanashiriki na maskini. Anaweza kuacha tu kabisa kununua vitu vizuri nyumbani kwake akatumia fedha yake kwa ajili ya masikini kabisa. Akawapa akaweza asomeshe watoto shule ambao sio wa kwake wala hawajui. Akawatibu watu wanaoumwa. Au unachukua tu anatoka nyumbani kwao kuzuri, nchi yake ni

So not all Westerners have little or no love. But Tanzanians perceive them as generally having little love for other people. This may have to do with the fact that Westerners are not as people-oriented as Tanzanians, but more task-oriented.

As a result of having little love, sometimes Tanzanians perceive Westerners as having very little *mercy*, as Leader 1 observes: "For example, we had a missionary. ... If you make a mistake he says, this is the end of your job forever. At this very hour. He has no grace time to explain her/him: 'If you continue like this you will lose your job.' But he says: 'No work anymore'."[263] Westerners can be very strict when you do not follow the system that is in place. According to my own experience and observations, it is true that for many Westerners, it is important to play by the rules. This has to do with the value of universalism.

In terms of being *faithful* to God, Tanzanian Leader 3 observes that Westerners do not fear God as much: "People [Westerners] respect money more than God which is different in Africa."[264] However in terms of money, Tanzanians believe that Westerners are more faithful than Africans: "I have been really happy to see how Westerners deal with money. Because if money comes in and they will be told this is for a specific purpose, it will be done. It will be used for this work" (Leader 5).[265]

Leader 4 makes a positive observation of how Westerners practise *humility*, as he testifies:

> I see [Western] pastors serving people food, for instance, when I studied at college. The principal, when his pastoral group is on duty to serve in the dining hall, he himself dresses in a way to carry things to the kitchen. He shares completely. We are sitting on our chairs. My principal comes to serve us. When I finish he comes to clear the table. He clears it. When the time comes to bring desert, he comes to serve us. Afterwards he washes the dishes. When he finishes, he puts the dishes away at their place. It is not only he but also the whole staff. But it is not that that they must do it. They are just willing to do that. Here I have really seen that they follow Jesus Christ.[266]

---

nzuri na anakuja hapa Tanzania kuna vumbi kuna kila kitu kuna magonjwa. Anatoa maisha yake kwa watu wengine.

[263] Translated from the original Swahili: Kwa mfano tulikuwa na mmissionari mmoja. ... Ukikosea anasema kazi kwisha kwa milele. Saa ileile. Hana grace time kumwambia: "Ukiendelea hivi utakosa kazi." Lakini anasema: "Kazi hapana."

[264] Translated from the original Swahili: Watu wanaheshimu sana pesa kuliko kumheshimu Mungu ambayo ni tofauti na sisi huko Afrika.

[265] Translated from the original Swahili: Lakini Wazungu kweli nimefurahi ni namna wanavyofanya kazi kwa kutumia fedha. Kwa sababu kama itaingia fedha na wataambiwa hii ni kwa ajili ya kitu fulani yatafanyika. Itatumika kwa ajili ya kazi ile.

[266] Translated from the original Swahili: Ninawaona wachungaji wakihudumia watu vyakula, kwa mfano niliposoma college. Mkuu wa chuo kama ni zamu ya pastoral group yake kuongoza katika mambo ya kuserve in the dining na yeye mwenyewe anavaa nguo ile ya kubeba vitu jikoni. Anagawa kabisa. Sisi tunakaa kwenye viti. Principal wangu amekuwa anakuja kutuhudumia. Mimi ninamaliza anakuja kuchukua. Anapeleka. Ikifika tena wakati wa kuleta desert tena anakuja kutuhudumia. Halafu anaosha vyombo kule ndani. Akimaliza anaweka vyombo

However, Westerners seem to have a problem with hierarchy: "Many Westerners when they see the environment of respecting elders, let's say submission, to submit to leaders, to submit to those who are higher in rank, to submit to leadership as the Bible teaches it, they see it as a law" (Leader 7).[267] Tanzanian Leader 7 continues to challenge the concept of servant leadership and its practice in the West: "It is true, servant leadership is preached a lot. But if you really look at it in the Western countries especially at leadership, it is like everyone is her/his own boss."[268] This again is a reflection of the high value of individualism in the West.

The *Western* respondents experience Tanzanian leadership as follows. Positive and negative examples were mentioned. Leader 9 shares the example of a Tanzanian pastor who reflects a Christ-like character humbly serving God and his people:

> What he does is, living like the people around him, but still being able to do extra things for his people, always an open house, not eating when his people cannot eat, being there whenever there is some one ill, never using any money for his own, unless it's needed and he will always involve the church elders in making decisions, but because he has such a vision, he will still lead them through the decision making.

This Tanzanian pastor truly exercises the biblical values of love, justice, mercy, humility and faithfulness. It was expressed by Westerners how important relationships and the value of *love* for Tanzanian leaders are: "Good [Tanzanian] leaders often take a personal interest in the people and even their families" (Leader 1). Leader 7 observes:

> A Tanzanian leader will always make her/his people feel cared for. S/he will try to help them in any way possible to meet their personal needs in terms of "school fees, housing, etc." for her/his team members. … S/he will always try to be available and s/he will not react in anger or in a way that people know they are disturbing him.

Theses examples suggest again that Westerners perceive Tanzanian leaders as people who consider people more important than work or plans. Western Leader 8 also gives an excellent example on how *justice* is exercised in Tanzania in terms of disciplining a staff member for professional misconduct:

> At a general staff meeting, the head of school talks about the offence in general terms, about its effects and why it is wrong. No one is named. Letters of warning may be given, but they are a general warning that is issued to all staff. A personal discussion may follow if the situation is

---

katika sehemu yake. Siyo yeye tu lakini staff wote. Lakini si kwamba sheria inawalazimisha. They are just willing to do that. … Hapa nimeona kabisa wanamfuata Yesu Kristo.

[267] Translated from the original Swahili: Wazungu wengi wanapoona ile hali ya kuheshimu wazee tuseme utii, kutii viongozi, kutii walio wakubwa, kutii uongozi ambao Biblia inatufundisha, wao wanaona ni kama sheria.

[268] Translated from the original Swahili: Kweli unahubiriwa sana servant leadership. Lakini ukiangalia hali halisi katika nchi za magharibi uongozi hasa yaani kila mtu ni kama boss of himself.

not resolved. Dismissal is rare. People are moved to a different place or given a different job.

This kind of behaviour seems to be typical for a shame-oriented society like Tanzania. By issuing a general warning, nobody loses face. Mercy prevails over justice. However, there are also other Tanzanian Christian leaders who address wrong behaviour directly and exercise justice openly, as Western Lay Leader 1 observes: "Some Tanzanian pastors I can think of do not shy away from confronting members of the congregation who are involved in a particular sin and therefore do well at speaking harsh words when necessary." It seems that some Tanzanian churches address wrong behaviour and implement discipline, especially in the rural areas, whereas others let *mercy* prevail over justice, as Leader 3 observes:

> Also, in Tanzania, leaders often let mercy over-ride justice. They will let grievous sins go unpunished by the church as long as the person says, "Please forgive me". ... But yet the minister constantly steals or misuses money specifically given to the church for a specific purpose. Other ministers know of the situation but yet say "We should forgive him, because the Bible tells us to forgive".

Some Westerners are disappointed regarding the level of *faithfulness* in Tanzanian leadership, as expressed by Leader 2:

> Integrity is a huge issue in the Tanzanian Church, temptations might be too many and the level of frustration with people one is responsible for too high. Fortunately there are some exceptions! It has been very disappointing for me though, to discover in many instances that the façade and good words would not hold what looked so promising.

In terms of *humility*, Western Leader 2 argues: "A Tanzanian bishop would hardly adopt the model of servant-leadership for himself. People probably would be confused if he did so." However, Leader 2 presents a different picture at the lower Tanzanian leadership level: "Tanzanian Christian leaders at the intermediate leadership levels are often very humble people, more so than we Westerners, I believe" because "humility grows (at least partly) through humiliation". This dissonance between different leadership levels may have to do with the fact that middle leaders exercise humility in the hope that one day they may be promoted. Once they receive a certain top position and the level of power and authority increases, their attitude may change. Thus, they may pretend humility which is again consistent with what Western Leader 3 observes when he challenges the kind of humility practised by Tanzanians: "In Tanzania, leaders are expected to appear humble and not 'rise' above other people. But this is not necessarily a heart value, but rather the perception of humility is important." However, there are also other Tanzanian Christian leaders who practise true humility that comes from the heart, as Leader 5 observes: "In Tanzania, a servant-heart can be expressed through feeding the poor; prayfulness always by praying for others no matter the circumstance; courage and empathy by battling corruption and listening to others". Humility is also expressed as a Tanzanian leader "will talk quietly not using loud words, because s/he does not want to show her/his influence and power by a forceful speech. ... S/he will not demand respect, but when people give it to her/him, s/he knows that s/he deserves it" (Leader 7).

It is difficult to present a general picture, because the respondents recognise that there are Western and Tanzanian Christian leaders who practise biblical values and others do not or they express it in a culturally different way. From the comparison of both leadership styles and the dialogue, the biblical values of love, justice, mercy, faithfulness and humility can be **prioritized** in the following order:

PRIORITIZED VALUES OF BOTH GROUPS	
WEST	TANZANIA
1. Justice	1. Love
2. Faithfulness	2. Mercy
3. Humility	3. Humility
4. Love	4. Faithfulness
5. Mercy	5. Justice

Figure 5.2

During the group discussion, each group prioritized the biblical values as presented above. Ideally the Westerners would put love at the top because they know it is important. But they admitted that in reality love is not practised so much. The Westerners and Tanzanians perceive the practice of the biblical values of each other in the same way as they were prioritized. The Tanzanians agreed: "We don't talk about justice." Western Leader 8 observes: "Often here in Tanzania it seems to me 'we are forgiven, therefore there are no consequences'." The Tanzanians replied: "Damages need to be tackled. The guilty one has to pay a goat and they have to eat together." "This is part one of the reconciliation. This is important. It is rebuilding the relationship but is not exercising justice." It is interesting that for Tanzanians the relationship overrides justice, whereas a Westerner would like to have seen compensation for the fault made. The Tanzanians challenged the Westerners really to practise love: "Westerners speak of love, but we practise it. We need to see emotions and actions to show love." I was also astonished about what one Tanzanian said in terms of how humility prevails over faithfulness in Tanzania: "I am prepared to lie to you as long as I practise humility." It seems that Tanzanians define humility from a cultural perspective. Humility is shown by the appropriate behaviour, which is an external rather than an internal humility. But if humility has to do with truthfulness and putting the other first, then an external humility is false. The Tanzanians agreed that faithfulness is a challenge for them, which they can learn from Westerners. However, they also said: "There are areas, where Africans are faithful. They are less faithful with time, material things and moral issues. As an African I am agreeing, because I don't want to hurt you. For us saying something directly is very difficult." From this dialogue it becomes clear that **the biblical values are strongly influenced by cultural values**. The value of justice and faithfulness is high in the West because of individualism. Love and mercy are low because people are not as important as they are in Tanzania. The opposite of cultural values in both societies is reflected in the different priorities of the biblical values.

How the biblical values are practised or not practised in the two societies is to a certain extent also an expression of how people understand good Christian leadership. During the group discussion, all the participants agreed that good Christian leadership as described by both groups in chapter three is an ideal that is impossible for one single person to fulfil. The Westerners noted that Tanzanians mainly consider a good Christian leader one who loves people, whereas having a vision is not as important. From a Western perspective "this is not a good leader at all, because this leader is not leading towards a goal", as one Western participant said. The Western leaders realised that they often did well in reaching a goal, but failed in the relation part. The difference between Christian and non-Christian leadership is "Christian leaders do not to put the goals above the relationships", says Western Leader 8. Tanzanian Leader 2 points out that the key to being a good leader in Tanzania is to have good relationships: "People can say about a bishop that he is not a good Christian, but he loves people. An African leader should first of all care about people."

When asked, *"Why is there such a dissonance between the ideal and actual practice?"* the participants responded that it is mainly because of our human nature and sinfulness. "This is human, that everybody has an ideal picture. Practice is hard because of the environment, [and] the motivation of a leader ..." (Leader 8). Other reasons were mentioned by the Tanzanians, such as the examples set by colonialists who, for example, had a driver and kept some distance from the people. On the other hand, from the discussion it appears that Tanzanians do not perceive such a big dissonance between servant leaders versus the leader as king; humility versus status symbols; accountability versus avoiding criticizing leaders; participatory leadership versus leaders who are expected to make decisions. The reasons are that they expect a leader to come from within their own group. The leader must know the environment, how people live and what their problems are. Then people will follow the leader. So participatory leadership for a Tanzanian means that the leader lives with the people and therefore is trusted and has credibility to lead. Because the leader participates in the community, s/he knows the problems of the people and can, therefore, make the appropriate decisions, which people accept and follow. As long as the Tanzanian leader touches base from time to time to build relationships, a certain distance and status symbols are accepted without any problems. The key to this whole issue is that Tanzanians define themselves in the relationship to others. In other words, they define themselves by **who they are**, whereas Westerners define themselves by **what they do**. Therefore, Tanzanians do not perceive this dissonance as long as the leader has a good relationship with them, as a Tanzanian participant says: "For it is not what you are doing that makes you a leader, but who you are!"

Other questions addressed during the group discussion were: *"Why is power exercised in different ways? Which is the dominant experience – positive or negative experience of power?"* It is interesting that Tanzanians view power generally as good, whereas Westerners are more suspicious of power. But then on the other hand, the Tanzanian dominant experience of power is changing and becoming more negative. More and more leaders are insecure and live in fear. Therefore they misuse power. Tanzanian Leader 2 says, in the past "Leaders used to be born leaders. Now you can get it with money!" Another Tanzanian participant adds: "Twenty years past [during the *ujamaa*-period] people were satisfied and not ambitious. Now they are ambitious and therefore there is more abuse of power." In other words, people find different ways and means, such as money, education or relationships, to get into leadership positions, whereas in the past people were leaders because of their good character. It seems that because abuse of power in the past was not a big issue among Christian leaders, today there are hardly any means to hinder power abuse. Whereas in the West many safeguards are employed in order not to give one person too much power to avoid the abuse of power. This may be a result of negative experience in the past. Thus, today the dominant experience of power from a Tanzanian perspective is positive.

The empirical data and the literature suggest that in some areas, there is not much difference between the Church and the secular world. Thus, the question was asked in the group *"Is the Church any different? Why not?"* From the responses given, even though love, mercy and relationships are valued, a key issue is that in fact we do not have Christian communities with strong personal relationships. Therefore, the Church is weak. In Africa, individualism is growing. So leaders are increasingly looking out for themselves. It seems that there is a change of values slowly taking place. Other reasons are that we cannot resist the cultural values and temptations, and also lack of spiritual leadership. This may be due to lack of moral and spiritual character formation.

If the Church is not much different then the question is *"How can bad leadership in terms of character and culture be changed?"* One of the Tanzanian participants made the point saying: "Christianity has been swallowed by the world. Efforts of Christianity are very clear. If we commit ourselves and stand firm, a lot of transformation can be made." In other words, Christians must have the courage to act and behave differently according to biblical values to be light and salt in this world. It was also noted that outside pressure and persecution purifies the Church, because there is no personal gain for Christian leaders in such a situation. The other important step is to address the issue of insecurity of leaders by sound discipleship and biblical teaching so that leaders not only understand that they are sons and daughters of God, but also experience his unconditional love.

5.1.3 Strengths and Weaknesses of Western and Tanzanian Leadership

Both leadership styles have strengths and weaknesses. As part of the dialogue, the interviewees were asked: *"How would you assess the strengths and weaknesses of Western and Tanzanian leadership?"* First, the strengths and weaknesses of Western leadership from a Western perspective and then from a Tanzanian perspective are presented. Following this, the strengths and weaknesses of Tanzanian leadership from a Tanzania perspective are presented and then from a Western perspective. Finally, the different strengths and weaknesses of Western and Tanzanian leadership are synthesized in a combined list to see the similarities and differences.

5.1.3.1   Strengths and Weaknesses of Western Leadership from a Western Perspective

According to the Western respondents, the *strengths* of Western leadership are: "Effective, clear, often with good examples from the leader himself" (Leader 1); "future minded, strategic towards success or fulfilment of goals" (Leader 4), "purpose driven" (Leader 5); "proactive" (Leader 3); "performance oriented" (Leader 8) and "high achievement" (Leader 9). Leader 7 points out that a Western leader "is as long in her/his position as s/he proves to be a good capable leader in order that the project moves towards its goals. S/he is constantly challenged to change and improve her/his skills." A number of respondents (Leader 3, 5 & 9) have emphasised the importance of accountability for Western leaders: "Leaders give account of their actions and decisions to those they are immediately responsible for" (Leader 8). It is interesting to note that most of the positive aspects mentioned are focused on achievement. Only a few strengths are about relationships such as "being facilitative, looking at development of the team people" (Leader 9), "providing followers opportunities for growth" (Leader 2), and "communication [and] caring for individuals" (Lay Leader 1).

One of the main *weaknesses* of Western leadership is that the task prevails over the person, as the majority of Western respondents (Leader 1, 3, 4, 5, 7 & 8) recognise: "[Western] leaders often tend to 'meet the bottom line' at all costs – no matter who gets hurt along the way" (Leader 5). However, it was also mentioned that some leaders are "too much worrying about being tactful" (Lay Leader 1). Sometimes leaders are not recognised as leaders because "Devolution of responsibility can result in the leader being seen to be doing not very much" (Leader 8) or "Leaders are often not highly respected" (Leader 5).

5.1.3.2   Strengths and Weaknesses of Western Leadership from a Tanzanian Perspective

According to the Tanzanian respondents, Western leaders have the following strengths and weaknesses. A Western leader is a leader because of her/his leadership qualities (Leader 6). "Westerners believe very much in themselves"[269] (Leader 6), which gives them a lot of self-confidence. "They [Westerners] have skilled manpower. ... The strength of Westerners is the work effort"

---
[269] Translated from the original Swahili: Wazungu wanajiamini sana.

(Leader 2)".[270] On the other hand, Leader 2 points out that this can also be a weakness since the work prevails over the person: "Western weakness is there where they do not respect a person like a person. When they only see her/his work that s/he does."[271] As a result, "They are not very relational. Not being relational means they are not very sympathetic" (Leader 6).[272] However, Leader 4 makes a different observation: "The strength of Western leadership in the church that I have seen is the love for people and to give people the freedom to express their thoughts. ... And the leader tries to know what their needs are and s/he ensures that they go where they want".[273] "Westerners have the strength to plan and use their time well" (Leader 5).[274] It is true that Westerners do a lot of planning. But there are also weaknesses related to planning because they either plan too far ahead or have difficulties changing their plan. "They look far ahead. And the view of a Tanzanian is short. So there is a weakness if you want to help this person to enable her/him you cannot plan very far" (Lay Leader 2).[275] "Westerners have the weakness of not changing the plan. They are faithful with money"[276] (Leader 5), but on the other hand, "they also want to assess themselves" [277] (Leader 1). Western leaders set an example, as Lay Leader 1 shares: "If a Westerner works s/he is close to the employees. Even though respect is there s/he works together with them. By doing so together, the work will be done well. Because s/he explains and sets an example how to do the work."[278] The closeness of Western leaders to their followers can be a strength but also a weakness, as Leader 7 points out: "A person can feel at home and forget totally that s/he is employed. S/he forgets her/his borders."[279] Leader 7 criticises the egalitarian value of Western leadership: "Western leadership is very useless here in Tanzania. Such leadership is useless because of our culture here. ... With such a leadership, it is very easy for a person to get used to losing the respect that is very important to keep

---

[270] Translated from the original Swahili: Nguvu ya wazungu ni bidii ya kazi.
[271] Translated from the original Swahili: Kwa wazungu udhaifu unatokea pale ambapo wanapokosa kumjali mtu kama mtu. Wanapojali tu kazi yake anayofanya.
[272] Translated from the original Swahili: Hawana utu sana. Kukosa utu maana yake ni they are not very sympathetic.
[273] Translated from the original Swahili: Nguvu ya uongozi wa kizungu kanisani ambayo nimeona nguvu yao ni kwamba ni upendo kwa watu na kuwapa watu uhuru wa kutoa mawazo. ... Naye kiongozi anajaribu kujua mahitaji yao ni nini na anahakisha anakwenda wanavyotaka.
[274] Translated from the original Swahili: Wazungu wana nguvu ya kufanya mpango na kutumia muda wao vizuri.
[275] Translated from the original Swahili: Wao wako mbali kwa mtazamo wa mbali. Na huyu mtanzania mtazamo wake ni mfupi. Kwa hiyo udhaifu vilevile upo kwamba kumsaidia huyu kumwezesha huwezi kupiga picha ya mbali sana.
[276] Translated from the original Swahili: Wazungu wana udhaifu wa kubadilisha mpango. Wazungu ni waaminifu na fedha.
[277] Translated from the original Swahili: Pia wao wanataka kujitathmini wenyewe.
[278] Translated from the original Swahili: Kwa mzungu akifanya kazi anakuwa karibu na wafanyakazi. Ingawa heshima inakuwepo ingawa anafanya kazi pamoja. Kwa hilo kama anafanya nao pamoja maana yake kazi itafanyika vizuri. Kwa sababu anawaelekeza anakaa nao pamoja kwa kuwaonyesha mifano anafanya kwanza anatangulia mbele.
[279] Translated from the original Swahili: Mtu anaweza kuelewa kama mtu wa nyumbani akajisahau kabisa kwamba ameajiriwa. Akasahau mipaka yake.

here."[280] In terms of communication, "They [Westerners] say it directly. And if s/he says it, s/he says really what s/he feels" (Leader 1).[281] "Westerners study a lot" (Lay Leader 3).[282] On the other hand, "They have not learned the African culture" (Leader 1).[283] Some Western leaders do not consider the context and environment in which Tanzanians live (Leader 2). The assessment of Western leadership shows that the Tanzanian respondents have different perceptions and experiences with Westerners. It also demonstrates that not all Western leaders are the same.

5.1.3.3 Strengths and Weaknesses of Tanzanian Leadership from a Tanzanian Perspective

How do the Tanzanian respondents assess their own leadership? They see the *strengths* of Tanzanian leadership as follows. A number of respondents (Leader 2, 5 & 6) emphasised the importance of people: "Tanzanians respect very much people. If a person comes unexpectedly s/he can change her/his plan and listens to the person's problem" (Leader 5).[284] "The Tanzanians' strength is that they can create an environment to motivate a person. That means to help her/him to give her/him an environment to work" (Leader 2).[285] This means paying not only the normal salary but also additional benefits such as housing, travel allowance and school fees. "They [also] hold meetings and decide together" (Leader 1).[286] Leader 7 points out another strength: "The Tanzanians' strength is s/he understands her/his environment from the beginning. Therefore, even if s/he grows up s/he understands that this is how things are."[287]

However, the Tanzanian respondents recognise that their leadership also has *weaknesses*. A number of respondents mentioned the problems that can result from a strong hierarchy and authoritarian leadership. "Weakness is there because the leader is at the top and behaves differently so that s/he [the follower] agrees easily to submit quickly because they will fear her/him. So things move forward, but the subordinate also does it because s/he fears, not because s/he

---

[280] Translated from the original Swahili: Uongozi wa kizungu haufai sana hapa kwetu. Uongozi wa aina hiyo unaweza usifae sana kulingana na utamaduni wa hapa ulivyo. ... Ila kwa uongozi wa aina hiyo ni rahisi sana hapa mtu kuwa na mazoea mpaka kupoteza heshima ile ya ambayo hapa ni muhimu sana ile heshima kuitunza.
[281] Translated from the original Swahili: Wanasema moja kwa moja. Na akisema anasema kweli yale aliyosikia.
[282] Translated from the original Swahili: Wazungu wanasoma sana.
[283] Translated from the original Swahili: Hawajajifunza mila za kiafrika.
[284] Translated from the original Swahili: Watanzania wanajali sana watu. Kama mtu anafika kwake ghafla anaweza kubadilisha mpango wake na kusikiliza shida za mtu.
[285] Translated from the original Swahili: Watanzania nguvu waliyonayo wanaweza kutengeneza mazingira ya kummotivate mtu. Kwa maana ya kumsaidia kumpa mazingira ya kufanya kazi.
[286] Translated from the original Swahili: Wanashirikisha vikao na kuamua mambo katika vikao kwa pamoja.
[287] Translated from the original Swahili: Nguvu ya watanzania mtu anaelewa katika mazingira yake tangu mapema. Kwa hiyo hata akikua anaelewa kwamba hivyo mambo ndivyo yalivyo.

knows what s/he is doing" (Lay Leader 1).[288] "A weakness is that we push people.[289] You pull and you push people to a place you like, to the direction you like" (Leader 4). "Sometimes they do not cooperate with the people. S/he can decide something without discussing it" (Leader 1).[290] "Our leadership often makes a lot of differences until we separate people and they feel degraded. Like at church if a person is together with an evangelist s/he does not eat with the pastors or bishops. You feel I am only a small person all the time. Now s/he does not have the freedom to share her/his thoughts or make a contribution" (Leader 7).[291] Even though the leader is in charge in some places, "If you have been employed, you can do what you want" (Leader 2).[292] This is consistent with what Western Leader 2 observed above that Tanzanian leaders sometimes are not consistent in executing regulating powers. A concern related to indirect communication has also been raised as a weakness: "Many Africans do not communicate directly. They are beating around the bush" (Leader 1).[293] Also "Tanzanians have the weakness not to plan their time well. ... Another weakness is how they handle money" (Leader 5).[294] "There are preferences, if the leader is from a certain ethnic group, many people will be from this group" (Leader 6).[295] "Another Tanzanian weakness is in terms of education. ... There is little knowledge" (Lay Leader 2).[296]

5.1.3.4 Strengths and Weaknesses of Tanzanian Leadership from a Western Perspective

How do Westerners see the strengths and weaknesses of Tanzanian leadership? Most Western respondents (Leader 1, 2, 4, 5, 7 & 8) emphasised people orientation as a *strength* of Tanzanian leadership. Tanzanian leaders care for people, as Leader 7 puts it: "My own responsibility is in the hands of somebody who cares for me." "[Tanzanian] leaders focus on relationships in decision-making" (Leader 5) and are "considering the whole group, society,

---

[288] Translated from the original Swahili: Udhaifu kwa sababu [kiongozi] akiwa juu atakuwa na tofauti ili amsaidie yeye na kukubali kirahisi. Kutii haraka kwa sababu watakuwa wanamwogopa. Kwa yale mambo yanakwenda, lakini pia huyu wa chini anafanya kwa sababu anaogopa sio kwa sababu anajua kile anachofanya.

[289] Translated from the original Swahili: Udhaifu ni tunawaburuza watu.

[290] Translated from the original Swahili: Mara nyingine hawashirikishi watu. Anaweza kuamua jambo bila kushirikisha.

[291] Translated from the original Swahili: Na sisi ni uongozi wetu unaweka sana hii tuseme unatofautisha sana mara nyingi tunawatenga watu kujisikia wanyonge pia. Kama kanisani mtu akiwa mwinjilisti hali na wachungaji na maaskofu. Unasikia mimi ni mdogo tu siku zote. Sasa hawezi kuwa na uhuru sana kutoa mawazo yake na kuchangia hoja.

[292] Translated from the original Swahili: Ukishaajiriwa sasa unaweza kufanya unavyotaka.

[293] Translated from the original Swahili: Kwa waafrika wengi hawaendi moja kwa moja. Halafu wanazunguka na mambo.

[294] Translated from the original Swahili: Watanzania wana udhaifu wa kupanga muda wao vizuri. ... Udhaifu mwingine ni jinsi ya kutunza fedha.

[295] Translated from the original Swahili: Kuna upendeleo, kama kiongozi ni wa kabila fulani basi watu wa kabila hili watakuwa wengi sana.

[296] Translated from the original Swahili: Udhaifu mwingine wa kitanzania ni upande wa elimu. ... Unakuta ujuzi ni mdogo.

church as a whole" (Leader 4), which means "time is less important than the process" (Leader 8). "Consensus and agreement are more important than the final decision" (Leader 8). "[Tanzanian] leaders are highly respected among their constituents" (Leader 5). "If the leader is good, s/he can achieve a lot, without asking too many questions" (Leader 7). A Tanzanian leader "tends to honour tradition" (Leader 3). Because of their group and shame orientation "people can keep their face" (Leader 2).

A number of Western respondents (Leader 1, 2 & 3) consider it as *weakness* that Tanzanian leaders put their own personal interests above the others' interest. In terms of authority and accountability the respondents raise the following concerns: "Those in authority have too much autonomy" (Leader 3). "[Tanzanian] leaders are often not held accountable for their actions" (Leader 5). They are "more vulnerable to corruption" (Leader 2) and not "consistent in executing regulating powers" (Leader 4). In terms of decision-making Tanzanian "leaders can be influenced easily resulting in poor choices or decisions" (Leader 5). "Decisions can be weakened or not made because not everyone agrees, [thus] progress forward can be slow" (Leader 8). As a result "a lot of 'work time' can be lost to meetings without the 'real job' being done" (Leader 8). Sometimes they are "depending too much on opinion and money from outsiders" (Leader 4). As a follower, "I am not asked and my opinion does not count either" (Leader 7). Consequently "if a leader is not good, everything is completely stuck" (Leader 7). Other weaknesses are "lack of communication [and] not treating church members as individuals" (Lay Leader 1).

The following figure 5.3 is a synthesis drawn from the assessment of both leadership styles.

	STRENGTHS AND WEAKNESSES OF BOTH GROUPS	
	WEST	TANZANIA
Strength	<ul><li>Leader because of leadership qualities</li><li>Self-confidence</li><li>Skilled man power</li><li>Achievement</li><li>Caring for people</li><li>Freedom to express thoughts</li><li>Knows needs of followers</li><li>Planning</li><li>Accountability</li><li>Close relationship with employees</li><li>Direct communication</li><li>Education</li><li>Facilitation</li><li>Helping people to grow</li></ul>	<ul><li>People orientation</li><li>Process is more important than time</li><li>Leaders are highly respected</li><li>Traditions are honoured</li><li>Can keep face</li><li>Being dogmatic when it is needed</li><li>Consensus oriented</li><li>Knowing environment</li></ul>

Weaknesses	• Task prevails over persons • Plan too far ahead • Difficulties in changing plan • Want to assess themselves • Not recognizing hierarchy • Little respect for leaders • Not learning the African culture and understanding the context	• Personal interests prevail over group interests • Hierarchical, authoritarian • Dependence on leader • Little accountability • Decision-making easily influenced • Little achievement • Vulnerable to corruption • Not consistent in executing regulating powers • Dependency on outsiders • Indirect and lack of communication • Not treating church members as individuals • Blind submission • Little time orientation • Preference for own ethnic group • Little education

Figure 5.3

In terms of strengths and weakness, the major differences between Westerners and Tanzanians are task versus people orientation, direct versus indirect communication, equality versus hierarchy. Every strength usually has a weakness. As both groups perceive the strengths and weaknesses of each other and also recognise their own strengths and weaknesses, they realise that it is important to have the right balance. During the group discussion, the question was asked: *"How can leaders from the West and Tanzania draw on the strengths rather than the weaknesses of their cultural paradigms and model recognisably Christian leadership in their contexts?"* From the discussion, this seems to be a real challenge because of the cultural pressure. A Christian is expected to be faithful, but "If I say something about another person, s/he would be kicked out of the job. S/he would lose the job and the relationship with her/him would be destroyed. The system does not do it and helps to be faithful. The system is rotten, therefore there is no use of being faithful", says Tanzanian Leader 2. Western Leader 8 says: "It is hard for a Westerner to learn from a Tanzanian, because issues are not talked about. Unless we read about it, we are not told and do culturally the wrong things." According to the participants during the group discussion, there seems to be very little that can be done other than having a cultural orientation for both groups, learning to read each other's body language, accepting the differences and apologizing if necessary. I do not find this solution very satisfying. Because, as discussed in chapter one (1.3 Christian Leadership, the Gospel and Culture) God is not only above but also through and in culture, I do believe that there are positive elements in each culture on which we can build and learn from each other such as Westerners expressing their love and visiting people or Tanzanians being good stewards in terms of handling money and possessions. Through this joint learning process, moral and spiritual formation can take place.

5.2 An Evaluation of Western and Tanzanian Leadership Styles in the Light of the Bible

As discussed in chapter one, it is the responsibility of Christian ethics not only to describe and understand the context and analyse the two leadership styles, but also evaluate them and propose possible practical action steps to promote change, liberation, salvation and transformation. "Christians believe that what is good is determined by the will of God, not by culture. The goal of ethics is not cultural conformity but transformation into the likeness of Christ" (Adeney 1995:15). As the Western and Tanzanian leadership styles are evaluated in light of biblical values and virtues, kingdom leadership and biblical use of power, the cultural context needs to be kept in mind. The aim of this Christian-ethical evaluation is to discover the positive aspects and also to identify the negative aspects of culture and unlock the cultural chains so that Christian transformational culture change can take place.

As the two leadership styles are evaluated, it is important to keep in mind that these are only patterns. Not all members of a culture will believe and react similarly. Within certain patterns or tendencies, individual personality and character still manifests itself (Lane *et al* 2000:29). As both leadership styles are evaluated, I will look at the main features of character, relationships, power and conflict. These features are key to leadership because they influence a leader's behaviour. A leader's character influences her/his leadership style. Leaders relate a lot to people. They exercise power on a daily basis and often need to deal with conflict situations.

5.2.1 A Christian-ethical Evaluation

In terms of *character*, the way Westerners ideally expect a good Christian leader to be seems very balanced between being people and task oriented. In reality, the task prevails over the relationship. Tanzanians emphasise the loving relationship a leader should have, listening and giving direction. For Jesus, it was important to have good, close and loving personal relationships with people, but he never lost sight of the task he had to accomplish. It is encouraging to see that both groups focus on the loving and serving attributes as being important and essential for a good Christian leader to have. These values are at the heart of a Christ-like character, as discussed in chapter one.

However, in both societies there is a gap between the ideal and actual practice. Westerners do well in being just and faithful. They recognise the importance of love and talk a lot about it. But often they do not always practise it in how they relate to others. Western leaders are challenged to demonstrate their love by visiting people, expressing a sincere interest in the personal life of others and showing affection (1 John 3:16+18). Because justice is such a high value in the West, there is very little mercy. This is influenced by the high value of individualism. Western leaders very much see what is right or wrong without necessarily considering the consequences for the relationship or the other person. On the other hand, because Tanzanians emphasise the value of love and mercy, they are much more concerned about the relationship and the consequences than what is right or wrong. Even though love is **the** core value in the Scripture, it seems to be a little overemphasised by Tanzanians whereas justice and faithfulness are lacking. What is required is a better balance of these values. Whereas Tanzanians are challenged to exercise justice and faithfulness, Westerners need to learn to value the other person more and practise love and mercy.

In terms of humility, both groups do need to continue to learn what it truly means to be a humble servant leader.[297] I have the impression that humility in Tanzania is very much an external cultural behaviour to show respect. Hence, it may be perceived as superficial. At the same time there is a huge gap between leaders and followers, which makes it difficult for a leader to show humility. On the other hand, Western leaders are expected to practise humility in such a way that sometimes they cannot lead anymore. Any picture has its difficulties. But turning the triangle or pyramid (see chapter 3 / section 3.3.1 Christ-Like Leadership) upside down in my view is not biblical because then the leader has little authority. The authority rests mainly with the followers. Thus, in my view the picture of a wheel with spokes is closer to the biblical image of servanthood. The leader is on the same level as the others. But because s/he is in the centre s/he still has the needed authority, which can be delegated from the centre to the edges. Whereas the triangle only reflects **servanthood**, the wheel with spokes is an image of **servant leadership**. The challenge for Western leaders is to exercise their authority as leaders in a humble way. Tanzanian leaders need to find ways to reduce the gap between them and their subordinates without losing respect. Margot Morrell and Stephanie Capparell (2001) point this out in their book *Shackleton's Way*. Chapter three is entitled "Creating a spirit of camaraderie". Only joining the ship in Buenos Aires, Sir Ernest Shackleton had to work hard to overcome divisions and laxness that had developed during the journey to Buenos Aires. He worked hard to set a routine and clarify each person's abilities. Most importantly was: "Everyone did not have exactly equal status, but each was valued equally and treated with equal respect … the resulting trust and camaraderie served them well in the more difficult times ahead … what counted was a man's proficiency" (Morrell & Capparell 2001:91-92). Status and responsibility may be different, but the humanity of each person is still important as we are all created in God's image.

Whereas in the West, task is more important than relationship, in Tanzania the relationship prevails over the task. Neither is sufficient alone. There ought to be a balance. For Jesus both the relationship and the task were equally important.

---

[297] In his book *Cross-Cultural Servanthood* Elmer (2006) describes the process and the challenges of how to implement servanthood in a cross-cultural context.

God is a God of community, which is reflected in the trinity. As Christians we are put together in community. We only function well as a **whole** body, not as separate pieces. At the same time from the very beginning God has had a vision. He wants everybody to have an intimate, personal relationship with him. So Jesus came with a mission to save and transform people. He had a mission and task to accomplish. Thus, whereas Westerners are asked to become more relational and people oriented, Tanzanians should not forget about the task that needs to be done, which is part of practising good stewardship. To become more people oriented for Westerners means, in fact, that they would be perceived as more loving and merciful. Part of this is that Westerners should value people as people instead of viewing relationships as instrumental. For Westerners, love is expressed in the task through deeds not just words. But emotions and relationships are also needed, not just the mind and deeds. As we have seen in chapter four, what someone does affects the level of trust in a relationship no matter in which society. To balance the relationship and the task is probably a big challenge for both groups, because it is at the heart of people's worldview.

Power is core to leadership. Because there is such a large power distance in Tanzania, certain groups within the society with less education, and women and children are oppressed. Once one reaches a leadership position of power, it is easy to misuse it. Some Tanzanian leaders misuse it because they try to protect their position and also seek personal benefits, whether it is in terms of status or economics. As discussed in chapter one, in the section on "Leadership and Power", the Whiteheads speak of five different faces of power. Tanzanian leaders emphasise power *on* and *over* others. In other words, they have a lot of autonomy and exercise their authority over others, with little accountability in some cases. I believe generally hierarchy is valid. Each society must have a structure in order to function. Exercising power over someone is needed in organisational leadership, as status and responsibility may be different. But the dignity of each person must be valued as we are all created in God's image. As we have seen in chapter one, leaders are also given power *for* others, to build them up. Jesus also shared his power *with* the disciples. He empowered them. That way followers experience mutuality and collaboration. Tanzanian leaders are at times afraid of sharing and delegating power and authority because they may lose their power. But partly it is also because followers expect a Tanzanian leader to exercise her/his authority. So for Tanzanian leaders to change, it is important that the expectations of subordinates also change and that they are willing to receive some authority and take responsibility for what they do. Power is not a private possession that only a few leaders have. It must be shared with others in an appropriate way, as Christ did. In many cases, Tanzanian subordinates are in a dependent relationship to their superiors. What is required is an interdependent relationship between them, which reflects a good level of maturity on both parts. Tanzanians also have to learn to exercise power *against* others so that people are liberated from evil and oppression. This is a real challenge for them because of their strong desire for harmony. In terms of authority and accountability, it seems there is a gap among Tanzanian leaders. This is also influenced by the low value of being faithful. Because relationship is so important, the value of harmony and love take in ethical terms the role of *prima facie* over the actual duty of faithfulness and honesty. Thus, if a relative is in desperate need, s/he must be helped even if the accounting is not absolutely accurate anymore. This cannot be, because from a biblical point of view leaders are expected to be good stewards. The other question is: Is this really love? Christians are asked to speak the truth in a spirit of love (Ephesians 4:15); love and truth ought not to be separated.

Westerners are strong in exercising power *on, over, against, for* and *with* others. This is easier for them because of being assertive and egalitarian. Western leaders exercise *power over* followers, give clear instructions and expect them to be carried out. If necessary and appropriate, they are also willing to confront people and take the consequences. They demonstrate adult competence, having personal esteem and exercising accountability. Westerners have a very tight accountability system, which is a reflection of their high value of faithfulness and justice, and also checks and balances in their cultural systems of politics and economics. If anything goes wrong it must have consequences; there is very little mercy, if any at all. The challenge for Westerners sometimes is that sharing *power with* subordinates is stressed too much. Western followers criticise and question their leaders very easily. In chapter one, it was argued that Jesus was the master and friend of the disciples. There is a place for a leader to consult with her/his subordinates. But there are also times when leaders must be able to make decisions without discussing everything, as Jesus did. There is certainly a place where leaders can and must be challenged in appropriate ways as part of the accountability system. But followers also need to understand and recognise that leaders have been given a position of authority, which must be respected.

Regarding *conflict* there is no one biblical way of dealing with conflict, as was discussed in chapter one. Jesus dealt with conflict both individually and in a group. Conflict can be a result of using power against someone. Because of their individualism Westerners deal with conflict rather on an individual basis than as a group. Tanzanians, on the other hand, because of their group orientation, prefer a mediator and expect a public act of repentance and reconciliation. Because of their strong desire for harmony, Tanzanians usually do not show anger or emotions. However, as we saw in chapter one how Jesus dealt with conflict, there is a place to show anger and emotion as long as this furthers the kingdom of God.

Cultural values must be challenged in both societies by biblical values because Christ transforms culture. In the life of a Christian leader, cultural values should not dominate biblical values. However, leaders can build on the positive cultural aspects to express biblical values, because God is in culture and works through culture, as argued in chapter one. At this point, it is important to consider practical steps in order to move forward so that true change and spiritual transformation can take place.

5.2.2 Practical Action Steps Forward

As can be seen from the description, comparison, dialogue and evaluation of the two leadership styles, culture seems to be dominant and has a strong influence on leadership behaviour. The theology and character of leaders is influenced by culture. Christian leaders from both societies have a biblical understanding of Christian leadership, which is biased by their culture. However, we have seen a lot of contradiction and dissonance between the ideal picture of Christ-like leadership and the actual practice in reality. This is because of the sinful nature of human beings. Christian leaders struggle in the same way as the apostle Paul (Romans 7:15-24), being in a constant battle of putting biblical knowledge into practice and implementing it day by day.

The first step in seeing leadership behaviour transformed is to **recognise and repent of** the negative aspects of cultural influence and bad character. Transformation begins with sincere repentance from the heart, as it is written in 2 Chronicles 7:14: "[I]f they pray to me and repent and turn away from the evil they have been doing, then I will hear them in heaven, forgive their sins, and make their land prosperous again." It is also important to be willing to let one's theology be challenged through an open dialogue.

Secondly, because character significantly influences leadership as it was argued in chapter one, the whole area of **spiritual and moral character formation** must be seriously considered. Leaders with a good moral character are more likely to lead well, resist temptations and have the courage to act against negative cultural values if they are in conflict with the Scriptures. To address bad leadership, character and behaviour and to challenge cultural values it is important for leaders to grow in their *spiritual maturity*. Spiritual maturity is a key aspect of a Christian leader's character. As we have seen in chapter one under the section on "Christian Leadership and Character Formation", spiritual maturity develops through spiritual formation. Whereas Westerners may need to emphasise spiritual formation in community where leaders are encouraged and critiqued by others, Tanzanian leaders need to stress the individual reflection so that the value of experience leads to ongoing changed leadership behaviour. Spiritual formation and maturity are essential for the moral character formation of a Christian leader. Spiritual formation takes place when the biblical values become the major grid through which one views culture. The Whiteheads (2003:74) describe this process in the following beautiful way: "To be seasoned as a Christian is to have the values of Jesus Christ seep all the way into us. No longer an external authority or set of rules, these values have been internalized and personalized. They have become us." The values of Jesus become part of a Christian. The *first* step to spiritual maturity is to recognise and accept who we are. God loves and accepts us as we are. This does not mean that a person does not need to change her/his life-style and become more mature. But self-acceptance is the beginning of a lifelong process. The *second* step is to take responsibility for who we are. It is easy for Christian leaders to blame culture, history, early missionaries or colonialists, who certainly had an influence on the leadership style. However, Magesa points out:

> Something is seriously wrong in the African Church if it is not ready and courageous enough to own up its own sinful history in this continent. One of its own sources of grace, the sacrament of Penance/Reconciliation, calls it to repent its past silences and doublespeak with regard to the slave trade, slavery, African religiosity, colonialism and neo-colonialism (2002:109).

Everyone has at least to take part of the responsibility for who they are. If people accept who they are, they feel secure, content and confident. Because they accept themselves, they are more ready to accept others as well. Any interpersonal relations begin with the self. The *third* step is to be willing to change and to be transformed through the Holy Spirit. This kind of spiritual maturity will influence the shape and direction of any collaboration. Spiritual maturity affects the relationships how people lead and work together in community. Sofield and Juliano (1987:67) put it like this: "When people are able to share faith, they usually experience a corresponding ability to work more collaboratively with one another." In other words, it enables people to deal with differences, tensions, misunderstandings and conflicts in an appropriate way. The Christian faith provides a tremendous foundation for people coming from different cultures like the West and Tanzania to share their lives and work together.

For spiritual formation and lasting change to take place, it is essential that people have access to the Bible in a language they understand best, love it and engage with it so that their lives can be transformed through the Holy Spirit (Scripture Impact Initiative 2004). In his research David Barrett (in Sanneh 1989:188), a Protestant missions researcher from the UK, identifies with great consistency the transformational impact that vernacular Scriptures have in a society. A few African theologians like Mbiti (1986:31) have recognised the importance of Bible translation into vernacular languages for the spiritual growth of Christians. Quarshie, a theologian from Ghana, argues:

> Biblical studies can, in effect, help to shape the use of the Bible and thereby those who use it on the African continent. The best way that Biblical Studies can do this – reaching most people on the continent in terms of numbers and in terms of psychological appeal – **is through working with the mother-tongue Scriptures** (2002:9). [my emphasis]

He (:12) continues: "Maximum use of the insights from mother-tongue Scriptures can be facilitated by the promotion of the use of the mother tongue at all levels of church life". Bible translation truly facilitates the contextualization of theology in Africa. Quarshie claims, to see true spiritual transformation in Tanzanian leaders,

> Africans must hear God speak to them in their own mother tongues, addressing their felt needs. For this to be achieved, the discipline of Biblical Studies has to be holistic in its study of mother-tongue Scriptures. **It must locate itself in the world-view of the mother tongue and its culture**, and must be guided by a desire to respond to the pressing needs of the African context (2002:13). [my emphasis]

From Kinoti's research and mine, it seems that some African traditional values and virtues, such as humanness, compassion, care, understanding, empathy, sharing and hospitality, honesty, truthfulness, humility and solidarity, are fading away. It is important for Tanzanian leaders to go back to their roots and discover their traditional values because "It is probably for its own survival and well-being that traditional society took pains to encourage its members to cultivate certain personality values. In traditional society certain personality characteristics were known to enhance community well-being and others not to" (Kinoti 1997:115). Nthamburi (2003:110) says: "The Church is constantly being reminded that it must overcome alienation from the vital forces of spirituality in its traditional heritage. Our traditional morality must inform our Christianity in order to regenerate our true spiritual anchor." "In Africa in general, the institution of the clan may be said to be the best expression of Jesus' commitment to egalitarian social relations" (Magesa 2002:81). Thus, Magesa (:81) suggests: "The clan may, consequently, be taken as a paradigm for relations within the Church and especially for Church government." Tanzanian Christian leaders recognise the gap between ideal Christlike leadership and actual practice. This is an important first step because it means hope for positive change and transformation, as Kinoti points out:

> [T]here is hope precisely because Africans are unhappy about their state of national and personal morality. There is hope because Africans are becoming self-critical and anxious to find solutions to their moral problems. There is hope because thinking Africans are realizing that they can only answer to the name *African*. There is hope because the rural majority is still close to the principles which guided the morality of past generations. There is hope because the African is still religious and in the mysticism of the East the African has to assert [her/]his authentic identity. There is hope because the African ear is sharp to hear the Good News of Jesus Christ amid the deafening voices of the contemporary world. ... There is hope in what the Church can do in calling Africans to maintain what is good in their culture for their integrity (2003:80-81). [her emphasis]

Another important step in changing the values of a community and consequently bad leadership behaviour, it is necessary to **raise the level of education**. Oppressive structures and behaviour can much better be maintained in societies like Tanzania where the level of education is generally lower than in the West. The educational system in Tanzania where "Instead of communicating, the teacher issues communiqués and makes deposits which the students patiently receive, memorize and repeat" (Freire 1993:72), sustains such oppression, which the Brazilian educator Paulo Freire (1993:71-86) calls the "banking" concept of education. To liberate people from oppressive structures and leadership behaviour, banking education must be changed into problem–posing education because:

> Banking education resists dialogue; problem-posing education regards dialogue as indispensable to the act of cognition which unveils reality. Banking education treats students as objects of assistance; problem-posing education makes them critical thinkers. Banking education in-

hibits creativity and domesticates (although it cannot completely destroy) the *intentionality* of consciousness by isolating consciousness from the world, thereby denying people their ontological and historical vocation of becoming more fully human. Problem-posing education bases itself on creativity and stimulates true reflection and action upon reality, thereby responding to the vocation of persons as beings who are authentic only when engaged in inquiry and creative transformation (Freire 1993:83-84). [his emphasis]

As we have seen from the interviews, the Tanzanian respondents with a higher level of education were much more critical than the others. So the way of thinking is slowly changing in Tanzania. However, if we want to see good and steady progress, more radical steps need to be introduced. Another effective way to increase the level of education is through a bilingual education system in which for the first three years children are taught in their mother tongue and then there is a transition into Swahili. "[R]esearch has shown that learners learn best in their mother tongue as a prelude to and complement of bilingual education approaches" (UNESCO 2003:6). Education is not just a matter of teaching in schools but also at church. "The pastor is not just a spiritual shepherd, he is also a teacher. As the good shepherd leads his flock to green pastures, so should a priest lead [her/]his congregation towards a better life on earth" (Mugambi 1989:111).

Not only formal but also informal education can change leadership behaviour. Living and working in a cross-cultural situation has great potential and offers many opportunities to question ones own values and learn from the other. Thus, an ongoing dialogue between leaders from the West and Tanzania provides such a learning environment, as argued earlier in chapter one. An important contribution for this to happen is that **Westerners living and working in Tanzania are willing to immerse themselves in Tanzanian society** as much as possible. To make this possible they need to balance their workload so that they have enough time and energy to visit Tanzanians at home and get involved in the local community and churches. That way Westerners will be able to gain better language proficiency and understanding of the environment and culture in which Tanzanians live. This practice would have a tremendous impact in terms of building close relationships and working together in a healthy way.

So far we have been looking at the questions: What does a true Christian-ethical leadership style look like and how do you get there? What leadership behaviour needs to change in each society? In the next section, the following question is considered: In what ways can kingdom leadership be appropriately contextualized?

5.3 Towards a Christian Leadership Style

Both leadership styles have strengths and weaknesses. Thus, it is obvious that there is great potential for Westerners and Tanzanians to learn from each other through dialogue. Western leaders can learn certain things from Tanzanians and Tanzanian leaders can learn from Westerners, which Freire

(1993:83-84) calls a "problem-posing education". Through this exchange of learning experiences a learning community is created that will facilitate a progress towards a more Christian leadership style in both societies, which reflects the biblical values and virtues more truly. Western and Tanzanian leaders are called to follow the footsteps of Jesus and authentically practise kingdom leadership using their authority and power biblically.

5.3.1 What can Westerners learn from Tanzanian Leaders?

"Can Western leaders learn from Tanzanians? If yes, what can they learn?" Basically, all respondents believe that Westerners can learn from Tanzanians. The *Western* respondents answered as follows: yes (9), sometimes (1). The *Tanzanian* responses were not as clear: yes (5), quite often (3), sometimes (1), not often (1). I was positively surprised that the majority of Western respondents believe they can learn from Tanzanians. This demonstrates a healthy attitude towards people from a different culture. The more differentiated answers by the Tanzanians suggest that they perceive Westerners as being in certain respects more advanced.

When asked, *"What do you think Westerners can learn from Tanzanians?"* the *Westerners* emphasised the value of people: "respect for others" (Leader 9), "to have more interest in the person they are working with" (Leader 1); "to be more considerate towards the staff and Christians in the church" (Leader 4); concern for others (Leader 8); being "sociable" (Leader 2); "people are more important than tasks" (Leader 7). Western Leader 7 says: "I think we can learn that we can trust somebody [a leader] and honour somebody and even submit to somebody". The importance of maintaining good relationships was mentioned by several respondents (Leader 2, 4, 5 & 9). "They [Westerners] should also learn when to say something and when to keep quite in order to keep harmony and discipline" (Leader 4). A number of respondents (Leader 6, 8 & 9) mentioned patience. "Tanzanians can teach Westerners how to do much with very little. They have built their country peacefully in the midst of wars, poverty, and famines" (Leader 6). "Westerns can learn the value of actually spending time discussing process rather than product" (Leader 8).

The *Tanzanian* respondents believe Western leaders can learn the following from them: "generosity" (Leader 6)[298], "humility" (Lay Leader 1 & 3)[299], "love" (Lay Leader 1)[300], "respect, ...[and] relationships" (Lay Leader 3)[301]. Leader 1 and Lay Leader 2 emphasised the importance for Westerners to learn the language and context in which Tanzanians live. "You as a Westerner should learn the Swahili language" (Leader 1).[302] I have seen a number of missionaries who are not proficient in Swahili, the national language of Tanzania. They have difficulties in communicating well. The importance of having good relationships with people has been mentioned by the majority of

---

[298] Translated from the original Swahili: ukarimu
[299] Translated from the original Swahili: ... unyenyekevu.
[300] Translated from the original Swahili: Upendo
[301] Translated from the original Swahili: Swala la heshima,... mambo ya binadamu
[302] Translated from the original Swahili: Wewe kama ni mzungu ujifunze lugha ya Kiswahili.

respondents (Leader 2, 3, 4, 5 6, Lay Leader 2 & 3). "A Westerner can learn from Tanzanians the value of people. S/he can also learn to accept a person the way s/he is and help her/him from where s/he is to move her/him forward" (Leader 2).[303] "Westerners can learn to respect a person more if s/he visits without having it planned" (Leader 5).[304] Western leaders can also learn how to exercise their authority, as Leader 7 puts it: "How to supervise the work well. ... For example, how to guard authority to protect the position."[305] "Then for Westerners it is important to learn more perseverance" (Leader 5).[306]

It is encouraging to see that there is agreement between both groups about what Westerners can learn from Tanzanians. The common features that Westerners can learn from Tanzanians are: To be more people and relationship oriented and loving, to be humble and show respect, to exercise authority, patience and perseverance. The responses suggest that the most important thing for Western leaders to learn is to be **more people oriented** since this is an **expression of love and mercy**.

Learning means changing attitudes and behaviour. The interviewees were asked: *"What kind of changes would you like to see in terms of Western leadership?"* Basically, the *Western* respondents would like to see a number of changes regarding their own leadership, which are related to the above. They want to learn humility and respect, caring for others, and patience. In addition, the Western respondents would like to see "more interest in raising others" (Leader 1) and less abuse of power (Leader 6). Leader 4 "would like to see Westerners in Tanzania being able to think more Tanzanian (walk in someone else's shoes)".

The *Tanzanian* respondents would like to see some additional changes regarding Western leadership. Western leaders should be transparent in money matters, planning and sharing their experience (Leader 2, 3 & Lay Leader 2). "Westerners should be transparent in what was received from somewhere. This much money came in for a certain purpose. And they should have a close relationship with the African leadership" (Leader 3).[307] Leader 2 suggests: "Maybe they can do as Paul did: when there is a Western leader, not only to train the African but also to appoint a person as her/his assistant to help her/him leading and passing on experience."[308] Practising more transparency

---

[303] Translated from the original Swahili: Mzungu anaweza kujifunza kwa watanzania thamani ya ubinadamu. Pia anaweza kujifunza kumkubali mtu jinsi alivyo na kumsaidia kutoka pale alipo na kumsogeza mbele.
[304] Translated from the original Swahili: Wazungu wanaweza kujifunza jinsi ya kujali zaidi, kama mtu anamtembelea bila kufanya mpango.
[305] Translated from the original Swahili: Namna ya kusimamia kazi vizuri. ... Kwa mfano namna ya kutunza madaraka, kutunza ile ngazi ya kazi.
[306] Translated from the original Swahili: Halafu kwa wazungu ni muhimu kujifunza uvumilivu zaidi.
[307] Translated from the original Swahili: Wazungu wawe tu wazi kwamba jamani kilichoingia ni hiki kutoka huko mahali. Imeingia kiasi hiki kwa ajili ya jambo hili na hili na hili. Na wawe na mahusiano ya karibu pamoja na uongozi wa kiafrika.
[308] Translated from the original Swahili: Labda wanaweza kufanya kama Paulo alivyofanya kwamba kiongozi mzungu anapokuwa katika kazi pamoja na kumsomesha mwafrika lakini

in this way may lead to more equality between the two groups. Tanzanian Leader 5 would like to see that "When Westerners and Africans work equally well, the Westerners should not give Africans a big work load and a small salary so that Africans feel they depend on Westerners."[309] This kind of equality could also be seen in a stronger attitude of humility, as desired by Lay Leader 1: "For a Westerner, I would be glad to see humility in a way if this person will try not to only decide and that's it. S/he should try even if the other is different, but s/he agrees because there is some truth in it."[310] In terms of how to relate to subordinates in Tanzania, Leader 7 cautions Westerners:

> Westerners should also not take everything too easy and trust their employees too much. In other words, some missionaries trust their house workers more than the pastor of the church. ... They should trust them like employees. But they should not share heavy things with them. ... They should continue to treat their employees well, which is good. ... But they should not raise them higher than their position is and trust them even more than the pastors or other leaders who are local citizens there.[311]

If Western Christian leaders sincerely follow Jesus and want to practise kingdom leadership, it is important that they engage in an ongoing learning process, grow and mature, and constantly change their leadership behaviour to become more like Christ. This means that they may need to go against the values of their culture or group expectations. The interviewees were asked: *"Do you think it is possible for a leader to go against the values of his/her culture or group expectations?"* The *Western* respondents answered as follows: yes (4), sometimes (2), not often (4). I am surprised that so many said that it is not often possible for leaders to go against the values of their culture. This means that even in the West, cultural values have a strong influence on leadership behaviour. However, even though it may be a challenge at times, it seems that because of the high value of individualism, it may still be easier for Western leaders than it is for Tanzanians to practise biblical values and virtues against the cultural values of their society.

---

ajaribu kumsaidia aweke mtu kama msaidizi wake kwa maana kumsaidia kuongoza, kumsaidia kumpa ujuzi.

[309] Translated from the original Swahili: Ningependa kuona wazungu na waafrika wakifanya kazi vizuri kwa usawa pasipo wazungu kuwapa waafrika mzigo mkubwa wa kazi na mshahara kidogo ili waafrika wasijisikie kuwategemea wazungu.

[310] Translated from the original Swahili: Kwa mzungu ningefurahi nikiona unyeyekevu na kwamba yule mtu atajaribu kuwa sio anaamua tu moja kwa moja tu amemaliza. Ajaribu kukubali hata kama liko tofauti lakini anakubali kwa sababu kati ya kile kitu kuna ukweli ndani yake.

[311] Translated from the original Swahili: Wazungu pia wasichukue kirahisi kila kitu na kuamini sana wafanyakazi wao. Maana wamissionari wengine wanaamini wafanyakazi wa ndani zaidi kuliko mchungaji wa kanisa. ... Wawaamini kama wafanyakazi. Lakini wasiwashirikishe mambo mengine mazito. Waendelee kuwahudumia wafanyakazi wao ambayo ni vizuri. ... Lakini wasiwainue kuliko kiwango chao na kuwaamini sana hata kuliko wachungaji au viongozi wengine ambao ni wa kizalendo ambao wako pale.

If leaders would go against the values of their culture or group expectations the question is: "If a leader wanted to change her/his behaviour contrary to accepted cultural values, how would that impact her/his relationships in the group s/he is part of?" The answers from the Western respondents to this question are quite mixed. It may have a negative impact as it may cause misunderstanding, create opposition and conflicts in relationships because the leader would break cultural standards (Leader 1, 2, 3, 4, 5, 6 & 9). "The people s/he works with will feel unloved and s/he will actually lose her/his efficiency in her/his cultural context" (Leader 1). So that would mean that people would not accept her/him (Leader 6). On the other hand, "for the long-term, people would honour her/him for who s/he is as a person and how s/he is able to move and change things" (Leader 4). The leader might experience a more committed group of followers, be accepted and successful (Leader 5, 6, 8 & 9).

5.3.2 What can Tanzanians learn from Western Leaders?

"Can Tanzanian leaders learn from Westerners? If yes, what can they learn?" Basically, all respondents believe that Tanzanians can learn from Westerners. The *Western* respondents answered as follows: yes (9), sometimes (1). The *Tanzanians* responded as follows: yes (4), quite often (6). Compared to the earlier response to the question *"Can Western leaders learn from Tanzanians?"*, Tanzanians are more confident that they can learn from Westerners than that Westerners can learn from them.

When asked, *"What do you think Tanzanians can learn from Westerners?"* (question 6.5) the *Tanzanians* mentioned the following: Time orientation (Leader 5, Lay Leader 1 & 3), work performance (Leader 2, 3 & Lay Leader 1), responsibility (Lay Leader 3), to have a good plan (Leader 3 & Lay Leader 3), to get education (Leader 2 & Lay Leader 2), to be truthful and have principles (Leader 6). Leader 3 summarises most of these things well: "What we Tanzanians want to learn from Westerners is to plan the work and also to be faithful in performance and time as you do. And also even being faithful in taking care of property of the project or the church. We also need to learn how to treat others justly."[312] Leader 1 believes Tanzanians should also learn the Western culture and language. Leader 7 and Lay Leader 2 express the importance of Tanzanian leaders learning how better to relate and communicate: "How to relate to their employees. How to respect a subordinate... Not to express authority too much" (Leader 7).[313] "They [Tanzanians] should learn how

---

[312] Translated from the original Swahili: Sisi watanzania kitu ambacho tunataka kujifunze kutoka kwa wazungu ni kupanga utaratibu wa kazi na vilevile kuwa waaminifu katika utekelezaji na katika wakati kama nyinyi mnavyofanya. Na vilevile hata kutunza mali za mradi aidha za kanisa tunatakiwa kuwa waaminifu katika kutunza hilo. Pia tunatakiwa tujifunze jinsi ya kutenda haki kwa wengine.

[313] Translated from the original Swahili: Namna ya kukaa na wafanyakazi wao. Namna ya kumheshimu mtu ambaye ni chini yako ... Kutojisikia madaraka sana.

to relate in terms of communication how to help each other" (Lay Leader 2).[314]

The *Western* respondents believe Tanzanian leaders can learn the following from them: "communication, caring for individuals" (Lay Leader 1); to put the common goals and benefits before their personal agenda; develop a broader vision (Leader 1); providing followers opportunities for growth (Leader 2); being proactive (Leader 3). "They can learn from us that things can be changed and should be changed if the leadership proves itself not to be trustworthy. They can also learn that members of a team can express their feelings without questioning the leadership" (Leader 7). A few respondents (Leader 3 & 5) mentioned the importance of learning to be held accountable. "They [Westerners] can also teach how better to manage finances and establish a good economy" (Leader 6), which leads to "good use of resources and honesty" (Leader 9). Tanzanians can learn the importance of "decision-making for the good of the people, not for a few" (Leader 5). In terms of achievement, Tanzanians can learn to be more "effective" (Leader 2). "Tanzanians can learn the importance of concluding a decision and moving on, as well as the more effective use of time" (Leader 8). "Tanzanians can learn to plan for the future and set certain goals. They can also learn to keep pressing on" (Leader 4).

It is encouraging to see that there is agreement between the two groups about what Tanzanians can learn from Westerners. The common features that Tanzanians can learn from Westerners are: time orientation, work performance, planning, education, honesty, faithfulness and accountability, justice and how to relate to subordinates. The responses suggest that the most important thing for Tanzanian leaders to learn is to be **faithful** and **accountable**. If faithfulness and accountability are practised, other things such as time orientation, work performance, planning, honesty and justice will consequently also improve.

Learning means changing attitudes and behaviour. The interviewees were asked: *"What kind of changes would you like to see in terms of Tanzanian leadership?"* Basically, the *Tanzanian* respondents want to see changes similar to those already expressed above. They can learn to be more time oriented, gain more education, practise transparency and faithfulness, work effort, to respect and value subordinates. Tanzanian leaders should be more careful how they exercise authority:

> The Tanzanian leader should try not to exercise authority too much. In other words, s/he should not feel that s/he is an important person. It is true I am a leader but s/he is also a person of people. S/he should easily cooperate with other people. S/he should not only talk like a leader, a great person (Leader 7).[315]

---

[314] Translated from the original Swahili: Wajifunze mahusiano kwa namna ya kuwa na mawasiliano jinsi ya kuweza kusaidiana.
[315] Translated from the original Swahili: Viongozi wa Tanzania wajaribu kutosimamia sana madaraka. Yaani, asiwe mtu anayesikia mimi ni fulani sana. Kweli mimi ni kiongozi lakini pia

Leaders should also pass on some of their authority to others (Leader 6 & Lay Leader 1). "Tanzanian leaders should not give preference to their relatives" (Leader 6).[316]

The *Western* respondents would like to see the following changes regarding Tanzanian leadership: "More humility and more interest in raising up others" (Leader 1); "less abuse of power" (Leader 6); less corruption (Leader 2); not seeking their own material benefit first (Leader 2 & 3); more accountability (Leader 5); more effectiveness (Leader 2, 8 & 9); more honesty (Leader 9). Tanzanian leaders are encouraged to communicate more openly and directly: "Tanzanians can be more open and say things even if it is not easy to express them in front of someone who is in opposition" (Leader 4). "I would like to see Tanzanians in the team really expressing what they think and feel" (Leader 7).

To practise kingdom leadership, Christian leaders may need to go against the values of their culture or group expectations. The interviewees were asked: *"Do you think it is possible for a leader to go against the values of his/her culture or group expectations?"* The *Tanzanian* respondents answered as follows: quite often (1), sometimes (5), not often (3), don't know (1). These answers suggest that the group pressure and expectations from the society to behave consistently with the cultural values may be higher in Tanzania than it is in the West.

If Christian leaders were to go against the values of their culture or group expectations the question is: "If a leader wanted to change her/his behaviour contrary to accepted cultural values how would that impact her/his relationships in the group s/he is part of?" The answers from the Tanzanian respondents are clear that the leader will face problems, but it is her/his responsibility to challenge cultural values and practise biblical values. "If the leader follows the Bible without respecting the culture, there will be conflict" (Leader 2).[317] "They will not listen to her/him!" (Leader 6).[318] "There won't be harmony among people ..." (Leader 4).[319] As a result "... her/his work will not be done. ... Often these people will not want to work with her/him. ... However, some culture or part of it is not good in one way or the other. It is necessary to oppose it" (Lay Leader 1).[320] "You as a leader need to have a position now. If you decide to oppose this, you should have clear reasons why you have opposed this, which are consistent with biblical values" (Lay Leader

---

ni mtu wa watu. Awe rahisi kushirikiana na watu wengine. Asizungumze kama ni kiongozi tu, mtu mkubwa.

[316] Translated from the original Swahili: Viongozi wa Tanzania waache upendeleo wa kindugu.
[317] Translated from the original Swahili: Kiongozi akifuata Biblia bila kujali mila inasemaje kutakuwa na mgogoro.
[318] Translated from the original Swahili: Hawatamsikiliza!
[319] Translated from the original Swahili: Hakutakuwa na harmony miongoni wa watu ...
[320] Translated from the original Swahili: Hakutakuwa na harmony miongoni wa watu ... Ingawaje utamaduni mwingine au mahali ya utamaduni wengine sio nzuri kwa njia moja au nyingine. Lazima upingane nao.

2).³²¹ "Now here her/his great task is to persuade people. S/he should have the ability to persuade people of her/his new position. S/he should have a way of communicating with these people so that they understand" (Leader 7).³²²

5.4 Leadership Styles and their Impact on Partnerships

Different leadership styles do have an impact on partnerships. As we have seen above, there are similarities and differences between Western and Tanzanian leadership. The more similarities there are, the less tension and friction there will be between the two groups as they work together. The similarities are especially in the expected character traits of a leader and the biblical understanding of leadership. However, as we have seen so far, the major differences are because of different cultural values. These differences create challenges and hindrances in any cooperation.

5.4.1 Challenges and Hindrances for Partnerships

Any partnership, no matter in which part of the world, faces challenges and hindrances. The interviewees were asked *"Which aspects of Western and Tanzanian leadership are hindrances in partnerships?"* (question 6.9). Question 6.11 *"Which aspects of Western and Tanzanian leadership do not foster partnerships?"* is closely connected to question 6.9. Therefore, the answers to both questions are presented together here. First, the Western view regarding their own leadership is presented and then the Tanzanian view of Western leadership is given. Second, the Tanzanian view of their own leadership is presented and then in turn the Western view of Tanzanian leadership is given.

The *Western* respondents consider the following issues of *Western leadership* as challenges and hindrances. Money seems to be a major issue.

> With the affluence of the West, it is always tempting to want a partnership in order to get some benefit out of it (more education, money), less for the relationship as such or for the "common" goal. The one who has the money "dictates" the goals, even if s/he thinks that s/he is trying genuinely to partner (Leader 2).

This kind of behaviour can create dependency (Leader 4). The way money is used can be another challenge: "Westerners will try to save money where Tanzanians would invest it (e.g. in decorations for celebrations, PR gifts and the like)" (Leader 1). "Because Western Christian leaders are strongly held accountable by their constituents, it is difficult to give 'control' over to Tanzanian leadership, especially in areas related to money and a quality product" (Leader 5). Thus, "to have to prove that you are trustworthy by outcomes is very hard for a Tanzanian" (Leader 7). According to the Western respondents,

---

³²¹ Translated from the original Swahili: Lazima wewe kiongozi uwe na msimamo sasa. Kama unaamua kupinga hiki uwe na sababu za msingi kwamba umepinga kwa sababu hii na zikubalike kufuatana na maadili ya dini inavyotaka.
³²² Translated from the original Swahili: Sasa hapo kazi yake kubwa ni kuwafanya watu wamkubali. Awe na uwezo wa kufanya watu wakubali katika msimamo wake huo mpya. Awe na njia ya kufanya mawasiliano na wale watu waelewe.

not only money but also how people relate may impact a partnership. "Insistence on standards and contracts can result in Western leaders being perceived as harsh and uncaring" (Leader 8). "Not caring for the partner" (Leader 1) and "not enough respect for family situations" (Leader 9) will hinder collaboration. "Lack of time with people gives the impression that the leader is not interested in the people on the project, just the results" (Leader 8). "The egalitarian nature of American relationships are difficult for Tanzanians" (Leader 3). The Western "feeling that doing it alone is good [and] insular world view" (Lay Leader 1) may also be a challenge. Western "critical [or] judgemental tendencies" and "not letting God be in control" (Leader 5) can also be hindrances.

The *Tanzanian* respondents see the following problems in Western leadership for partnerships. The majority of respondents pointed out the issue of **independence**. "You [Westerners] do not like to be helped at all" (Leader 1).[323] "It is possible that the difference in wealth and ability creates a gap" (Leader 5).[324] This gap may cause Westerners to say: "I have everything. I'm self-sufficient. I don't need you. ... I'm doing what I want" (Leader 4). Because of the attitude of being independent Westerners do not give many opportunities to Tanzanians: "They [Westerners] like to have their own supervisors. We would like that they take our people to be taught so that when they leave, they [the Tanzanians] can do the work" (Leader 6).[325] This in turn creates a lack of transparency. "For instance, if a decision is made they [Westerners] do it very much on their own." (Leader 7).[326] The lack of transparency is also reflected in the fact that often Tanzanians are not invited to meetings of Westerners: "If they [Westerners] have their staff meetings, they do not want even one Tanzanian to be there" (Leader 1).[327] The attitude of independence and task orientation also impacts relationships. "Because ... you work how you like until Africans think this work is yours" (Leader 2).[328] "If a Westerner is in her/his office s/he does not want to be disturbed by anyone ..." (Leader 1).[329] "There a Westerner can say: 'If it is like this, I cannot work with you if you deal with family problems more than with work'" (Leader 2).[330]

---

[323] Translated from the original Swahili: Nyinyi hamtaki kabisa kusaidiwa.
[324] Translated from the original Swahili: Tofauti wa mali na uwezo inawezekana inaleta ufa.
[325] Translated from the original Swahili: Wanapenda na wasimamizi wa kutoka kule kwao. Sisi tungependa wawachukue watu wetu halafu wafundishwe, ili wao wanapoondoka waweze kushika.
[326] Translated from the original Swahili: Kwa mfano kama ni maamuzi wanafanya sana wao.
[327] Translated from the original Swahili: Lakini wao wanakuwa na mission staff hawataki mswahili hata mmoja aingie kwenye mission staff.
[328] Translated from the original Swahili: Kwa sababu ... mnavyopenda kazi mpaka waafrika wanafikiri hiyo kazi ni ya kwenu.
[329] Translated from the original Swahili: Halafu kwamba mzungu anataka akiingia ofisini asisumbuliwe na mtu ...
[330] Translated from the original Swahili: Kwa hiyo mzungu anaweza kusema: "Kama ndiyo hivyo. Basi, siwezi kufanya kazi na nyinyi mnavyotaka kushughulika matatizo ya familia zaidi kuliko kazi."

The *Tanzanian respondents* consider the following issues of *Tanzanian leadership* as challenges and hindrances. The majority of respondents pointed out the issue of **accountability** and **faithfulness**. "If you observe the work guidelines, which should be followed, we [Tanzanians] do not follow them. ... Another thing is the misuse of money." (Leader 3).[331] "They [Tanzanians] should learn to be self-motivated and work without being supervised" (Leader 6).[332] "Often s/he thinks about the salary, not the responsibility" (Lay Leader 1).[333] Another hindrance is education. "The educated consider [the uneducated] to be useless. They have no good contribution to make." (Leader 4).[334] Another challenge is the difference in wealth: "If a Tanzanian sees that her/his economic situation is bad, s/he gives up" (Leader 5).[335] Other hindrances are "denominational differences"[336] (Leader 7), "communication"[337] (Lay Leader 1), "people are more important than work"[338] (Leader 2), and different "time orientation"[339] (Lay Leader 3).

The *Western respondents* see the following difficulties in Tanzanian leadership for partnerships. "It is hard for them to not misuse the Western influence just for money matters, but to focus on spiritual things in partnerships. It is hard for them to stick to agreed goals if there are changes in circumstances" (Leader 7). "On the other hand, Africans might be willing to change appointments and adapt their calendars for reasons not easily understood by a Westerner (funerals, weddings, etc.)" (Leader 1). Thus, "too much time with people can be perceived as avoidance of work. Lack of accountability can give the impression that things are not being handled transparently" (Leader 8). "Putting their personal agenda above mutual agreed goals will not prove helpful" (Leader 1). "Tanzanian leaders might hold back with their knowledge and experience as this might be part of their being able to stay in power" (Leader 2). "The insistence upon rank or status inhibits relationships" (Leader 3). "It is difficult for some Tanzanian leaders to understand and accept specific Western leadership values of humility, vulnerability, servanthood, which go somewhat against their view of 'a respected leader'" (Leader 5).

The various leadership challenges for both groups can be summarized as presented in the following figure 5.4.

---

[331] Translated from the original Swahili: Sasa ukitazama zile kanuni ambazo za kazi zinaweza kuzifanya na sisi hatuzifanyi. ... Lingine ni hayo mambo ya ufujaji wa pesa.

[332] Translated from the original Swahili: Wajifunze kufanya kazi kwa kujituma bila kusimamiwa.

[333] Translated from the original Swahili: Mara nyingi anafikiri juu ya mshahara, si wajibu wake.

[334] Translated from the original Swahili: Wenye elimu wanaona [wasio na elimu] hawafai. Hawana mchango wa mawazo mazuri.

[335] Translated from the original Swahili: Mtanzania anajiona wa chini hali yake ya uchumi ni mbaya anakata tama.

[336] Translated from the original Swahili: ... dhehebu hadhi dhehebu ...

[337] Translated from the original Swahili: Mawasiliano

[338] Translated from the original Swahili: ... binadamu ni muhimu sana kuliko kazi.

[339] Translated from the original Swahili: Swala la muda

LEADERSHIP CHALLENGES FOR BOTH GROUPS	
WEST	TANZANIA
Too independent	Too dependent
Too wealthy	Too poor
Expect strong accountability	Need to be more accountable
Desire for control	Holding on to position and power
Lack of transparency (with Tanzanians, but not Western donors)	Lack of transparency to share plans and knowledge
Need to be more people oriented	Need to be more task oriented
Need to be more event oriented	Need to be more time oriented
Need to be more authoritarian	Need to be less authoritarian
Need to share their education and expertise more	Need to gain more education

Figure 5.4

It is interesting to note that most challenges and hindrances of the two leadership styles are in contrast to each other and in reference to cultural values. Both groups lack transparency to each other, which I believe is basically a power issue because information **is** power. However, it needs to be understood by everybody "the greater truth is that *shared* information is many times more powerful" (Addicott 2005:53).

During the group discussion the participants agreed that these differences do influence cross-cultural partnerships and making mistakes cannot be avoided. Because of the colonial history Westerners cannot fully become insiders in Tanzania and vice versa. The perceptions of superiority and inferiority are still there. This should not be underestimated. It is important to recognise these differences and then deal with them appropriately, as outlined below.

5.4.2 A Way to Foster Partnerships

It is helpful to see the similarities and differences of the two leadership styles. The more similarities there are, the easier it is to work together. It is also good to recognise differences in a partnership. However, differences should not be the focus because they divide people. They need to be talked about, recognised and it should be understood why they are there so that they can be dealt with appropriately and it is possible to learn from each other. Otherwise they remain obstacles rather than a learning curve for both. To foster partnerships, the focus should be on similarities and common values because they unify people rather than separating them. The interviewees were asked *"Which aspects of Western and Tanzanian leadership foster partner-*

ships?" First, the Western view is presented and then, in turn, the Tanzanian view is given.

The *Western* respondents identified a number of aspects such as relationships, spiritual unity and common goals, which are essential in fostering partnerships. According to the majority of respondents (Leader 1, 4, 5, 7, 8 & Lay Leader 1), first of all it is essential to build strong personal **relationships** through "social time together" (Leader 8), "mutual visits and private contacts, talking to one another and eating together" (Leader 4). Tanzanians are very people oriented (Leader 7 & Lay Leader 1). "The interest in personal friendships by Tanzanians can help build an intimate relationship that helps the partnership" (Leader 1). Building relationships in such a way facilitates "good communication" (Leader 5). Through these relationships and good communication, "an awareness of the cultural difficulties [can be created]. This would give greater understanding of perceptions and reduce misunderstandings" (Leader 8). The second area in fostering collaboration is **spiritual unity** (Leader 2). Spiritual unity can be encouraged through "prayer together" (Leader 5), "humility [and] love" (Leader 6). From experience it appears that often the level of spiritual unity is deepened through "hard experiences, which carry the whole group through" (Leader 4). Going together through difficulties can lead people into "prayer, intercession, help [and] encouragement" (Leader 4). The third area of importance in moving a partnership forward is to have a common **goal**. "[The] ... goal [must be] truly wanted by both of them" (Leader 2). Western "goal-orientation might help to develop a broader vision in Tanzanians" (Leader 1). Having a common goal helps "being creative together, [and] planning and searching for solutions together" (Leader 4).

The *Tanzanian* respondents mainly identified the two areas of relationships and having goals as critical in fostering partnerships. Spiritual unity was also mentioned. In terms of **relationships**, it is important to have "love"[340] (Lay Leader 2). Love is demonstrated in "how people work together in love"[341] (Leader 3). To make this cooperation work, "They should see where they differ and where they agree. Then they reduce these differences" (Leader 2).[342] "The close relationships that Tanzanians have ... [and] also respecting and listening to everyone – as a team"[343] (Leader 3) helps to strengthen the collaboration. It is also useful to have meetings together (Leader 1) where people "can advise and help each other as needed" (Leader 5).[344] Through joint meetings, the level of transparency may increase and the relationship be strengthened, as Leader 6 points out: "When people are open, it is easy to get to know a person and cooperate with her/him."[345]

---

[340] Translated from the original Swahili: Upendo

[341] Translated from the original Swahili: ... watu wanafanya kazi kwa pamoja kwa upendo.

[342] Translated from the original Swahili: Waone wanagongana wapi na wanapatana wapi. Halafu wanaondoa ile migongano.

[343] Translated from the original Swahili: ... yale mahusiano ya karibu waliyokuwanayo watanzania. ... Tena kumjali na kumsikiliza kila mmoja ...

[344] Translated from the original Swahili: Kushauriana na kusaidiana inapobidi.

[345] Translated from the original Swahili: Watu wanapokuwa wazi ni rahisi kumfahamu mtu na kuweza kushirikiana naye.

I was surprised that only one respondent (Lay Leader 3) mentioned spiritual things such as "teaching one another the Scripture", which may lead to **spiritual unity**.[346]

According to the Tanzanian respondents, the second aspect in fostering partnerships is having a **goal**. "If you have a good programme, you will cooperate ..." (Leader 1).[347] "Common issues bring people together" (Leader 4).[348] Several respondents (Leader 3, 6, Lay Leader 2 & 3) pointed out that to reach the goal they appreciate if Westerners build capacity: "When they help us, teaching us how to do the work so that it will be successful, this is where we see that our colleagues share with us what we need to be successful" (Leader 3).[349] This kind of capacity building will enable both groups "to work equally, planning and implementing together" (Leader 5).[350] However, capacity building not only means that Tanzanians learn from Westerners but also the other way round, as Lay Leader 1 puts it: "A Tanzanian agrees to learn. Or a missionary agrees to learn from a Tanzanian."[351] Learning from each other is also an expression of humility: "To agree to be subordinate. To see another time that your colleague knows something more that s/he can teach me. Another time you should know that you know this and I know that. If we put it together, we'll succeed" (Lay Leader 1).[352]

From my personal experience in facilitating partnerships for many years, I have seen that building **strong personal relationships, spiritual unity** and **common goals** are foundational and key to any successful and healthy cooperation. It is interesting that North American partnership consultant Daniel Rickett (2002) emphasises in his book *Making Your Partnership Work* the importance of having trusting relationships and a common vision in order to produce meaningful results. Ernie Addicott (2005:43), a Protestant partnership consultant, argues, "Strong, healthy personal relationships are the ultimate foundation of an effective partnership ..." The investment in strong, personal, trusting relationships pays off in the long run because these personal relationships create strong ties through which mutual understanding can happen and difficulties be overcome. Christianity is a religion of restored relationships. Throughout the whole Bible, it can be seen that God is a God of community. God calls people into an intimate and loving relationship with him and one another (Matthew 22:37-38).

---

[346] Translated from the original Swahili: ... mambo ya kufundishana maandiko ...
[347] Translated from the original Swahili: Ukiwa na programme nzuri mtashirikiana ...
[348] Translated from the original Swahili: Common issues hapa zinaweka watu pamoja.
[349] Translated from the original Swahili: ... wanapotusaidia labda kutufundisha wakati fulani kufanya kazi labda katika utaratibu fulani ili ile kazi iwe na ufanisi ni kwamba hapo tunaona kwamba hapo wenzetu wanatushirikisha yale ambayo tunatakiwa labda kuifanya ili tuwe na mafanikio.
[350] Translated from the original Swahili: Kufanya kazi kwa usawa ikiwemo kupanga na kutekeleza pamoja.
[351] Translated from the original Swahili: Mtanzania kukubali kujifunza. Au mmissionari akubali kujifunza kutoka kwa mtanzania.
[352] Translated from the original Swahili: Ni kukubali kuwa chini. Kuwa kuona mwenzako anafahamu zaidi kwa wakati uliopo. Kwamba anaweza kunifundisha kitu fulani. Na sehemu nyingine kwamba ujue unafahamu hiki na mimi nafahamu hiki. Tukiweka pamoja tutapata kitu.

Partnership is based on *interdependence*. As people and also relationships grow and mature they move progressively on a continuum from dependence to independence to interdependence (Covey 1989:49). In fact, Covey (:49-51) argues that to become interdependent, it is necessary first to become independent. He (:51) claims: "Interdependence is a choice only independent people can make." According to Covey (:49), independent people are self-reliant. They are able to get or accomplish what they want through their own effort. This is a fairly narrow definition. I agree with Covey to the point that a person needs to go through the various stages from dependence to independence to interdependence. However, I prefer the Whiteheads' (2000:117-118) understanding of independence. To be dependent on others helps people to recognise the strength of others. Dependence means to rely on other people's resources. According to the Whiteheads (:117), independence means that people recognise their own strength. Leaders have some confidence in their own resources, which gives them a certain autonomy. They feel adequate and confident to make a contribution. Thus, independence is a positive achievement of a healthy self-awareness and self-esteem. Independent leaders are willing to express their ideas, expect things of others, assume responsibility and take charge (:119). Mature leaders in the West and in Tanzania who are self-confident are able to depend on the resources of other people as well as their own (:117). They recognise they do not possess everything that brings meaning, joy, and accomplishment to their lives. They are willing to give and receive. They are motivated by values larger than self-interest and goals more significant than personal benefit (:121). The Whiteheads (:121) point out: "People at this stage welcome interdependence. Partnership in power – the ability to enjoy *mutual* influence and *mutual* empowerment – now becomes real." To move towards true, genuine interdependence for some Christian leaders in the West, it may be necessary to admit that they cannot do everything alone and learn to depend on others, whereas Tanzanians may need to recognise their abilities and strengths and gain more self-confidence so that they can shift from dependency to true independence and then healthy interdependence. "Interdependence requires that I be able to depend on others; it also demands that I be able *to let others depend on me*" (Whitehead & Whitehead 2003:159) [their emphasis].

This is very much in line with Stephen Dent (1999:189), a North American partnership consultant, who defines interdependence as "two (or more) independent entities working together as partners without losing their separate identities". Interdependence involves counting on the complementary contribution of others to achieve something none of us could do alone. When this attribute of interdependence is lacking, we believe that we alone can do what is best, or we prefer to accept lesser outcomes that do not require us to interact with or depend on others (:187-198). I do believe that together, Westerners and Tanzanians can achieve much more and of higher quality than alone.

Sometimes interdependence is understood as being equal. I prefer the biblical emphasis on humility to the secular idea of equality (Philippians 2:1-8). Interdependence does not necessarily mean to be equal in terms of ability, possessions, skills and knowledge. It rather means that each party has its own unique role and task in making a contribution towards the partnership (Kim 1991:138). Neither an attitude of dependence nor one of independence is appropriate in biblical terms (Wannemacher 2001:3). Interdependence is the essence of partnering, a tribute to God's grace and a reflection of God's character (Ephesians 4:16). A relationship is alive when both parties, Westerners and Tanzanians, give and receive. At the same time, these parties "must face the implicit as well as the explicit weaknesses of each other" (Sookhdeo 1994:54). Interdependence is one of the factors that promote healthy, quality partnerships. The strong partner is not dominant or superior, neither is the weaker partner inferior or ever submissive, as the Whiteheads point out:

> Mature relationships between adults are characterized by mutuality, even where strict "equality" is neither necessary nor possible. We cannot be exactly equal in intelligence, physical strength, social graces, and other abilities. The challenge of mutuality invites us to become engaged with each other's strengths and weaknesses. Such mutuality neither demands nor pretends to be a total equality. By recognizing and even celebrating differences of strength, we protect ourselves from the genuine imbalances of paternalism and dependency (2003:158).

Recognising each other's strengths and weaknesses provides an opportunity to build loving relationships among people by complementing one another. Life is so complex and people need each other, as Brown points out:

> The importance of these interdependent needs lies in the fact that life is complex and if we are to have a moral life, whether in community or as individuals, we need other people from whom we can learn and with whom we can explore ideas about the kind of world we want and the kind of people we want to be (1998:132).

Westerners can learn from Tanzanians and Tanzanians can learn from Westerners what Christian-ethical leadership means. Together we can explore ideas of what Christian-ethical leadership should look like and what kind of leaders it requires. This will enable people to grow in their understanding of leadership. Brown continues:

> This interdependence is not a social convenience. It is part of being human that we are social beings. We need each other if we are to grow and reflect more of our true humanity, and for this reason we have a responsibility to work against those things that will divide and prevent us from recognizing each other's worth and acting interdependently (1998:133).

In other words, people live in community and have a responsibility to act and communicate in a respectful way that builds trust. Interdependence is an important aspect of Christian-ethical leadership, as it recognises the dignity of the other person.

True genuine interdependence can lead to *spiritual unity*, which is core to any Christian relationship. Jesus desires unity among his followers: "I pray that they may all be one. Father! May they be in us, just as you are in me and I am in you. May they be one, so that the world will believe that you sent me"

(John 17:21). How is spiritual unity created? Spiritual unity grows through moral and spiritual formation, which is part of discipleship. First, spiritual unity among Christians is a result of a close, intimate relationship that people have with God. Second, unity grows when people recognise their brokenness and repent. Third, it is important to identify, own and articulate the common values that bind people together. Fourth, spiritual unity is created through suffering, encouragement and prayer (Bush 1991:12-14). Challenges, difficulties and suffering bring Christian leaders from the West and Tanzania together, because they recognise they cannot deal with them on their own. They need each other. As they encourage one another and pray together, they may be able to see a spiritual breakthrough. Spiritual unity does not grow among morally weak and selfish leaders. As has been discussed above in the section on "Practical Action Steps Forward", spiritual unity grows stronger as Western and Tanzanian Christian leaders mature spiritually individually and in community and practise kingdom leadership.

On the firm foundation of strong personal relationships and authentic spiritual unity Christian leaders from both groups are able to plan together and implement these *goals* using a transparent accountability system. Common goals in turn foster relationships and unity, as demonstrated in figure 5.5.

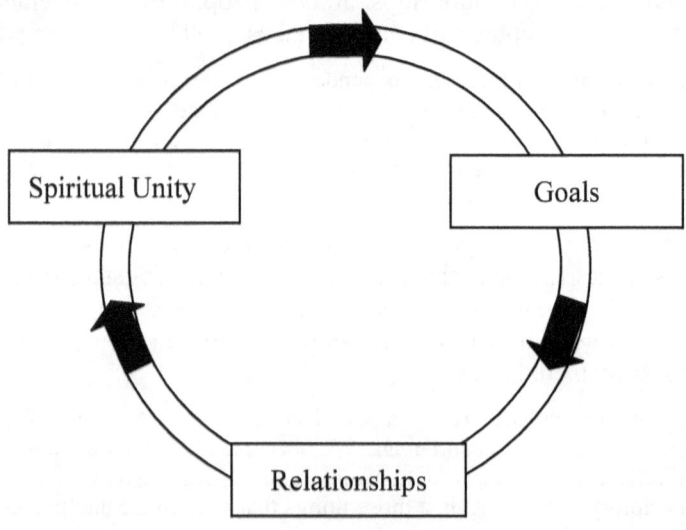

Figure 5.5

This partnership formation process is an ongoing journey from exploring and building strong and close personal relationships, praying and interceding together to build spiritual unity. Out of this spiritual fellowship, joint plans can be developed that glorify God.

Christian leaders from the West and from Tanzania are together on a spiritual journey. Through strong personal relationships where a dialogue can take place, they form a learning community where they can support, encourage and critique each other practising kingdom leadership. Through this learning pro-

Chapter 5: A Christian-Ethical Dialogue and Evaluation

cess, the existing gap between them may be progressively closed and the similarities prevail over the differences. As Christian leaders from both groups truly practise Christian-ethical leadership, the picture of a preferred future as expressed 15 years ago by the Methodist theologian Zablon Nthamburi of Kenya will, it is hoped, become a reality sooner rather than later:

> [T]he African church was calling for a partnership that is based on **equality** and **mutuality**. It was calling for a commitment by the whole community of God's people to build each other up by building up of communities that are founded on **dignity, self-reliance and the maximizing of participation and mutual accountability**. ... This means North and South sharing a mission. It will also mean greater sharing across denominational, cultural, racial and socio-economic barriers. Sharing does not only involve personnel and resources but includes **sharing of life through worship, study and actions that enhance the building of authentic unity**. Such sharing includes sharing of information and decision making processes (1991:79). [my emphasis]

It is encouraging to see that there is openness by Westerners and Tanzanians in the context of Christian organisations and churches to enter into dialogue and to learn from one another. They see positive and negative issues in each other's leadership style. Both groups have a growing awareness of their strengths and weaknesses and what they can learn from each other. This is a good foundation on which church leaders and leaders from various organisations from the West and Tanzania can draw on the strengths rather than on the weaknesses of their cultural paradigms and model recognisably Christian leadership in their contexts. Basically, both groups need to find a better balance. Leaders from churches and other organisations can learn from this study that culture strongly influences leadership. Because of the cultural influence certain values gain more weight than others, such as relationships versus task. A strength can easily become a weakness if it is over emphasised. They can also learn that it is extremely important to listen to one another and learn from each other. In any society, spiritual and character formation is essential for good leadership. The differences in leadership are certainly a challenge in cross-cultural partnerships. Recognising these differences is the first step. Knowing about the differences can help in making fewer mistakes. However, these differences can be overcome to a certain degree by building strong, trusting, personal relationships and friendships. Because some of the differences are so deep and significant, they cannot be completely overcome. Hence, it is unavoidable that mistakes are made from time to time. Therefore, it is important to exercise grace and mercy, recognising our humanness and to being constantly willing to ask for forgiveness and also to forgive. In this way leaders from the West and Tanzania will be able to continue to live and work together in unity, it is hoped with less friction, so that God may be glorified.

Conclusion

In conclusion, the main arguments from chapters one to five are summarised and conclusions are drawn in terms of leadership in the West and in Tanzania and its impact on cross-cultural partnerships.

In chapter one, Christian ethics was defined and it was discussed how this relates to leadership. Ethics is a reflection upon human actions, attitudes and character, how they are perceived and what ought to be. Ethics does not stop here, but calls for a change and transformation of individuals and communities. Christian ethics in particular is Christ and God centred. Christian ethics conforms to the will of God and fulfils human nature. The Christian ethical worldview is shaped by the Bible and the community. Christian leaders are called to let their worldview be transformed because it shapes their norms, values and virtues. Leaders act and base their decisions on these norms, values, virtues and moral consequences.

For this study, the biblical values of love, justice, mercy, faithfulness and humility were identified as being the key to Christian leadership. Jesus applied these norms and values in modelling kingdom leadership and challenging the cultural values of his time. Jesus demonstrated that kingdom leadership is more than servanthood. It is stewardship. Stewardship exercises authority and responsibility with an attitude of humility. Christian leaders need to be transformed and become more like Jesus to have an impact within the society, challenging the cultural values of their time. A step further is to apply kingdom ethics not only within one's own life, organisation and society but cross-culturally.

Core to kingdom leadership is the appropriate use of power. Power and authority are given by God. Therefore, Christian leaders must submit to the authority and will of God. If power is abused as a private possession, authority becomes unaccountable, a special status and self-serving. The appropriate use of power as Jesus practised it will result in Christian leaders who are stewards and servants of God for others.

The appropriate use of power often is a result of leaders with integrity. Hence, Christian virtues and spiritual character formation are essential for Christian leaders. Even though a leader's character has been formed during childhood certain character traits can still be changed later on. Character is formed individually, in community and through engagement with the Scriptures. Christian leaders must acquire Christian virtues and make them a habit to become an integrated part of their character. As a leader's character is not only formed but also transformed through the Holy Spirit s/he becomes a spiritually mature leader.

Not only theology and character influence our leadership behaviour but also culture. Culture and worldview influence how people understand and interpret the Bible. Biblical values such as love, mercy and faithfulness are universal but may be applied differently in different societies. However, since God is not only above and works through culture, but is also in culture, he can transform culture from within. As culture and the Bible are taken seriously, a transformation process can take place in dialogue with other Christians and the Bible. This research is a contribution to such an ongoing dialogue.

Chapter one provides a theoretical framework for a cross-cultural dialogue on Christian leadership. Such a cross-cultural dialogue results in a better understanding of what Christian leadership means and hopefully influences the spiritual and character formation of leaders in this contemporary world. Subsequently, the spiritual transformation of leaders is the foundation for healthy and fruitful cross-cultural collaboration among partners.

In chapter two, the research design and methodology were discussed. Since this research relating to different cultures is rather complex, a combination of different methods and data sources was employed, such as literature, interviews, participant observations, case studies and a group discussion. This combination provides a sound empirically and theoretically grounded argument.

It should not be underestimated how much the cultural values impact a leader's character, theology and leadership behaviour. Culture is interwoven into every aspect of life, including leadership. Hence, it is essential to understand well the cultural context in which leaders operate. To interpret and analyse the cultural context generated through the data, the cultural value systems by Hofstede, Trompenaars and Hampden-Turner were applied. These two theoretical models are complementary and provide a framework to analyse and compare the cultural contexts of leadership styles in the West and in Tanzania and position them on a value continuum. It is essential to understand which cultural norms and values are similar and which are different so that the two groups can enter into a dialogue with each other and the Scripture to unlock the negative aspects of their respective cultures. Based on these cultural value models, a questionnaire was designed and the following key themes relevant to leadership were extracted: personal information, character, relationships, power and conflict.

Data related to these themes were obtained through the interviews and a group discussion. Western and Tanzanian leaders of different ages, gender, educational levels, occupations and denominations were interviewed in order to have a broad cross-section with different perspectives represented. The generated data have made it possible to identify how cultural values and also how Christian norms, values and virtues are understood and applied in each society. Chapter two provides a method for understanding the context of both leadership styles.

In chapter three, the cultural contexts, personal background and character of Western and Tanzanian leadership was presented. Culture and history influences leadership, and some leadership behaviour can only be understood well in its historical and *cultural context*.

The *personal background* of the interviewees is important as it influences their understanding of leadership. Younger and more educated people expect a more participatory leadership approach than older and less educated people. Leaders with a higher level of education are also more critical. Whereas

Westerners consider egalitarian leadership as good leadership, Tanzanians expect strong leadership but stress that good leaders value and respect people.

One of the keys to good leadership is a leader's moral and spiritual *character*. The ideal picture of a good leader is similar in the West and in Tanzania. Both groups appreciate the same leadership qualities such as listening, loving and serving. Tanzanians and Westerners identified the same biblical, ethical values of love, humility, faithfulness, justice and mercy as important to leadership, as discussed in chapter one. Even though these values are universal because they reflect God's character, they are applied differently in different cultures. Whereas Westerners focus on how Jesus fulfilled his mission, Tanzanians emphasise how he related to people. Whereas Westerners stress servanthood, Tanzanians emphasise the importance of providing leadership with a serving attitude.

However, there is a dissonance between the ideal picture and the reality because cultural values dominate. In reality, among Westerners justice and faithfulness prevail over love and mercy. For Tanzanians love and mercy are the most important. The challenge is how to close the gap between the ideal picture and actual practice through character formation. Westerners consider character formation as more important than Tanzanians because they emphasise the ascribed status. To become a good leader, Westerners consider it as important to have a learning attitude, to hold good values and to practise self-reflection. In contrast, Tanzanians believe it is important for someone to become a good leader to have a calling, education, to gain experience and to be mentored well. Whereas in the West, character formation takes mainly place individually, in Tanzania it happens in community.

Chapter three demonstrates that if true spiritual transformation has not taken place, the cultural values dominate over the biblical values in the life of a leader. Leaders with a good character are willing to act against their culture. To understand partnership challenges it is essential to know in which way our culture impacts on the biblical values of Christian leaders and consequently their leadership behaviour. It can be dangerous when people who collaborate assume the other understands and practises love or honesty the same way as they do. Therefore, these basic concepts need to be put on the table and discussed openly to create at least a common understanding, reduce unnecessary surprises and come to a deeper theological understanding of what these biblical values really mean in this contemporary and global world.

In chapter four, the features of relationships, power and conflict in terms of leadership in the West and in Tanzania are described, compared and analysed. It can be noted that these areas of leadership are strongly influenced by the social environment in which leaders live and its cultural values. In reference to *relationships*, whereas Westerners are task oriented and individualistic, Tanzanians are people and group oriented. In other words, Westerners focus on the end result and Tanzanians on the process. Both groups feel a certain tension between having good relationships and achieving a task. Tanzanian leaders consider the relationship as more important than the task, whereas for Westerners it is just the opposite. Tanzanians view the organisation they work for like a family. Subordinates expect their superiors to help them, even with personal issues. Westerners are time oriented, whereas Tanzanians are event oriented. Tanzanians can easily adjust to a new or changing situation if necessary. In Tanzania and in the West, trust is built and also breached in similar ways. For both groups it is important that people do what they say. However, whereas Westerners emphasise good communication, in Tanzania a person who is trustworthy conforms to group values. In terms of self-disclosure, Western information sharing is purpose driven. In contrast, Tanzanians constantly share information with other people. It is interesting and encouraging to see that both groups are trying to adjust their values to be more balanced. This is really important, since in a partnership the key is the relationship. If the relationships are healthy a certain task can be more easily accomplished.

Westerners and Tanzanians consider *power* as good if used well. However, power abuse increases when leaders are insecure or have a bad character. Whereas equality and egalitarianism are highly valued in the West, the organisational and church structure in Tanzania is rather hierarchical. Consequently, power distance in Tanzania is much higher than in the West. This can also be seen in the fact that the use of titles is really important in Tanzania. It appears that power distance is connected to accountability. The larger the power distance is, the more difficult it is to exercise accountability because it is difficult to critique leaders. Hence, it is easier to abuse power in Tanzania. Thus, sometimes Westerners are careful when they collaborate with Tanzanians. In such a partnership it is important for both groups to have a transparent accountability system in place so that people can trust each other. To make a partnership successful, it is essential to understand the use of power in different societies as it influences the way meetings are conducted and decisions made. Even though there are a number of similarities in relation to how meetings are conducted in the two societies, there are some differences that can cause tension when working together. For instance, because of the hierarchical system a chairperson has more power in Tanzania than in the West. Whereas Western delegates have the authority to make a decision during the meeting, in Tanzania usually only the top leader has the authority to make a decision on the spot. Thus, if a partnership meeting is called, it is extremely important who is invited. Delegates from both groups must have a certain position of authority within their organisation or church. Otherwise they are not taken seriously or a decision cannot be made. Also Western leaders must be very patient in such cross-cultural partnership meetings, as it can take a long time before a decision is made. They do need to learn that the decision-making process is as important as the outcome. If the process is satisfying to most people, it is more likely that the outcome will have stronger support.

There are major cultural differences between the West and Tanzania, which can create *conflict* in a cross-cultural partnership. Hence, it is essential to know how leaders deal with conflict in each society. Since Westerners are specific and assertive, they tend to be more confrontational. On the contrary, Tanzanians have a strong desire for harmony where direct confrontation can destroy a relationship. Another contributing factor in conflict is non-verbal communication if this is not understood. The challenge in a cross-cultural partnership for Westerners is to read between the lines, especially to understand the non-verbal clues, to discover the true message. At the same time Tanzanians should not be offended too quickly and be merciful when Westerners are a bit blunt and direct. If possible at all Westerners try to restore a relationship on an individual basis. Their main concern is to see justice happening. In contrast, for Tanzanians the aim is to rebuild relationships and restore harmony within the group. They experience reconciliation as a group.

There is no question that cultural values influence leadership behaviour. Most of these cultural values are different between the West and Tanzania. In a partnership, it is important to be aware of these differences so that they can be handled appropriately without causing too much friction. However, it is important to keep in mind that culture is not static, but constantly changes.

In chapter five, both groups enter into a dialogue. Both leadership styles were evaluated. In the discussion of what they can learn from each other, a composite picture of a Christian leadership style is drawn. The ways in which the different leadership styles affect cross-cultural partnerships and how healthy collaboration can be fostered are presented. Through the *dialogue* it was confirmed that most leadership differences relate to cultural values. Because of the strong cultural influence, there is a dissonance between the ideal picture and actual practice. The cultural values have a strong impact on the biblical values. Because of their cultural values, Westerners and Tanzanians prioritize the biblical values of love, mercy, humility, faithfulness and justice differently. Because of the high value of individualism in the West, justice prevails over love and mercy. On the other hand, for Tanzanians love is most important because they are so strongly people oriented. That mercy is more important than exercising justice is a result of the high value of relationships in Tanzania. This is also reflected in the fact that Tanzanians define who they are in relationship to others, whereas Westerners define themselves by what they do. Through the dialogue both groups recognised that it is important to learn from each other and find a balance. That way it is possible to build on the positive cultural aspects and model recognisably Christian leadership in each context.

Through the *evaluation* of the two leadership styles, it becomes clear that both Westerners and Tanzanians have strengths and weaknesses. Cultural values must be challenged by Scripture so that culture can be transformed and consequently our leadership behaviour become truly Christ-like. Since Jesus was both task and people oriented, Westerners need to focus more on relationships and Tanzanians more on the task. Spiritual transformation of leadership behaviour, first of all, takes place by recognising and repenting of the negative cultural aspects and bad character. A leader's character must be formed spiritually and morally through sound biblical teaching in a language people understand well. Character formation should take place individually and in community. Also leaders and followers should have a certain level of education to avoid oppression and the abuse of power. For cross-cultural workers, it is essential to learn about the historical and cultural context of the people one works with.

Moving towards a Christian leadership style, it is important that both groups recognise that they can learn from each other. Most important for Westerners is to learn to be more people oriented, loving, merciful, and be willing to depend on others. Tanzanian leaders can learn to be more faithful, accountable and independent. It takes courage for leaders of both societies to go against the values of their culture to model a Christ-like leadership. For Tanzanians, it is more difficult because of high group pressure and expectations. Leaders with a good character are more likely to be willing and have the courage to act against the negative aspects of their culture.

The different leadership styles in the West and in Tanzania have an *impact on cross-cultural partnerships*. Some of the main factors are how people handle money, the way they relate to others, dependency versus independence, accountability and faithfulness. To overcome these differences and challenges, it is essential to build strong personal relationships, foster spiritual unity, have common goals and a transparent accountability system in place. Healthy collaboration must be built on an interdependent relationship in which all parties can make an important contribution.

Through this research, it has been identified that leadership styles are influenced by culture, theology and character. Through the cross-cultural dialogue and evaluation of both leadership styles, it has been identified which leadership aspects are merely Western or Tanzanian and which are essentially Christian. As the areas of culture, theology and character continue to influence each other in dialogue, a more Christ-like leadership is developed. This is an important step in moving towards kingdom leadership and healthier and more fruitful partnerships.

Appendix

Questionnaire:
Leadership Styles in the West and in Tanzania

1. Personal Information

1.1 Name
1.2 Into which age group do you fall?
 ❑ 20-30
 ❑ 31-40
 ❑ 41-50
 ❑ 50+
1.3 What is your nationality and ethnic group?
1.4 Which denomination are you from?
1.5 What formal education have you had?
1.6 What is your current occupation and work experience?
1.7 What is your own leadership role?
1.8 What is your experience of the leadership of others and assessment of it? Which aspects have been positive? Which have been difficult? Give an example.
1.9 What is your evaluation of how you have functioned as a leader? Can you give a personal example?

2. Character and Leadership

2.1 How would you describe a good Christian leader?
2.2 Which Bible persons or passages do you consider to be key to Christian leadership? Why?
2.3 Who do you consider to be a good leader? For what reasons?
2.4 How does one become a good leader?
2.5 What are the features of authentic leadership as modelled by Christ?
2.6 How are these features of Christ-like character expressed in the West and in Tanzania? Give an example of each.
2.7 Which biblical, ethical values related to leadership are important to you? For example, one such value is compassion. Name five to ten more examples.
2.8 How do you understand servant leadership? What picture would you use to describe servant leadership?

2.9 Is leadership influenced by culture? Tick one.
- ☐ Yes
- ☐ Quite often
- ☐ Sometimes
- ☐ Not often
- ☐ No
- ☐ Don't know

2.10 If so, in which way is leadership influenced by culture? Can you give an example?

2.11 Which Christian virtues or aspects of character do you consider important for leaders to have? One example is honesty. List eight more.

2.12 How do Western and Tanzanian Christian leaders practise the biblical values of love, justice, mercy, faithfulness and humility in their ministry? Comment on any similarities and differences. Can you give two examples from your own experience?

2.13 Which biblical values are universal and which are culture specific? Why? Give one example of each.

3. Relationships and Leadership

3.1 Describe the structure of the organisation or church in which you work.

3.2 What roles exist? How do the various roles interrelate? Who jokes with whom?

3.3 Imagine that you have prepared yourself to go shopping or it has rained for three days and you want to prepare the fields to plant. Visitors come from the neighbourhood. What would you do? Tick one.
- ☐ Ask them to come back another time.
- ☐ Ask a family member to visit with them and leave.
- ☐ Visit with them a short time and then excuse yourself.
- ☐ Visit with them and go to town or to the field another day.
- ☐ Other _____

3.4 What do you expect from your employer? Tick one – or as many as apply.
- ☐ Salary according to performance
- ☐ Social security/benefits such as housing, medical etc.
- ☐ Employer cares for me like a family member
- ☐ Encouragement
- ☐ Anything else _____

3.5 How do you build trust? How do you know that you can trust a person?

3.6 How is trust breached? Describe a situation where trust has been broken.

3.7 If you have a conversation with somebody, are there certain things you share more easily than others?

3.8   If yes, what kind of information do you feel more or less comfortable to disclose? Give an example of each.

3.9   The organisation has been given an assignment to finish by a certain deadline. Unfortunately one of the family members of an employee becomes sick. What would you do? Tick one.
❏ Allow the employee to take care of the family member, taking the risk of not meeting the deadline of the assignment.
❏ Allow the employee to take care of the basic needs of the sick family member and return as soon as possible back to work.
❏ Allow the employee to take an hour to arrange for somebody else to take care of the family member.
❏ Expect the employee to continue her/his work so that the deadline can be met and insist that somebody else should take care of the sick family member.
❏ Other _____

3.10 How are tasks and goals achieved? Tick one.
❏ People ideally achieve alone and assume personal responsibility.
❏ People ideally achieve in groups, which assume joint responsibility.
❏ Other _____

3.11 If you have a contract with someone and the circumstances change, what would you do? Tick one.
❏ Keep the contract.
❏ Adjust the contract to the circumstances.
❏ Try to change the circumstances in order to keep the contract.
❏ Ignore the contract in the light of changing situations.
❏ Other _____

3.12 If you have an appointment and a visitor comes to see you unexpectedly, what would you do? Tick one.
❏ Keep the appointment.
❏ Be late for the appointment.
❏ Spend time with the visitor and not keep the appointment.
❏ Other _____

3.13 What attitudes and actions do followers expect from leaders? List two of each.

4. Power and Leadership

4.1   What is power?
4.2   Next question: Is it a good or a bad thing? Why?
4.3   What gives a person power?
4.4   What kinds of people have more power than others?
4.5   In your context, how are women perceived as leaders in terms of their status and role? Give an example.
4.6   How are authority and accountability exercised?

4.7 How do leaders relate to their subordinates? Tick one.
❑ In a friendly way as friends or peers
❑ Friendly but keeping some distance
❑ With social distance but polite
❑ With social distance according to the position
❑ Other _____

4.8 As subordinate I expect (Tick one.)
❑ to be consulted and my opinion to be seriously considered and incorporated.
❑ to be consulted and my opinion to be considered.
❑ to be consulted but the boss to make the final decision.
❑ to be told what to do.

4.9 Can you think of an instance where power was exercised positively?

4.10 How often is the abuse of power an issue in the West? Tick one.
❑ Very often
❑ Quite often
❑ Sometimes
❑ Not often
❑ Never
❑ Don't know

4.11 How often is the abuse of power an issue in Tanzania? Tick one.
❑ Very often
❑ Quite often
❑ Sometimes
❑ Not often
❑ Never
❑ Don't know

4.12 How is power abused in your home country? Can you give an example?

4.13 What is the role of the chairperson in a meeting?

4.14 Do you always introduce someone using their title, e.g. Rev., Dr, Chairperson, Teacher, Director? Tick one.
❑ Yes
❑ Quite often
❑ Sometimes
❑ Not often
❑ No
❑ Don't know

4.15 What is the task of a representative before, during and after a meeting?

4.16 What authority do delegates have in a meeting? In which way are delegates empowered?

4.17 How are decisions made? What process is followed? Can you give an example?

5. Conflict and Leadership

5.1 If somebody expresses a different opinion in a meeting, what do you think is the best way of dealing with it? Give an example.

5.2 How do you restore peace after a disagreement or conflict? Can you recall an incident?

5.3 Are harmony and consensus ultimate goals? Tick one.
❑ Always
❑ Quite often
❑ Sometimes
❑ Not often
❑ Never
❑ Don't know

5.4 Aggression and emotions should not be shown. Do you agree? Tick one.
❑ It is never appropriate to show aggression and emotions.
❑ Quite often it is not appropriate to show aggression and emotions.
❑ Sometimes it is not appropriate to show aggression and emotions.
❑ Sometimes it is appropriate to show aggression and emotions.
❑ It is appropriate to show aggression and emotions.
❑ Don't know.

5.5 Aggression and emotions may be ventilated at proper times and places. Do you agree? Tick one.
❑ Yes
❑ Quite often
❑ Sometimes
❑ Not often
❑ No
❑ Don't know

5.6 If you have a different opinion, is it important for you to keep face and be willing to submit for a certain purpose? Tick one.
❑ Always
❑ Quite often
❑ Sometimes
❑ Not often
❑ Never
❑ Don't know

5.7 What form should a leader's communication take? Tick one.
❑ Direct, to the point, purposeful in relating, precise
❑ Transparent and providing background information
❑ Elaborative and giving examples
❑ Indirect, circuitous, evasive and tactful
❑ Other _____

6. Assessment of Leadership

6.1 Do you think there are any differences in Western and Tanzanian leadership styles? Tick one.
❑ Yes
❑ Quite often
❑ Sometimes
❑ Not often
❑ No
❑ Don't know
If you do perceive differences, can you give examples of at least two?

6.2 How would you assess the strengths and weaknesses of Western and Tanzanian leadership? List two of each – a total of eight.

6.3 Do you believe Westerners can learn from Tanzanians? Tick one.
❑ Yes
❑ Quite often
❑ Sometimes
❑ Not often
❑ No
❑ Don't know

6.4 Do you believe Tanzanians can learn from Westerners? Tick one.
❑ Yes
❑ Quite often
❑ Sometimes
❑ Not often
❑ No
❑ Don't know

6.5 What do you think Westerns and Tanzanians can learn from each other? List two things each group can learn from the other.

6.6 What kind of changes would you like to see in terms of Western and Tanzanian leadership?

6.7 Do you think it is possible for a leader to go against the values of his/her culture or group expectations? Tick one.
❑ Yes
❑ Quite often
❑ Sometimes
❑ Not often
❑ No
❑ Don't know

6.8 If a leader wanted to change her/his behaviour contrary to accepted cultural values, how would that impact her/his relationships in the group s/he is part of?

6.9 Which aspects of Western and Tanzanian leadership are hindrances in partnerships? List two.

6.10 Which aspects of Western and Tanzanian leadership foster partnerships? List two.

6.11 Which do not? List two.

7. Comments and Feedback

7.1 Do you have any other comments you wish to make?

7.2 Do you wish to receive some overall feedback concerning this questionnaire?
❏ Yes
❏ No

7.3 Do you wish to receive further information concerning the successful completion of my dissertation?
❏ Yes
❏ No

Thank you very much for assisting me by answering these questions.

R. I. Schubert

Bibliography

Addicott, E. 2005. *Body Matters: A Guide to Partnership in Christian Mission*. Edmonds, USA: Interdev Partnership Associates.

Adeney, BT. 1995. *Strange Virtues: Ethics in a Multicultural World*. Downers Grove, Illinois: InterVarsity Press.

Adeyemo, T. 1993. Christian Leadership in Africa, in *Perspectives on Leadership Training,* edited by VB Cole, RF Gaskin & RJ Sim. Nairobi: NEGST Faculty.

Amirtham, S & Pryor, R (eds). 1989. The Iona Document on spiritual formation, in *Resources for Spiritual Formation in Theological Education*. Geneve: WCC Programme on Theological Education, 146-164.

Anderson, WB. 1977. *The Church in East Africa 1840-1974*. Nairobi, Kenya: Uzima Press Limited, Dodoma, Tanzania: Central Tanganyika Press, Kampala, Uganda: Centenary Publishing House.

Avery, GC. 2004. *Understanding Leadership: Paradigms and Cases*. London: Sage Publications.

Bam, B. 1991. Seizing the Moment: Women and the New South Africa, in *Women Hold Up Half the Sky: Women in the Church in Southern Africa*, edited by D Ackermann, JA Draper & E Mashinini. Pietermaritzburg: Cluster Publications, 363-368.

Bell, RH. 2002. *Understanding African Philosophy: A cross-cultural approach to classical and contemporary issues*. New York, London: Routledge.

Bennett, DW. 1993. *Metaphors of Ministry. Biblical Images for Leaders and Followers*. Eugene, Oregon: Wipf and Stock Publishers.

_____. 2005. A Call to Develop Christ-like Leaders. *Lausanne Occasional Paper No. 41*. Lausanne: Lausanne Committee for World Evangelization and its National Committees around the world.

Bevans, SB. 2002. *Models of Contextual Theology*. Revised and expanded edition. Mariknoll, New York: Orbis Books.

Birch, BC. & Rasmussen, LL. 1989. *Bible and Ethics in the Christian Life*. Minneapolis: Augsburg Fortress.

Bonhoeffer, D. 1954. *Life Together: The Classic Exploration of Faith in Community*. USA: Harper & Row Publishers.

_____. 1959. *The Cost of Discipleship*. New York: Simon & Schuster.

Boon, M. 1998. *The African Way: The Power of Interactive Leadership*. 2nd edition. Johannesburg: Zebra Press.

Bosch, DJ. 1991. *Transforming Mission: Paradigm Shifts in Theology of Mission*. Maryknoll, New York: Orbis Books.

Brown, C. 1998. *Crash Course on Christian Ethics*. London: Hodder & Stoughton.

Bush, L. 1991. In Pursuit of True Christian Partnership, in *Partners in the Gospel: The strategic role of partnership in world evangelization,* edited by JH Kraakevik & D Welliver. USA: Billy Graham Center, Wheaton College, 3-16.

Chinchen, D. 1995. The Patron-client system: A Model of Indigenous Discipleship. *Evangelical Missions Quarterly*. Wheaton: Evangelism and Missions Information Service, October: 164-173.

_____. 2001. Let my people lead: Indigenous African Management Styles. *Evangelical Missions Quarterly*. Wheaton: Evangelism and Missions Information Service, April: 164-173.

Chiwanga, SE. 2001. Beyond the Monarch/Chief: Reconsidering the Episcopacy in Africa, in *Beyond Colonial Anglicanism: The Anglican Communion in the Twenty-first Century*, edited by IT Gouglas & K Pui-Lan. New York: Church Publishing Incorporated, 297-317.

Clinton, RJ. 1988. *The Making of a Leader*. Colorado Springs: VavPress.

_____. 1996. *Der Werdegang eines Leiters: Lektionen und Stufen in der Entwicklung zur Leiterschaft*. 2nd edition. Greng-Murten: Verlag für kulturbezogenen Gemeindebau.

Coenen, L, Beyreuther, E & Bietenhard, H (eds). 1971. *Theologisches Begriffslexikon zum Neuen Testament*. Wuppertal: R. Brockhaus Verlag.

Connors, RB Jr & McCormick, PT. 1998. *Character, Choices & Community: The Three Faces of Christian Ethics*. New York: Paulist Press

Covey, SR. 1989. *The 7 Habits of Highly Effective People: Restoring the Character Ethic*. USA: Fireside.

_____. 1991. *Principle-Centered Leadership*. New York: Free Press.

Dale, RD. 1986. *Pastoral Leadership: A Handbook of Resources for Effective Congregational Leadership*. Nashville: Abingdon Press.

Dent, SM. 1999. *Partnering Intelligence: Creating Value for Your Business by Building Strong Alliances*. Palo Alto, CA: Davis-Black Publishing.

De Pree, M. 1989. *Leadership is an Art*. New York: Dell Publishing.

Eitel, KE. 1986. *Transforming Culture: Developing a Biblical Ethic in an African Context*. Nairobi: Evangel Pubishing House.

Elmer, DH. 2006. *Cross-Cultural Servanthood: Serving the World in Christlike Humility*. Downers Grove, Illinois: InterVarsity Press.

Frankena, W. 1973. *Ethics*. 2nd edition. Upper Saddle River, New Jersey: Prentice Hall.

Freire, P. 1993. *Pedagogy of the Oppressed*. 30th Anniversary Edition. New York, London: continuum.

Gordon, RG Jr & Grimes, BF (eds). 2005. *Ethnologue: Languages of the World*. 15th edition. Dallas: SIL International.

Gosling, J & Mintzberg, H. 2004. Die fünf Welten eines Managers. *Harvard Business Manager: Führung SPEZIAL*. April: 46-59.

Groves, P. 1998. The Least in the Community of Jesus as Examples for Leadership Today. *ANVIL*, 15(1):13-21.

Grün, A. 2001. *Menschen führen – Leben wecken: Anregungen aus der Regel des heiligen Benedikts von Nursia*. 3rd edition. Münsterschwarzach: Vier-Türme-Verlag.

Guba, EG & Lincoln, YS. 1994. Competing Paradigms in Qualitative research, in *Handbook of Qualitative Research*, edited by NK Denzin & YS Lincoln. Thousand Oaks, London, New Delhi: Sage Publications, 105-117.

Gunderson, D. 1997. *The Leadership Paradox: A Challenge to Servant Leadership in a Power Hungry World*. Seattle: Youth with a Mission Publishing.

Hall, ET. 1981a. *The Silent Language*. New York: Anchor Books.

_____. 1981b. *Beyond Culture*. New York: Anchor Books.

_____. 1982. *The Hidden Dimension*. New York: Anchor Books.

Hall, ET & Hall, MR. 1990. *Understanding Cultural Differences: Germans, French and Americans*. USA, UK: Intercultural Press, Inc.

Hampden-Turner, C & Trompenaars, F. 2000. *Building Cross-Cultural Competence: How to create wealth from conflicting values*. West Sussex, England: John Wiley & Sons.

Harris, PR, Moran, RT & Moran, SV. 2004. *Managing Cultural Differences: Global Leadership Strategies for the 21st Century*. 6th edition. Amsterdam, Boston, Heidelberg, London, New York, Oxford, Paris, San Diego, San Francisco, Singapore, Sydney, Tokyo: Elsevier Butterworth Heinemann.

Hauerwas, S. 1981. *A Community of Character: Toward a Constructive Christian Social Ethic*. Notre Dame: University of Notre Dame Press.

Hefley, J & M. 1995. *Uncle Cam: The story of William Cameron Townsend Founder of the Wycliffe Bible Translators and the Summer Institute of Linguistics*. Huntington Beach, CA: Wycliffe Bible Translators.

Helander, E & Niwagila, WB. 1996. *Partnership and Power: A Quest for Reconstruction in Mission*. Erlangen: Verlag der Ev.-Luth. Mission.

Hersman, LR. 1995. *Grid-group Analysis of National Structures for International Mission Teams*. USA: Fuller Theological Seminary. http://wwwlib.umi.com/dxweb/gateway.

Hesselgrave, DJ. 1991. *Communicating Christ Cross-Culturally: An introduction to missionary communication*. 2nd edition. Grand Rapids, Michigan: Zondervan Publishing House.

Hiebert, PG. 1999. *Missiological Implications of Epistemological Shifts: Affirming Truth in a Modern/Postmodern World*. Harrisburg, Pennsylvania: Trinity Press International.

Hill, H & friends. 2002. SIL Culture. *Ethno-info*. Nairobi: SIL Africa Area Anthropology Department, 50: 3-8.

Hofstede, G. 1997. *Cultures and Organizations: Software of the Mind*. UK: McGraw-Hill.

_____. 2001. *Lokales Denken, globales Handeln: Interkulturelle Zusammenarbeit und globales Management*. 2nd edition. München: Deutscher Taschenbuch Verlag.

House, RJ, Hanges, PJ, Javidan, M, Dorfman, PW & Gupta, V (eds). 2004. *Culture, Leadership, and Organizations: The Globe Study of 62 Societies*. Thousand Oaks, California: Sage Publications.

Huddleston, T. 1995. The Person Nyerere, in *Mwalimu: The Influence of Nyerere*, edited by C Legum & G Mmari. UK: Britain-Tanzania Society, 1-8.

Isichei, E. 1995. *A History of Christianity in Africa: From Antiquity to the Present*. Grand Rapids, Michigan: William B. Eerdmans Publishing Company, Lawrenceville, New Jersey: Africa World Press Inc.

James, RM. 2003. Women's Participation in Church-based Organizations, in *Quests for Integrity in Africa*, edited by G Wamue & MM Theuri. Nairobi: Acton Publishers.

Johnson, F. 1939. *A Standard Swahili-English Dictionary*. Nairobi, Dar es Salaam: Oxford University Press.

Jones, DC. 1994. *Biblical Christian Ethics*. Grand Rapids, Michigan: Baker Books.

Kammer III, CL. 1988. *Ethics and Liberation: An Introduction*. Eugene, Oregon: Wipf & Stock Publishers.

Kasenene, P. 1994. Ethics in African Theology, in *Doing Ethics in Context: South African Perspectives*, edited by C Villa-Vicencio & JW de Gruchy. Maryknoll, New York: Orbis Books, Cape Town and Johannesburg: David Philip, 138-147.

Käser, L. 1998. *Fremde Kulturen: Eine Einführung in die Ethnologie*. 2nd edition. Bad Liebenzell: Verlag der Liebenzeller Mission; Erlangen: Verl. der Ev.-Luth. Mission.

Kato, BH. 1985. *Biblical Christianity in Africa*. Theological Perspectives in Africa: No. 2. Ghana: Africa Christian Press.

Kayonga, AMM. 2003. African Women and Morality, in *Moral and Ethical Issues in African Christianity: Explorative Essays in Moral Theology*, edited by JNK Mugambi & A Nasimiyu-Wasike. 3rd edition. Nairobi: Acton Publishers.

Kelly, GB & Nelson, FB. 2003. *The Cost of Moral Leadership: The Spirituality of Dietrich Bonhoeffer*. Grand Rapids: Eerdmans.

Kessler, V & M. 2001. *Die Machtfalle: Machtmenschen in der Gemeinde*. Gießen: Brunnen Verlag.

Kim, MH. 1991. Principles of Two-Thirds World Mission Partnership, in *Partners in the Gospel: The Strategic Role of Partnership in World Evangelization*, edited by JH Kraakevik & D Welliver. USA: Billy Graham Center, Wheaton College, 125-140.

Kinoti, G. 2003. *Hope for Africa and What the Christian Can Do*. 3rd edition. Nairobi, Kenya: International Bible Society – Africa.

Kinoti, HW. 1997. Well-Being in African Society and the Bible, in *The Bible in African Christianity: Essays in Biblical Theology*, edited by HW Kinoti & JM Waliggo. Nairobi, Kenya: Acton Publishers.

_____. 2003. African Morality: Past and Present, in *Moral and Ethical Issues in African Christianity: Explorative Essays in Moral Theology*, edited by JNK Mugambi & A Nasimiyu-Wasike. 3rd edition. Nairobi, Kenya: Acton Publishers.

Klopfenstein, DE. 1989. Research in Leadership. *Christian Education Journal*, 9(2):41-54.

Kraft, C. 1979. *Christianity in Culture: A Study in Dynamic Biblical Theologizing in Cross-Cultural Perspective*. USA: Orbis Books.

Kretzschmar, L. 1993. *Theological Ethics: Previous Study Guide for TEA100-4*. Pretoria: University of South Africa.

_____. 1994. Ethics in a Theological Context, in *Doing Ethics in Context: South African Perspectives*. edited by C Villa-Vicencio and JW de Gruchy. Maryknoll, New York: Orbis Books, Cape Town and Johannesburg: David Philip, 2-23.

_____. 1995. The Bible and Power: An Ethical Perspective on the Abuse of Power, in *Baptist Faith Witness: The Papers of the Study and Research Division of the Baptist World Alliance 1990-1995*, edited by WH Brackney & LA (Tony) Cupit. Birmingham, Alabama USA: Samford University, 197-203.

_____. 2001. The Resurgence of Christian Ethics and Spirituality, in *Towards an Agenda for Contextual Theology: Essays in Honour of Albert Nolan*, edited by MT Speckman & LT Kaufmann. Pietermaritzburg: Cluster Publications, 279-305.

_____. 2002. Authentic Christian Leadership and Spiritual Formation in Africa. *Journal of Theology for Southern Africa*, 113: 41-60.

_____. 2004. *Ethics and Life: Only Study Guide for CMM111-P*. Pretoria: University of South Africa.

Lane, HW, DiStefano, JJ & Maznevski, ML. 2000. *International Management Behavior: Texts, Readings and Cases*. 4th edition. UK: Blackwell Publishing.

Lausanne I. 1974. *The Lausanne Covenant*. http://www.gospelcom.net/lcwe/statements/covenant.html.

Lausanne Committee for World Evangelization. 1978. *The Willowbank Report: Report on a Consultation on Gospel and Culture*. http://www.gospelcom.net/lcwe/LOP/lop02.htm.

Lewis, RD. 2003. *When Cultures Collide: Managing Successfully across Cultures*. London: Nicholas Brealey Publishing.

Lingenfelter, SG. 1996. *Agents of Transformation: A Guide for Effective Cross-Cultural Ministry*. Grand Rapids, Michigan: Baker Book House.

_____. 1998. *Transforming Culture: A Challenge for Christian Mission*. Grand Rapids, Michigan: Baker Book House.

Lingenfelter, SG & Mayers, MK. 1986. *Ministering Cross-Culturally: An Incarnational Model for Personal Relationships*. Grand Rapids, Michigan: Baker Book House.

Linthicum, R. 2003. *Transforming Power: Biblical Strategies for Making a Difference in Your Community*. Downers Grove, Illinois: InterVarsity Press.

Magesa, L. 2002. *Christian Ethics in Africa*. Nairobi: Acton Publishers.

Maletzke, G. 1996. *Interkulturelle Kommunikation: Zur Interaktion zwischen Menschen verschiedener Kulturen*. Opladen: Westdeutscher Verlag.

Mason, J. 2002. *Qualitative Researching*. 2nd edition. London: Sage Publications.

Maxwell, JC. 1999. *The 21 Indispensable Qualities of a Leader: Becoming the Person Others will Want to Follow*. Nashville: Thomas Nelson Publishers.

Mayer, C, Boness, C & Thomas, A. 2003. *Beruflich in Kenia und Tansania: Trainingsprogramm für Manager, Fach- und Führungskräfte*. Göttingen: Vandenhoeck & Ruprecht.

Mayers, MK. 1987. *Christianity Confronts Culture: A Strategy for Crosscultural Evangelism*. Grand Rapids, Michigan: Zondervan Publishing House.

Mbiti, JS. 1974. *Afrikanische Religion und Weltanschauung*. Berlin: Walter de Gruyter & Co.

_____. 1986. *Bible and Theology in African Christianity*. Nairobi: Oxford University Press.

McDonald, JIH. 1995. *Christian Values: Theory and Practice in Christian Ethics Today*. Edinburgh: T&T Clark.

Mhogolo, GM. 1996. *Huduma ya Kanisa*. Dodoma: Central Tanganyika Press.

_____. 2004. Bible study on 7 April. Dodoma.

Miller, DL & Guthrie, S. 2001. *Disciplining Nations: The Power of Truth to Transform Cultures*. Seattle, WA: YWAM Publishing.

Mmari, G. 1995. The Legacy of Nyerere, in *Mwalimu: The Influence of Nyerere*, edited by C Legum & G Mmari. UK: Britain-Tanzania Society, 176-185.

Mncube, B. 1991. Sexism in the Church and in the African Context, in *Women Hold Up Half the Sky: Women in the Church in Southern Africa*, edited by D Ackermann, JA Draper & E Mashinini, E. Pietermaritzburg: Cluster Publications, 355-362.

Morrell, M & Capparell, S. 2001. *Shackleton's Way: Leadership Lessons from the Great Antarctic Explorer*. London: Nicholas Brealey Publishing.

Moyo, A. 2003. Material Things in African Society: Implications for Christian Ethics, in *Moral and Ethical Issues in African Christianity: Explorative Essays in Moral Theology*, edited by JNK Mugambi & A Nasimiyu-Wasike. 3rd edition. Nairobi, Kenya: Acton Publishers.

Mugambi, JNK. 1989. *African Christian Theology: An Introduction*. Nairobi: East African Educational Publishers.

_____. 2003. The Problems of Teaching Ethics in African Christianity, in *Moral and Ethical Issues in African Christianity: Explorative Essays in Moral Theology*, edited by JNK Mugambi & A Nasimiyu-Wasike. 3rd edition. Nairobi, Kenya: Acton Publishers.

Mugambi, JNK & Nasimiyu-Wasike, A (eds). 2003. *Moral and Ethical Issues in African Christianity: Explorative Essays in Moral Theology*. 3rd edition. Nairobi: Acton Publishers.

Müller, KW. 2003. *Interkulturelles Management*. AcF: Gummersbach.

Mwikamba, CM. 2003. Changing Morals in Africa, in *Moral and Ethical Issues in African Christianity: Explorative Essays in Moral Theology*, edited by JNK Mugambi & A Nasimiyu-Wasike. 3rd edition. Nairobi, Kenya: Acton Publishers.

Mwombeki, FR. 2004. *Uongozi wa Usharika*. Arusha: Scripture Mission.

Ngara, E. 2004. *Christian Leadership: A Challenge to the African Church*. Nairobi: Paulines Publications Africa.

Niebuhr, HR. 1951. *Christ and Culture*. USA: Harper San Francisco.

Nouwen, HJM. 1989. *In the Name of Jesus: Reflections on Christian Leadership*. New York: Crossroad Publishing Company.

Nthamburi, Z. 1991. *The African Church at the Crossroads: A Strategy for Indigenization*. Nairobi, Kenya: Uzima Press.

_____. 2003. Morality in Public life, in *Moral and Ethical Issues in African Christianity: Explorative Essays in Moral Theology*, edited by JNK Mugambi & A Nasimiyu-Wasike. 3rd edition. Nairobi, Kenya: Acton Publishers.

Nürnberger, K. 1988. *Theological Ethics: Previous Study Guide for TEA100-4*. Pretoria: University of South Africa.

O'Donovan Jr., W. 2000. *Biblical Christianity in Modern Africa*. UK: Paternoster Press.

Oduyoye, MA. 1986. *Hearing and Knowing: Theological Reflections on Christianity in Africa*. Maryknoll, New York: Orbis Books.

Parsons, T, & Shils, EA. 1951. *Towards a General Theory of Action*. Cambridge, Mass: Harvard University Press.

Pike, KL. 1996. *With Heart & Mind: A Personal Synthesis of Scholarship and Devotion*. 2nd edition. Duncanville: Adult Learning Systems, Inc.

Quarshie, BY. 2002. Doing Biblical Studies in the African Context – The Challenge of Mother-tongue Scriptures. *Journal of African Christian Thought*, 5(1):4-14.

Richardson, N. 1994. Ethics of Character and Community, in *Doing Ethics in Context: South African Perspectives,* edited by C Villa-Vicencio & JW de Gruchy. Maryknoll, New York: Orbis Books, Cape Town and Johannesburg: David Philip, 89-101.

Rickett, D. 2002. *Making Your Partnership Work*. USA: Winepress Publishing.

Rodrigues, C. 2001. *International Management: A Cultural Approach*. 2nd edition. Ohio: South-Western College Publishing.

Roembke, L. 1998. *Building Credible Multicultural Teams*. edition afem, Mission Academics Bd. 4. Bonn: Verlag für Kultur und Wissenschaft.

Sanders, OJ. 1994. *Spiritual Leadership: Principles of Excellence for Every Believer*. 2nd revision. Chicago: Moody Press.

Sanneh, L. 1989. *Translating the Message: The Missionary Impact on Culture*. Maryknoll, New York: Orbis Books.

Schroll-Machl, S. 2003. *Doing Business with Germans: Their Perception, our Perception*. Göttingen: Vandenhoeck & Ruprecht.

Schubert, R. 2002. *The Core Ideology of a Leader in Tanzania*. Unpublished essay. Gummersbach: Akademie für christliche Führungskräfte.

Scripture Impact Initiative. 2004. *The Four-fold Nature of Scripture Impact: Access to, Love for, Engagement with, & Transformation by the Word of God for All Peoples*. Unpublished document. SIL International and Wycliffe International.

SIL International Conference & Wycliffe Bible Translators Convention. 1999. *Joint Resolution of Vision 2025*. Waxhaw, US.

Sofield, L & Juliano, C. 1987. *Collaborative Ministry: Skills and Guidelines*. Notre Dame: Ave Maria Press.

Sookhdeo, P. 1994. Cultural Issues in Partnership in Mission, in *Kingdom Partnerships for Synergy in Missions,* edited by WD Taylor. Pasadena, California, USA: William Carey Library, 31-42.

Taasisi ya Uchunguzi wa Kiswahili. 1981. *Kamusi ya Kiswahili Sanifu.* Dar es Salaam, Nairobi: Oxford University Press.

_____. 1996. *English-Swahili Dictionary: Kamusi ya Kiingereza-Kiswahili.* Dar es Salaam: Taasisi ya Uchunguzi wa Kiswahili (TUKI).

TANU. 1967. *The Arusha Declaration.* http://www.allwomencount.net/arusha_declaration.htm.

Transparency International. 2005. *Transparency International Corruption Perceptions Index 2005.* http://www.transparency.org.

Trompenaars, F & Hampden-Turner, C. 2002. *Riding the Waves of Culture: Understanding Cultural Diversity in Business.* London: Nicholas Brealey Publishing.

UNESCO. 2003. *Education in a Multilingual World.* Paris: UNESCO.

Vest, N. 2000. *Desiring Life: Benedict on Wisdom and the Good Life.* Cambridge, Boston, Massachusetts: Cowley Publications.

Villa-Vicencio, C. 1994. Ethics of Responsibility, in *Doing Ethics in Context: South African Perspectives,* edited by C Villa-Vicencio & JW de Gruchy. Maryknoll, New York: Orbis Books, Cape Town and Johannesburg: David Philip, 75-88.

Wannemacher, M. 2001. *A Synopsis of Selected Literature on Partnership and Funding with Particular Application.* Unpublished document.

Whitehead, EE & Whitehead, JD. 2000. *The Promise of Partnership: A Model for Collaborative Ministry.* US: iUniverse.com, Inc.

_____. 2003. *Seasons of Strength: New Visions of Adult Christian Maturing.* US: St. Mary's Press.

Wilkes, CG. 1998. *Jesus on Leadership: Discovering the Secrets of Servant Leadership from the Life of Christ.* Wheaton, Illinois: Tyndale House Publishers.

Wycliffe International. 2004. *General Statistics.* Unpublished document.

www.ingramcontent.com/pod-product-compliance
Lightning Source LLC
Chambersburg PA
CBHW020651230426
43665CB00008B/389